GIRL

ON

GIRL

GIRL ON GIRL

How Pop Culture Turned

a Generation of Women

Against Themselves

Sophie Gilbert

PENGUIN PRESS · NEW YORK · 2025

PENGUIN PRESS
An imprint of Penguin Random House LLC
1745 Broadway, New York, NY 10019
penguinrandomhouse.com

Set in Plantin MT Pro
Designed by Cassandra Garruzzo Mueller

Library of Congress Cataloging-in-Publication Data

Names: Gilbert, Sophie (Sophie G.), author.
Title: Girl on girl : how pop culture turned a generation of women
against themselves / Sophie Gilbert.
Description: New York : Penguin Press, 2025. |
Includes bibliographical references and index.
Identifiers: LCCN 2024056378 (print) | LCCN 2024056379 (ebook) |
ISBN 9780593656297 (hardcover) | ISBN 9780593656303 (ebook)
Subjects: LCSH: Anti-feminism—United States—History—21st century. |
Feminism—United States—History—21st century. | Women in
popular culture—United States—History. |
Feminism and mass media—United States—History.
Classification: LCC HQ1421 .G535 2025 (print) |
LCC HQ1421 (ebook) | DDC 305.42—dc23/eng/20250127
LC record available at https://lccn.loc.gov/2024056378
LC ebook record available at https://lccn.loc.gov/2024056379

Printed in the United States of America
1st Printing

The authorized representative in the EU for product safety and
compliance is Penguin Random House Ireland, Morrison Chambers,
32 Nassau Street, Dublin D02 YH68, Ireland, https://eu-contact.penguin.ie.

For all the girls, Lily most of all.

(And for Henry and John, who make things so much fun.)

Contents

Introduction

Re-vision—the act of looking back, of seeing with fresh eyes, of entering an old text from a new critical direction—is for us more than a chapter in cultural history: It is an act of survival. Until we can understand the assumptions in which we are drenched we cannot know ourselves.

ADRIENNE RICH (1972)

Woman is not born: she is made.

ANDREA DWORKIN (1981)

In 1999, the year I turned sixteen, there were three cultural events that seemed to define what it meant to be a young woman—a girl—facing down the new millennium. In April, Britney Spears appeared on the cover of *Rolling Stone* lying on a pink bed wearing pink panties and a black push-up bra, clutching a Teletubby doll with one hand and a phone with the other. In May, a sixty-foot-tall naked image of the children's-television presenter Gail Porter was projected onto the Houses of Parliament in London—where fewer than one in five MPs were women at the time—in a viral caper to promote a men's magazine. And in September, DreamWorks Pictures released *American Beauty*, a movie in which a middle-aged man has recurring sexual fantasies about his teenage daughter's best friend; the film later won five Academy Awards, including Best Picture.

All three texts now seem to me suffused with a kind of winking, postmodern irony. (Fuchsia satin sheets? A *Teletubby doll* to signal transgression?) In the Spears profile, the interviewer weaves back and forth between lust—the logo on her Baby Phat T-shirt, he notes, is "distended by her ample chest"—and detached observation that the sexuality of millennial teen idols is all just a "carefully baited" trap to sell records to suckers. The projection of Porter's image, executed without her knowledge or consent by a marketing agency called Cunning Stunts, was sold at the time as one big hilarious prank, while nevertheless seeming to affirm that women belonged in softcore photo shoots, not in government. In *American Beauty*, Lester's fixation on an underage girl is sold as a textbook midlife crisis, even as the movie itself turns the character of Angela into a highly eroticized floral centerpiece.

At sixteen, though, I didn't discern any of this. What *was* obvious to me was that power, for women, was sexual in nature. There was no other kind, or none worth having. More crucially, the kind of power being fetishized in popular culture on the cusp of the twenty-first century wasn't the sort you accrue over a lifetime, in the manner of education or money or professional experience. It was all about youth, attention, and a willingness to be in on the joke, even if we were ultimately the punch line.

I started thinking about writing this book early in the 2020s, in a moment when time no longer seemed linear, progress no longer felt inevitable, and every ugly trend I'd come of age with as a Y2K teen had looped its way right back around. Hillary Clinton's failed presidential campaign in 2016, followed by the explosion of testimony regarding sexual abuse and harassment that manifested as the #MeToo movement a year later, made certain realities self-evident. The recreational misogyny of the aughts was back, this time with new technology and a cult figurehead, Andrew Tate, who'd once appeared on the reality series *Big Brother* while under investigation for rape. Wives-and-girlfriends tabloid obsession had been reinvented for TikTok, where doll-like women murmured in affectless monologues about living the financially dependent dream of a "soft, feminine life." The body-positivity movement, which had done its utmost to claim space for normal bodies in media and retail, was rapidly being shunted out of favor by the rise of weight-loss medication and a whole new crop of women with whittled-down waists and jutting rib cages.

Everything old was new again, and yet things were also darker and more disengaged. In 2022, the overturning of *Roe v. Wade* marked the most tangible rollback of women's rights in half a century. Culturally, the motif of the moment was impossible to avoid, and it seemed to pinpoint how small our collective ambitions had become. Women my age were suddenly trading friendship bracelets and decoding messages supposedly embedded in pop lyrics with the intensity of CIA cryptographers. We went on girl trips, traded girl talk, had "hot girl summers," and picked at girl dinners. In 2023, I put on my best millennial-pink blazer—the one I wear for panel discussions—and stood in a line of women all equally psyched to have our photos taken in an adult-sized doll box, as if a moment of visual solidarity could make up for losing our reproductive rights. The Barbie world, with its all-female Supreme Court and hegemonic femininity, only made it clear that we were all still playing with scraps of power. At the end of 2024, once again, a competent, accomplished, empathetic woman was beaten in the US presidential race by a failed businessman and convicted felon whose platform was elevated by some of the most proudly vicious misogynists and white supremacists in modern memory. Who wouldn't want to be a girl again, given the alternative?

So much of this malaise felt familiar. There was a moment at the beginning of the twenty-first century when feminism felt just as nebulous and inert, squashed by a cultural explosion of jokey extremity and technicolor objectification. This was the environment that millennial women were raised in. It informed how we felt about ourselves, how we saw each other, and what we understood women as a collective to be capable of. It colored our ambitions, our sense of self, our relationships, our bodies, our work, and our art. I came to believe that we couldn't move forward without fully reckoning with how the culture of the aughts had defined us.

With this book, I wanted, from the position of a critic, to excavate how and why every genre of entertainment at this time—music, movies, TV, fashion, magazines, porn—was sending girls the same message, one that we internalized with rigor.

I wanted to understand how a generation of young women came to believe that sex was our currency, our objectification was empowering, and we were a joke. Why were we so easily persuaded of our own inadequacy? Who was setting the agenda? Why, for decades and even now, has virtually every cultural product been so insistently oriented around male desire and male pleasure?

I didn't necessarily expect to find all the answers. My main goal was to reframe recent history in a way that might enhance my own perspective. But what became clear was how neatly culture, feminism, and history run on parallel tracks, informing, disrupting, and even derailing each other. I also became fascinated by the echoes—connections, repetitions, and trends across time and genres. They're still reverberating now, as we continue to seesaw erratically between progress and backlash.

AS I LOOK BACK, all these trends, and the culture they stood for, now seem inextricable from the rise of postfeminism. Less an explicit ideology than a mechanism to attract media attention and sell things, postfeminism emerged in the 1980s and 1990s as a reaction to women's activism, bolstered by the sense that second- and third-wave feminists were somehow inhibiting our collective freedom. In *The New York Times Magazine* in 1982, Susan Bolotin observed that young women were suddenly disavowing a personal connection with feminism despite acknowledging what it had achieved. A smear campaign against the women's movement appeared to have done its job; younger women, Bolotin noted, interpreted feminists as being "unhappy" and "shrill," even as they embraced the new opportunities that the efforts of other women had given them.

Postfeminism was vague; it seemed to define itself mostly in opposition to a boogeyman version of feminism, encouraging women to embrace casual sex, spend with abandon, and be as stereotypically girly or overtly sexy as they desired. All these things were insistently sold as being *empowering*, a word that now makes me deeply suspicious any time I encounter it in the wild. Over the course of the 1990s, postfeminist ideals slowly saturated popular culture. It wasn't a coincidence that the decade began with the ferocious activist energy of riot grrrls and ended with the hypercommercialized Spice Girls, whose genius, as the journalist Caity Weaver wrote in 2019, was in "depicting a young girl's idea of adulthood . . . sleepover antics turned career." To be deprived of ambition is to be infantilized. One defining postfeminist avatar was *Sex and the City*'s Carrie Bradshaw, a doll-like consumerist with a rainbow-colored shoe collection whose Upper East Side apartment was one big dress-up box. In literature and later in film, Bridget Jones pioneered an enduring new female archetype: the trainwreck. (The book, a *New York Times* review noted in 1998, "captures neatly the way modern women teeter between 'I am woman' independence and a pathetic girlie desire to be all things to all men"—the paradox of postfeminism in a nutshell.)

Up until this moment, the women's movement had been gaining momentum. The publication of Susan Faludi's *Backlash* in 1991, and the shock of Anita Hill's Senate testimony at confirmation hearings for Clarence Thomas in the same year, helped shape feminism's third wave, a movement that was really trying to be inclusive, sex-positive, and hopeful about the future. What stunned me while researching this book is just how efficiently this energy was blunted by mass culture. In music, rock's angry women were sidelined throughout the decade and replaced by pop's much-younger, much-less-opinionated girls. In fashion, powerful supermodels who demanded to be paid what they were worth and supported each other were phased out in favor of frail, passive teenagers. As the 1990s went on, culture gradually redefined feminism from a collective struggle to an individual one. Instead of an inclusive movement that acknowledged intersections of race, class, and gender, we got selective upward mobility and rampant consumerism. All these modes would continue to play out throughout the decades to come, through the corporate feminism of *Lean In*, the girlboss moment, and the "I'm not here to make friends" ruthlessness of reality TV.

This inversion of protest was how the aughts began. The trick postfeminist mass media had pulled off, as Natasha Walter argued in her 2010 book *Living Dolls*, was that it had co-opted words such as *liberation* and *choice* to sell women "an airbrushed, highly sexualized, and increasingly narrow vision of femininity"—one in which we were expected to *choose* a life of being both willing objects and easy targets.

TO ME, THE SHIFTING CULTURAL ideals for womanhood in the 1990s help clarify why the aughts were quite so cruel, as the tenets of postfeminism became mandates that none of us could really opt out of. There was only one way to exist in public, and it was a trap. As emerging stars got younger and younger— "It's Totally Raining Teens!" a notorious *Vanity Fair* cover from 2003 declared—the pressure on them to check all the wildly divergent boxes required to make it only intensified. Seventeen-year-olds were expected to be sexy virgins, girls with porn-star looks and purity rings, able to sell anything to any demographic. This is not a balancing act that anyone can pull off for long. And the more visibly expressive or submissive women became in their sexuality throughout the decade, the more was demanded of us in turn.

I've structured this book chronologically, from the 1990s to the present, as a way of trying to parse what was happening in culture against the backdrop of what was happening in history. And, as you'll see, virtually every era, art form, historical moment, trend, and icon reflects the influence of the genre that became, over the past twenty-five years, more ubiquitous than any other mode of entertainment. The title *Girl on Girl* was initially supposed to be a joke—a wry nod to all the ways in which women seemed to have been turned against themselves and each other, handicapped as a collective force over the course of my adult life. But the more research I did, the more porn seemed to have filtered its way through absolutely everything in mass media.

The influence of porn charges through music: in the opening interlude of Lil' Kim's *Hardcore*, in Fiona Apple's unsettling video for "Criminal," and in the moment in 2003 when Snoop Dogg arrived at the MTV Video Music Awards (VMAs) with two adult women on leashes. It's in art and fashion: in Jeff Koons's explicit *Made in Heaven* series, in David Bailey and Rankin's 2003 photographic series that the pair nicknamed the "pussy show," in the work and life of Terry Richardson, and in the Y2K obsession with the visible G-string. Porn is behind the near-extinction of pubic hair as well as the proliferation of dangerous Brazilian butt lifts, and it's at least partly behind the ballooning rates of cosmetic surgeries over the past quarter century. It's literally present, grainy and muffled, in the opening scene of *American Pie* and thematically there in the wave of teen sex comedies that imitated it. Porn is behind the art-house trend for movies that married explicit sex with emotional and physical brutality. It's there in the upskirt pictures of young female stars published in the late 2000s and in the ways in which sex tapes featuring young female celebrities were stolen and disseminated across the internet. It's heavily discernible in the perplexing sexual relationship between Hannah and Adam on *Girls*. It's even in politics: Just days after the 2008 Republican

National Convention, Hustler Video started production on a hardcore movie titled *Who's Nailin' Paylin?*, featuring actresses parodying Sarah Palin, Hillary Clinton, and Condoleezza Rice.

There are plenty of other subjects under consideration in the chapters that follow: the limiting and regressive conception of women on reality television, the rise of female auteurs and auto-fiction, and how the girlboss era turned the individualistic ethos of postfeminism into gold, among others. But it fascinates me that so much of what I was trying to figure out kept coming back to porn. It's the defining cultural product of our times—the thing that has shaped more than anything else how we think about sex and, therefore, how we think about each other. "Porn does not inform, or debate, or persuade," Amia Srinivasan wrote in her 2021 book *The Right to Sex*. "Porn trains." It has trained a good amount of our popular culture, as you'll discover in this book, to see women as objects—as things to silence, restrain, fetishize, or brutalize. And it's helped train women too. In a 2013 study, the social psychologist Rachel M. Calogero found that the more women were prone to self-objectification—the defining message of postfeminism and porn alike—the less inclined they were toward activism and the pursuit of social justice. This, to me, goes a long way toward explaining what happened to women and power in the twenty-first century.

In no way is this book complete. I've left out more than I was able to include, mostly because I wanted to make connections and understand patterns. The historical moment I've considered was largely defined by heteronormativity, gender essentialism, and a rigid binary—all of which has limited my ability to write outside those frameworks. This is just a small piece of a much larger project of reappraisal. Analyzing history together is, above all, an expression of hope: We try to understand all the ways in which things went wrong so that we can conceive of a more powerful way forward.

GIRL

ON

GIRL

CHAPTER I

Girl Power, Boy Rage

Music and Feminism in the 1990s

I heard someone from the music business saying they
are no longer looking for talent, they want people with a
certain look and a willingness to cooperate.

JONI MITCHELL (2004)

When will this caveboy shit end?

DREAM HAMPTON (1991)

In 2003, the music critic Jessica Hopper published an essay
in *Punk Planet* titled "Emo: Where the Girls Aren't," detailing the alienation she felt from one of the most influential artistic genres of the era. "Girls in emo songs today do
not have names," she wrote. "Our actions are portrayed solely
through the detailing of neurotic self-entanglement of the boy
singer—our region of personal power, simply, is our impact on
his romantic life. We're vessels redeemed in the light of boy-
love. On a pedestal, on our backs."

Many of us could sense this dynamic at the time, even if we
couldn't quite rationalize it. What Hopper was articulating

about emo was true of much music in the aughts: The most popular anthems of the decade were sticky, leaden strip-club soundtracks, full of rote clichés about male sexual prowess and devious, grasping women. In my late teens and twenties, I danced in clubs to Sisqó's "Thong Song," Christina Aguilera's "Dirrty," and 50 Cent's "P.I.M.P." without realizing that something had shifted. It's impossible to analyze millennial culture without first going back to the 1990s, where flash points in music would uncannily anticipate and inform what was coming. During that decade, music was the site of some of our most crucial battles over sex, power, and feminism. It was where provocateurs and rebels came to play and to protest. Women in music in the 1990s were angry and abrasive and thrillingly powerful. And then, just like that, they were gone—replaced by girls. The backlash that banished them would reverberate across all forms of media, so relentlessly and persuasively that people of my generation would hardly think to notice what we'd lost.

At the tail end of 1990, Madonna released a video to accompany her new single, "Justify My Love," that set the tone for the coming decade: audacious, wildly sexual, a little bit trollish. The song was a hypnotic, trip-hoppy declaration of lust; the video was a conceptual, wildly sexual exploration of fantasy and desire that detonated pre-internet popular discourse. Madonna, shot in black-and-white, is seen walking down a hotel hallway toward an assignation, limping slightly in heels and a black raincoat, clutching her head as if in pain. As she passes different doorways, we see fleeting glimpses of the people occupying various rooms, watching us watch them. The star is joined by her lover (played by her real-life boyfriend at the time, the amiable lunk Tony Ward); a man laces a woman into a rubber corset; a dancer in a unitard contorts into shifting positions; Ward watches Madonna with another partner, his expression a picture. More people arrive; Ward gets trussed up in fetish netting; everyone tests the amorphous boundaries of sexuality, gender, and dominance. Finally, Madonna puts on her coat and leaves, laughing, renewed and jubilant, no longer tired.

The brazen, unnerving sexuality of the video was the whole point. By the end of that year, the AIDS epidemic had claimed more than 120,000 lives in the United States, one-fifth of which were in New York, the epicenter of fashion, art, music, media, and advertising. Cultural anxiety regarding the idea that sex could literally kill you had led to two wildly divergent schools of thought in media. One, nicknamed the New Traditionalism, preached a revival of old-fashioned family values, where women went home and stayed there. (The 1987 movie *Fatal Attraction* made this fear of a corrupted American culture literal, in the form of Glenn Close's sexually adventurous, bunny-boiling career woman, the fling who won't be flung.) The other, the New Voyeurism, embraced sex, but as a spectator sport. "At a time when doing it has become excessively dangerous, looking at it, reading about it, thinking about it have become a necessity," a *Newsweek* feature on Madonna declared in 1992. "AIDS has pushed voyeurism from the sexual second tier . . . into the front row."

For the rest of the 1990s, culture would be shaped by the push-pull of these two opposing forces. The New Traditionalism and the New Voyeurism seemed at odds, but both were essentially promising women the same thing: that fulfillment and prosperity lie in catering to men's desires. Music, though, was where women were pushing back. The "Justify My Love" video reads now as a brazen affirmation of sexual freedom in a turbulent era. But there was a twist. The subject of the video was Madonna—the fantasies, the imagery, the pleasure all hers. If it was alienating to men, or to mainstream audiences, she didn't care. The video ended with words on a screen: "Poor is the man / Whose pleasures depend / On the permission of another."

Madonna must have anticipated mass outrage, and she got it. But she also helped ignite a sex-positive wave of music that put women's desires front and center. In 1993, Janet Jackson released *Janet*, a silky, carnal record all about lust. The video for her track "Any Time, Any Place" teases the same voyeuristic impulses at play in "Justify My Love"; people spy on each other through peepholes and letterboxes and an elderly neighbor looks on, disapprovingly, as Jackson pushes her lover's head down while he's on top of her—a revolutionary assertion of sexual power and equality that would later be echoed in videos and lyrics by TLC, Mary J. Blige, and Lil' Kim.

At the time, music videos were still a novel art form. The 1990s predilection for voyeurism wasn't just a response to AIDS: Images became more ubiquitous and more freighted because consumers now had the ability to *watch* music as well as listen to it. When MTV launched in 1981, it turned the nature of pop and rock stardom inside out. What you looked like as an artist became, overnight, as crucial as the sound you made. Artists such as Madonna, Cyndi Lauper, and Tina Turner, whose unique aesthetics made them immediately recognizable on-screen, flourished in the new medium. But Madonna and Jackson both also seemed to recognize all the ways in which video made women targets. Twelve days after the launch of MTV, Duran Duran began production on the video for "Girls on Film," a six-minute short in which topless models had pillow fights, mud wrestled, kissed, poured champagne over each other's breasts, and straddled an oversized pole covered in shaving cream—adapting hokey sexist imagery for a new technological era.

Madonna's and Jackson's videos openly challenged the idea of women's performing for men's pleasure. In the 1986 video for "Open Your Heart," which incorporates a vast nude painting by the Polish artist Tamara de Lempicka, Madonna played a peep-show dancer in front of an audience of leering, dead-eyed onlookers. The following year, a study found that while rock videos were "cable's first real contribution to entertainment programming on television," the majority of videos shown on MTV depicted women as sex objects or two-dimensional stereotypes. Madonna was more pro-sex than possibly anyone else alive, but for her, sexuality was synonymous with power. Her 1992 coffee-table erotica book *Sex* was another manifestation of *her* fantasies: surreal in parts, kinky in others, sometimes outright comical. The author Mary Gabriel argues that it "may have been the first major book of female sexual imagery ever published that was not created to titillate a heterosexual man." And yet the message the entertainment industry would end up taking away from the book was that it was sexual—and that it sold, and sold, and sold.

IN SOME WAYS, the story of what happened to the feminist movement during the 1990s can be told by tracing the evolution of a single slogan. In 1991, Kathleen Hanna was in Olympia, Washington, in her final semester of college, preoccupied with the fanzine she was making for her punk band, Bikini Kill. Hanna had been reading some of the feminist psychologist Carol Gilligan's work on adolescent girlhood, confidence, and resistance and was brainstorming titles for her next zine with Bikini Kill's drummer, Tobi Vail. "Let's put a word with 'girl' that doesn't usually go with 'girl,'" Hanna recalls suggesting in her 2024 autobiography, *Rebel Girl*.

"Power," Vail replied. "Girl Power."

By the end of the 1990s, Girl Power would be a universally familiar slogan, and yet the more it was recited, the less it seemed to stand for. Girl Power as an early-1990s ideology was intensely, intentionally political. It filtered punk's rage through lived experience, demanding more space and respect for women at live shows and throughout the industry as well as creating radical texts that often resembled—with their use of collage, drawings, and block letters—a girl's diary. One flier Hanna wrote for a Bikini Kill show featured a list of imperatives titled "The Revolution Starts Here + Now Within Each One of Us" and included exhortations such as "Resist the internalization of capitalism, the reducing of people + oneself to commodities meant to be consumed." Other contemporary zines associated with the nascent movement that would be named "riot grrrl" explored subjects such as postmodernism, bisexuality, inclusivity in feminism, and the work of the surrealist French playwright Antonin Artaud.

There was no political *Teen Vogue* during the 1990s. The magazine I read as a tween in the United Kingdom was *Just Seventeen*, a heavily consumerist, boy-obsessed glossy named after the Beatles' lyric about dating a teenager. It offered leg workouts, twenty reasons to call your crush, even explicit sex tips, but nothing about Artaud or self-commodification. The writer Olivia Laing, also growing up in Britain that decade, was luckier: They discovered riot grrrl via a blistering performance by the punk band Huggy Bear on Channel 4's *The Word* and immediately sent off a stamped-addressed envelope to claim their own zine. "It's easy to be dismissive about teenage girls— frivolous, vapid, superficial—but looking again at these secret texts, what I'm struck by is their intensity of thought," they wrote in *The Guardian* in 2018. "Early zines discuss ways to empower girls, to stay safe, to reclaim streets and mosh pits. . . . But the potential self-righteousness is undercut by an avant-garde irreverence of style. Mainstream culture is literally chopped up and rearranged, embroidered for good measure with a doodling of guns and stars."

I've always wondered why people diminish girlhood as somehow cosseted or twee, when the reality of coming-of-age as a young woman is so raw, filled with emotional violence and literal blood. Do girls not suffer enough to be taken seriously? In *Rebel Girl*, Hanna recounts the experiences that led her to punk activism: her abusive father, whom she and her sister once had to talk out of shooting both them and himself; an unplanned pregnancy and abortion that, because she was underage, she had to write *an essay* to be granted; the time her ex-boyfriend papered her college library with pictures of her naked; her experience volunteering at a women's shelter after her roommate was violently assaulted by a stranger; her time as a dancer at a gentleman's club; and her rape at the hands of an intimate friend whom she trusted. She remembers thinking that the kind of feminism she was looking for might not exist. The name "Bikini Kill" was a reference to Bikini Atoll, the coral reef in the Marshall Islands where the US government tested nuclear weapons after forcibly repatriating inhabitants. The military, Hanna writes, "taped a picture of Rita Hayworth to the side of one of the bombs, an act against Hayworth's will that left her known as a 'bombshell.'"

What charged the riot-grrrl movement from the beginning was anger at this kind of diminishment and abuse. In the late

1980s, punk music was thriving in Washington, DC, and in the Pacific Northwest, but it made little space for women and girls who felt marginalized within the music scene and unsafe in their day-to-day lives. By the early 1990s, bands such as Babes in Toyland, Bikini Kill, Heavens to Betsy, Excuse 17, 7 Year Bitch, and Bratmobile were coalescing as a ferocious but nebulous movement. In 1991, Hanna and Vail published the "Riot Grrrl Manifesto," arguing that visibility, encouragement, and safety were necessary for women artists to thrive, and that an "angry grrrl rock revolution" was coming that would seek "to save the psychic and cultural lives of girls and women everywhere." As bands toured, they disseminated this message all over the country, leading to riot-grrrl chapters nationwide.

In 1992, the *Chicago Reader* examined the riot-grrrl scene, noting that one of its earliest political acts wasn't a song but a list of men who date-raped women, scrawled on the wall of a restroom at Evergreen State College. The idea of secrecy—that the movement was empowered both by public expression and private discourse among its followers—was pivotal to riot grrrl's early popularity, while also contributing to its downfall. Without a formalized structure, the coalition was splintered and vulnerable to charges that it was juvenile, precious, and not sufficiently inclusive. Many punk fans felt left out: The musician Ramdasha Bikceem founded her own zine, *GUNK*, at the age of fifteen, where she wrote about feeling doubly excluded from both the music she loved and the riot-grrrl scene that she characterized as "white middle class punk grrrls."

By 1993, frustrated with the condescension with which riot

grrrl had been portrayed in the media, Bikini Kill had stopped doing interviews, which limited riot grrrl's influence. But Hanna's "Girls to the Front" ethos also forcibly carved out space for both female punk fans and baby feminists outside the music scene, and the spirit of creativity and confession contained in zine culture would be reborn online in the years to come. By 1996, independent riot-grrrl conventions had taken place in a dozen cities across the United States, as well as in Europe and Asia, when the movement's "Girl Power" slogan was appropriated by an all-new girl band several thousand miles away.

The riot-grrrl movement and the Spice Girls were sharply at odds. Riot grrrl evolved organically out of art women were making on their own to signal their presence as an engaged, political fandom. The Spice Girls were created by a father-and-son producer team who put an ad in a trade paper announcing auditions. Riot grrrl was a creative manifestation of third-wave feminism. The Spice Girls pioneered and embodied postfeminism and its messaging: Feminism was over, having achieved all it needed to; women were free to dress and adorn themselves however they wanted; any individual choice could be empowering if someone declared it to be so; consumerism was the path to self-fulfillment. If the emerging model for pop stars was "sexy teenager," the Spice Girls were sexy women who behaved like toddlers at a wedding: grabbing things at random, spinning round and round and round, throwing food on the floor. They embodied "freedom" if you understood that concept as "total absence of impulse control." They made you want to immediately go shopping. And they talked, often, about Girl Power.

In 1997, the Spice Girls published a book with that very title, a text that borrowed zine aesthetics, but with a more polished production value. In it, they defined "Girl Power" as including elements such as "You believe in yourself and control your own life" and "You and your mates reply to wolf whistles by shouting, 'Get Your Arse Out!'" On one page, Victoria Beckham (Posh Spice) was quoted as saying: "We want to be a household name. We want to be a Fairy Liquid or Ajax." Geri Halliwell (Ginger Spice) explained that the Spice Girls self-categorize as types because they're "about freedom of expression, which is why we wanted to retain our own personalities." There was no one way to be a Spice Girl, because Girl Power as an ideology was as malleable as Play-Doh. It was for everyone.

If that made it feel like a movement full of opportunity, the reverse was actually true, as the sociologist Jessica K. Taft argued in 2004. The Spice Girls' version of "Girl Power," she wrote, was constructed in such a way as to neutralize feminism—to loudly and deliberately replace it with a more modern alternative—and to "make no indication that this alternative [was] a model for social or political change." Taft interpreted Girl Power as having four distinct tenets: antifeminism, postfeminism, individual power, and consumer power. The relentless positivity of its content, the idea that women could achieve anything as long as they were willing to present themselves the right way and hustle, anticipated the girlboss moment of the 2010s, and was just as myopic regarding structural inequities in society. But Girl Power was irresistible. "You can be a leader, you can be strong, you can be confident," an ad for Space Camp Barbie read in 1999, capturing the mood. "Girls can do it all."

Girl Power was almost instantly appropriated by brands, who saw in it a powerful new consumer demographic. The December 1997 issue of *Fortune*, Taft noted, contained a six-page spread on Girl Power and marketing, which explained that 88 percent of girls between thirteen and seventeen "just love to shop." For millennial girls, buying things was suddenly being presented as a political act—one that negated the need for other kinds of activism. To invert a quote from *The Handmaid's Tale*, the riot-grrrl movement wanted women to have freedom *from*: sexual violence, abuse, injustice, fear. The Spice Girls embodied freedom *to*: have fun, earn money, pursue pleasure. There are no prizes for deducing which ideology was easier to package and sell.

By 2001, the movie *Josie and the Pussycats*—one of my favorites—was ruthlessly satirizing the ways in which teens were being manipulated by pop culture into spending their disposable income on consumer goods in order to prop up the American economy. In the film, subliminal messages are hidden in pop songs to dictate trends and must-have items, and if unwitting stars discover the truth, they're quickly dispatched in plane crashes. In reality, nothing so underhanded was necessary. Within eighteen months of releasing "Wannabe," the Spice Girls would sign endorsement deals with companies including Pepsi, Polaroid, Cadbury's, Chupa Chups, and Hasbro. By the end of 1997, they'd collectively earned around half a billion dollars from marketing deals alone. "Life is different in Spiceworld," *Slate*'s David Plotz wrote that year. "If there is a product that 12-year-olds use, there will be a Spice Girls version of it in your mall by Thanksgiving." Girl Power was everywhere you looked, in technicolor block-capital letters that stood for not much at all.

WHAT MADE RIOT GRRRL and records such as *Janet* and Madonna's *Erotica* seem so radical in the early 1990s was partly what women artists dared to do and partly what they were rebelling against: not just the novelty misogyny of "Girls on Film" and women cavorting on cars in Whitesnake videos but an emerging taste for tracks that were hateful, violent, and even abusive. During the 1990s, hip-hop—an art form that had evolved in part out of disenfranchisement and social protest—was rapidly gaining commercial power. But as the money at stake grew exponentially, the genre's charged antiestablishment energy was in need of a safer, more profitable target.

Even before Madonna's "Justify My Love" was banned from MTV, debates about sexual content in music were raging. After the Moral Majority 1980s, the 1990s were emerging as a new decade of sexual liberation, where looking was sanctioned because it was so much safer than touching. But the act of looking requires an object, and in mainstream culture, at least, its object was women. In 1989, the Miami dirty-rap group 2 Live Crew released its third album, *As Nasty As They Wanna Be*—a record replete with braggadocious, exhaustively explicit storytelling that quickly ignited a moral panic. A Florida judge declared *As Nasty As They Wanna Be* officially obscene, citing its "violence" and "perversion," and banning it from sale. In June 1990, when the group performed a handful of tracks at a club in Broward County, the rappers were arrested, kicking off a national conversation about censorship, art, racism, and musical tradition that largely evaded the significant details of 2 Live Crew's musical treatment of women—specifically Black women.

In the pages of *The New York Times*, and subsequently in court, the 2 Live Crew rappers were defended by the academic and historian Henry Louis Gates Jr., who declared that they were simply engaging in "heavy-handed parody, turning the stereotypes of black and white American culture on their heads." He argued that they were "acting out, to lively dance music, a parodic exaggeration of the age-old stereotypes of the oversexed black female and male." Moreover, Gates wrote, it was hard not to deduce that 2 Live Crew was being targeted specifically because its members were Black and, therefore, were being interpreted as more threatening to American culture than were contemporary White rock musicians or comedians whose artistic output was just as provocative.

Most other public intellectuals agreed. And yet in defending 2 Live Crew from charges of obscenity, as the law professor and civil rights advocate Kimberlé Crenshaw countered in the *Boston Review*, Gates was disregarding something crucial: the striking misogyny and sexual violence in the group's lyrics and what they represented. "The first time I listened to 2 Live Crew, I was stunned," Crenshaw wrote. "The issue had been distorted by descriptions of *As Nasty As They Wanna Be* as simply 'sexually explicit.' *Nasty* is much more: it is virulently misogynist, sometimes violently so. Black women are cunts, 'ho's,' and all-purpose bitches: raggedy bitches, sorry-ass bitches, lowdown slimy-ass bitches. Good sex is often portrayed as painful and humiliating for women."

In 1989, Crenshaw had coined the term "intersectionality" to describe how women of color experienced overlapping forms of discrimination that mainstream discourse often overlooked; just a year later, a cultural flash point was proving her thesis. Black women, Crenshaw wrote in the *Boston Review*, the most frequent targets in rap, were being asked to choose between an antiracist defense of the group that ignored its misogyny and an indictment of the group's violent sexism that could be construed as racist. (She was also "deeply skeptical about the claim that the Crew was engaged—either in intent or effect—in pursuing a postmodern guerilla war against racist stereotypes," a repudiation of the ironic-sexism defense that was way ahead of its time.)

As Nasty As They Wanna Be is ribald, comic, and lyrically grotesque. A scene from the song "Bad-Ass Bitch" in which Brother Marquis describes spit-roasting a woman with two of his friends now feels intentionally cruel and dehumanizing to me in the way that much online porn does, no matter how technically impressive the contortions. But it was also representative of a turn that rap had taken at the end of the 1980s, starting on the West Coast and quickly gaining momentum. Some historians and critics have theorized that as hip-hop became a bigger business, major labels demanded that artists depoliticize their work. As a result, the anger and frustration once aimed at injustice in America was simply redirected toward women. But by the time 2 Live Crew appeared in court, hardcore depictions of sex were also more prominent in US culture than they had ever been, thanks to VHS technology, and their popularity would continue to surge throughout the 1990s. In 1985, there were roughly 75 million adult-film rentals per year in the United States, most from brick-and-mortar video stores. A decade later, the number was 665 million.

Women artists emerging in this moment, particularly in hip-hop, were faced not only with a culture that disparaged women as bitches, "chickenheads" (a derisive term for a woman giving oral sex whose head bobs up and down), and gold diggers but also an industry enamored with video that prized women for their sexuality as much as their talent. Rap, the feminist cultural critic Michele Wallace wrote in 1990, was seen by some women at the time as "basically a locker-room with a beat." It hadn't always been this way. In 1986, Salt-N-Pepa had become the first female rap act to reach platinum status in the United States with "Push It," a pulsating, exuberant track that burned with sexual power. (Years later, Cheryl "Salt" James told *The Guardian* that according to someone she met who worked in an aquarium, whenever they played "Push It," sharks started mating.) In 1988, the seventeen-year-old MC Lyte's album *Lyte as a Rock* asserted both her force as an artist ("I Am Woman") and her emotional vulnerability ("Paper Thin").

But with the 1990s came a palpable shift. In 1991, the year Anita Hill testified to a Senate committee—with Crenshaw on her legal team—that Clarence Thomas had sexually harassed her, the N.W.A. rapper and producer Dr. Dre pleaded no contest to physically assaulting the TV host Dee Barnes in a nightclub in Hollywood. (The subsequent *Rolling Stone* headline read: "N.W.A.: Beating Up the Charts.") In an article for *The Source* that year, the journalist dream hampton—whose music writing throughout the 1990s was pivotal in honoring hip-hop as an art form while laying out its failures—argued that the "verbal and mental abuse" directed at women in hip-hop was evolving into real, physical violence. The article was so controversial when it came out, she told *The Atlantic* years later, that Spike Lee offered to get her a bodyguard.

In America, 1992 was dubbed "The Year of the Woman," as women ran and were elected to office in record numbers. "To me, the [1991 Senate] hearings were not about determining whether or not Clarence Thomas did in fact harass Anita Hill," the feminist Rebecca Walker wrote in an article for *Ms.* titled "Becoming the 3rd Wave." "They were about checking and redefining the extent of women's credibility and power." In hip-hop, male artists seemed to be engaged in a similar effort. As Kathy Iandoli writes in *God Save the Queens*, 1992 was replete with sexist and outright hateful tracks that were wildly popular:

Boogie Down Productions' "13 and Good" ("That's statutory rape / But she was GOOD"), Dr. Dre's "Bitches Ain't Shit" ("Bitches ain't shit but hoes and tricks / Lick on these nuts then suck the dick"), Too $hort's "Hoes" ("Who said that hoe ain't old enough? / If she could bleed then she could fuck"). These were lyrics that record labels had actively condoned, preferring sexually violent imagery against women to more combustible language directed at police or the state. And the success of these records underscored a question once posed by the author and academic bell hooks: "How many disenfranchised black males would not surrender to expressing virulent forms of sexism, if they knew the rewards would be unprecedented material power and fame?"

Michele Wallace described the bind Black women found themselves in: "Feminist criticism, like many other forms of social analysis, is widely considered part of a hostile white culture," she wrote in *The New York Times*. "For a black feminist to chastise misogyny in rap publicly would be viewed as divisive and counterproductive," even leading to accusations of "collaborating with a racist society." But music itself allowed more room for contradiction and dissent. In 1993, the year Janet Jackson proclaimed her own sexual power, Queen Latifah released *Black Reign*, featuring the Grammy-winning "U.N.I.T.Y.," a track that directly challenged how Black women were derided, harassed, and abused in popular culture. "Who you calling a bitch?" she demanded furiously. That same year, Salt-N-Pepa released "Shoop," a breezy, swaggering song that turned the tables on catcalling, reaching number four on the *Billboard* singles chart and helping the group's album sell more than five million copies.

"Shoop," *Black Reign*, and Mary J. Blige's *What's the 411?* helped coalesce what the writer Joan Morgan later labeled "hip-hop feminism": a movement that centered Black women's voices and storytelling; acknowledged intersectionalities of race and gender; and was pro-sex, pro-pleasure, and conscious of the ambiguities for women who made and loved music and who wanted the space to be able to champion and critique it at the same time. (In a sign of how complicated gender dynamics were within the industry, *What's the 411?* was produced by Sean "Diddy" Combs, who in 2024 was arrested for charges including sex trafficking and hit with dozens of lawsuits regarding allegations of sexual assault that dated as far back as 1990.) "I needed a feminism that would allow us to continue loving ourselves *and* the brothers who hurt us without letting race loyalty buy us early tombstones," Morgan wrote in her 1999 book *When Chickenheads Come Home to Roost: A Hip-Hop Feminist Breaks It Down*. In the absence of an ideology that supported her, she figured one out for herself.

SO MUCH OF THE MUSIC created by women in the early 1990s was responding to, and enraged by, real, systemic injustices. Sonic Youth's "Swimsuit Issue," written by Kim Gordon, was inspired by a sexual-harassment suit against an executive at Geffen Records, the group's label, and alluded to Anita Hill's Senate testimony. "Don't touch my breast / I'm just working at my desk," Gordon spat, against violent, jagged guitar chords. In 1992, Sinéad O'Connor, fervent even as her hands shook slightly, tore up a picture of the pope on *Saturday Night Live* to protest sexual abuse within the Roman Catholic Church. Tori Amos wrote "Cornflake Girl" after a discussion with a friend about female genital mutilation. Hole's "Miss World," the Juliana Hatfield Three's "Supermodel," PJ Harvey's "Dress," No Doubt's "Just a Girl," and Bikini Kill's "Lil Red" raged against oppressive beauty standards and approved markers of femininity for women. Skunk Anansie's debut album, *Paranoid & Sunburnt,* indicted everything from racism and child abuse to organized religion and condescending men. ("He tried to intellectualize my blackness. . . . Motherfucker don't you lecture-ize me.") In 1999, at the tail end of the decade, Kelis delivered "Caught Out There," one of the most explosive tracks about infidelity of all time, complete with pain-soaked expressiveness and intermittent primal screams.

The anger expressed on these records was sharp, and it pointed at an industry and a culture that wanted women to be pretty, passive, and powerless. "A lot of what the '90s was about was this huge question of 'How do we live as women within some kind of idea of the feminine but not have it wreck us?'" is how the music critic Ann Powers once characterized the era. Liz Phair's 1993 *Exile in Guyville* was a low-fi, song-by-song response to the Rolling Stones' *Exile on Main Street* that chewed up musical sexism and spat it back out in songs such as "Explain It to Me" and "Flower." ("I want to fuck you like a dog / I'll take you home and make you like it.") Alanis Morissette's *Jagged Little Pill*, produced by Madonna's Maverick imprint after most other major labels passed on it, turned one woman's reaching her breaking point into thirty-three million records sold and five Grammy Awards.

Women were making music about abortion, about sexual assault, about domestic violence. They were spelling out all the ways in which they felt belittled and diminished as artists, in an industry where it was silently forbidden to play two songs in a row by female acts. The media responded with coverage much like *NME*'s 1992 interview with Tori Amos, which bore the headline "Ginger Nut," and *Q*'s May 1994 cover feature on PJ Harvey, Bjork, and Tori Amos that blasted: "Hips. Lips. Tits. Power."

But the more women vocalized their objections, the more male artists seethed in response. The nodded-out angst of grunge soon gave way to the toxic masculine wasteland of nu metal. Songs such as Korn's 1996 "Kunts" ("Fuck you titty sucking two balled bitch / with a fat green clit, my big cornhoto bitch / oh shit, fucking ass licking piss sucking cunt") and Limp Bizkit's 1997 "Sour" ("Mellow out! / Bitch") took all the most misogynist elements of hip-hop and added gleeful middle-school immaturity to the mix. And the irony-as-defense motif was tweaked with new ingenuity by Eminem, a skinny White rapper from Detroit whose creation of a persona, Slim Shady, allowed him to fantasize about killing his girlfriend and disposing of her corpse, about drugging and raping a fifteen-year-old, and about ripping Hillary Clinton's tonsils out. (In a throwback moment, Eminem also joked on "Guilty Conscience" with Dr. Dre, who produced *The Slim Shady LP*, about the time Dre beat up the rapper and TV host Dee Barnes.)

Music is just music, the justification goes. Eminem was, in the tradition of hip-hop artists before him, giving voice to a marginalized faction of society immersed in disaffection and despair. (Like most rageful artists from the 1990s, he's also long since softened, tweeting in 2022 that he was outraged by the Supreme Court's erasure of reproductive rights.) But music isn't inert or always innocently detached from the ways in which we might interpret it. In 2006, a study by sociologists in Munich found that men who listened to sexually violent and aggressive lyrics—Eminem's "Superman" and Offspring's "Self-Esteem" were two of four songs included—were more predisposed to think negatively about women and to have thoughts of vengeance directed at them. Men in the study who listened to misogynist songs, when asked to make sandwiches for women and men, put more hot chili sauce in the sandwiches intended for women, suggesting a subconscious desire to punish them.

This theory had already been proven to some extent at Woodstock '99, a festival made notable for its dearth of female artists, extortionate prices, and horrific planning, as well as its eruptions of arson, rioting, and sexual assault. At the original Woodstock, as the feminist writer Ellen Willis observed in 1969, "the most exhilarating intoxicants were the warmth and

22

fellow-feeling that allowed us to abandon our chronic defenses against other people." At its sequel thirty years later, a lineup loaded with swaggering male acts scored an event where female attendees were reportedly harassed, groped, assaulted, and even gang-raped. The concert's ethos could be captured in a single song, which Limp Bizkit played that weekend: "Break Stuff."

ALSO IN 1999, one of music's defining feminist protests came to an end. Lilith Fair, the traveling festival founded by Sarah McLachlan, called it a day after three years of shows, $10 million raised for women's charities, and relentless derision from the media (some industry insiders reportedly referred to it as "Lesbapalooza"). McLachlan declared in a media conference that the festival's performers were "well into our 30s now, and we decided we wanted to have babies," demonstrating that even some of the most visible and empowered third-wave feminists in media were struggling to have it all. But there had also been a quiet restructuring in music that made some of the artists who'd played Lilith feel suddenly homeless in the industry. "It was like, Wow. Where did all the girls go?," the critic and writer Rob Sheffield told *Vanity Fair* in 2019. "You turn on rock radio, and there are no women at all. It wasn't gradual. It was a very abrupt backlash between '97 and '99. All over the music industry." Music's women had, almost overnight, been replaced by pop's girls.

Different theories abound as to how this shift happened. The musician Jaime Brooks argued that the new reliance on technology in music was giving more power to (almost exclusively male) producers and undermining the status of performers and songwriters. The Spice Girls' explosive financial success had certainly emboldened scouts and music executives to prioritize pop acts, particularly ones that could appeal to a teenage fan base. The spirit of camaraderie and collaboration that Lilith had embodied was also fundamentally at odds with the individualistic, soundbitey essence of Girl Power 2.0. But the singer-songwriter Meredith Levande, in a 2008 essay published in *Meridians*, pointed to a different target: the 1996 Telecommunications Act. With media companies liberated to own as many different broadcasting outlets as they wanted, she argued, the same networks that owned music channels also had a vested interest in playing more sexualized content that could point people to their own highly profitable pay-per-view networks. Music channels were, in Levande's theory, a gateway to porn. The more sexualized female artists were, the better.

Porn was an increasingly prominent cultural force in the late 1990s, before it became the default stylistic mode of the early 2000s. Around the mid-1990s, N.W.A.'s DJ Yella worked on the first of more than three hundred pornographic movies he'd direct over the course of his postmusic career. In 1996, Lil' Kim's debut record, *Hardcore*, opened with an interlude featuring a man going to an adult theater and paying for a ticket to a porn movie, unzipping his pants, and audibly masturbating as soon as Kim appears. (Kim told bell hooks in 1997 that her upfront schtick was about reclaiming power over her own sexuality, saying: "When you're younger, it's like, 'I don't want you to tell your family. No, don't tell your friends if we have sex.' But now it's like, 'We havin' sex. Tell whoever—make sure you tell 'em how good I did it!'") In 1998, the tired porn trope of the sexy schoolgirl was defibrillated by the video for "Baby One More Time," in which the sixteen-year-old Britney Spears thrust her hips with an intensity that, now, I find more unsettling than her exposed midsection. The video works because Britney seems so earnest, so unaware of how people might be reading her. She looks so *young*. This is teen sexuality as postmodern spectacle: a mishmash of transgressive allusions transmuted into a product that can't possibly be interpreted as serious.

By 2001, Britney was of age, Snoop Dogg was hosting the top-selling hardcore pornographic video in America, "Snoop Dogg's Doggystyle," and no one had to feign innocence anymore. That was the year Britney appeared in a TV ad for Pepsi, dancing so mesmerizingly in stonewashed jeans and a balconette bra that the world could only watch. (At the end of the ad, the former presidential candidate and noted Viagra spokesperson Bob Dole said, "Easy boy," and the joke was that he was addressing both his dog and his penis at the same time.) The following year, a Russian double act created by a child psychologist with a porn fixation debuted a pop video that adapted multiple fetishes at once: underage girls, school uniforms, wet T-shirts, and girl on girl. If lesbianism manifested in 1990s culture as a group singalong to "Closer to Fine" onstage at Lilith Fair, by 2002, it was something more sinister: sixteen-year-old t.A.T.u. kissing in the rain while being watched by adults and other schoolkids from behind a wire fence.

I can't help but read the arc of music in the 1990s as an explicit response to women's taking control of their art, their image, and their careers. Madonna became, throughout the decade, one of the most vilified public figures in history, deemed responsible for everything from unbridled commercialism to the excesses of celebrity culture. Janet Jackson's pillorying came later, when the appearance of her nipple during the 2004 Super Bowl halftime show offered an opportunity to redirect American outrage away from the Iraq War. After women rappers broke out on (relatively) equal terms during the 1980s, as Clover Hope argues in her 2021 book *The Motherlode*, from the mid-1990s onward, they were presented as being under the patronage of more powerful men: Lil' Kim and Notorious B.I.G., Eve and Dr. Dre, Nicki Minaj and Lil Wayne. "This system of control," Hope writes, "allowed men to keep power and promote women they considered worthy while keeping male approval as the key to success." And as outspoken women proved their power commercially and collectively as touring acts, they were replaced on the radio and in the media by teenagers who didn't—or couldn't yet—complain.

CHAPTER 2

Show Girl

Overexposure in the New Millennium

We need newness and excitement in fashion. That's what it's about—
that's what puts the fun in fashion. . . . We're always questioning people's
values. How much can you provoke? How much are they willing to show?

CALVIN KLEIN (1994)

In times of backlash, images of the restrained woman
line the walls of the popular culture's gallery.

SUSAN FALUDI (1991)

In 2004, the Deitch Projects gallery in downtown New York
debuted a splashy exhibition of new work by the photographer Terry Richardson, accompanied by the publication of
a book, both titled *Terryworld*. Richardson, by that point, was
the torchbearer and mascot for an aesthetic that was irresistible
at the beginning of the twenty-first century: a tacky, sweaty
mode of portraiture that gave Hollywood stars and random
passersby the same high-flash, semisurprised, not-quite-human
aura. *Terryworld* featured images of Kate Moss, sitting smiling
at a gold piano, her hair curled as if for prom; Pharrell Williams,

head tilted laconically as an unseen figure pulls on his tie; and Dennis Hopper, his face shrouded in smoke. Its most reliable subject, though, was Richardson's erect penis, which he captured in different settings: poking out of boxer shorts emblazoned with guns, pointing down at the head of a seemingly passed-out model whom Richardson holds by the hair; choking another model whose eyes display what appears to be discomfort.

Terryworld was printed by Taschen, the German art publisher whose opulent coffee-table books span everything from children's fairy tales to modern architecture to high-concept erotica. Priced at sixty dollars, or several times more for a signed, limited-edition copy complete with its own Richardson teddy bear, the book resisted categorization. It was not quite art or porn or fashion photography but a hybrid of all three that kept insisting it was also a big joke. It was the perfect emblem for the decade's defining aesthetic: porno chic. *Terryworld* the book began with a short biography and interview with Richardson in which he explained his mission. "I don't want to work in the porn industry," he told his editor, Dian Hanson. "If I was working for *Barely Legal* it wouldn't be a challenge. When you work in the fashion industry you can make things that are seen by so many people. That's the most subversive thing; to be out in the mainstream and get away with it."

The tone of Richardson's work—the way it flattens all its subjects into two-dimensional beings seen through the photographer's sweaty, cynical lens—might feel discomfiting now, but the substance of it, in that moment, wasn't unusual. In 2004, popular culture was consumed with porn, fixated on its trappings and tropes and aesthetics. That summer, the adult-film actress Jenna Jameson's memoir, *How to Make Love Like a Porn Star*, spent six weeks on *The New York Times* bestseller list. In May at the Cannes Film Festival, the British director Michael Winterbottom debuted his latest movie *9 Songs*, the story of a young couple's relationship that contained multiple scenes of unsimulated sex.

The peak of the year's X-rated activity came around New York Fashion Week in the fall, when a parade of A-listers came to take in what *The New York Times* described as fashion's current "erotic infatuation." The *Terryworld* opening was attended by Sonic Youth's Kim Gordon and the film director Vincent Gallo, who'd himself captured Chloë Sevigny performing oral sex in his 2004 movie *The Brown Bunny*. In a new book titled *Louis XV*, Juergen Teller documented himself in full-frontal flagrante with the actress Charlotte Rampling in a Paris hotel room, a series distinguished by the fact that Rampling remained largely clothed while Teller exposed everything. In October, stars including Ben Stiller and Rachel Weisz attended the opening of Timothy Greenfield-Sanders's *XXX*, a photographic series featuring porn actors that was accompanied by an HBO documentary. "Fashion has tremendous influence on how the culture changes," Greenfield-Sanders told a *Times* reporter. "And porn has had a tremendous influence on fashion."

He wasn't overstating things. Porn's dominance in popular culture came much like Ernest Hemingway's description of bankruptcy: first gradually, then suddenly. One of the consequences of the AIDS crisis was that explicit representations of sex were no longer taboo—they were vital for education and public health. Media reveled in its newfound freedom. By the end of the 1990s, a nation had been obliged to consider what stains on a blue dress signified; what, exactly, Hugh Grant was doing on the Sunset Strip; and whether John Wayne Bobbitt got what he deserved; while also wondering whether a person might sell themselves for a million dollars, as Demi Moore did in *Indecent Proposal*. Throughout the same decade, fashion photography had played with transgression: younger models, thinner models, heroin chic, S&M, a half-covered breast in the hallowed pages of *The New Yorker*. (It was Kate Moss's, photographed for a Calvin Klein ad.) Fashion, Guy Trebay wrote in *The New York Times*, had begun championing porno chic "even before art, video, music, and Hollywood got in on the trend, infatuated with the genre's flat lighting, its affectless subjects, its pine-paneled rec rooms and ugly consumerism."

By 2003, as if in active opposition to the abstinence-only conservatism of the George W. Bush presidency, sex had broken out from hipster magazines and edgy perfume ads into the mainstream. What felt novel was how *cool* it was, how supposedly empowering and liberating and potentially lucrative. In 2003, Moss pole danced—just a few months after giving birth to her daughter—in a black brassiere and panties in the video for the White Stripes' "I Just Don't Know What to Do with Myself," prompting a frenzied new craze for striptease workouts. That year, the British tabloid newspaper *The Sun* offered a £50,000 prize for the first couple to have sex on camera on the reality show *Big Brother*, and no one seemed to care that a journalistic institution was essentially commissioning sex or to find the offer even slightly unsettling.

At this point, pornographic imagery and tropes had also been wholly absorbed by popular culture. Not long after the British photographer Rankin was commissioned in 2001 to capture Queen Elizabeth II, he collaborated with David Bailey on a show devoted to female genitalia. Bailey, whose documentation of the swinging sixties had influenced the Michelangelo Antonioni film *Blow-Up*, was one of the most iconic names in British culture. Rankin was a cutting-edge portraitist and publisher. "It was all Rankin's suggestion," Bailey explained on the website for *Rankin and Bailey: Down Under*. "He'd seen a pussy photograph on the wall and we thought, 'Oh shit, let's do a pussy show together!'" The models for Bailey's extreme close-ups were a combination of student nurses and sex workers. For Rankin's series, high-profile models including Jodie Kidd and Laura Bailey were supposedly posed as though "engaged in sexual activity with Rankin and his camera," in order to assert their "dominance and control" and their "female sexual power." The exhibition, like *Terryworld*, featured an accompanying coffee-table book, priced at £350 a copy. (It's fair to assume that, as so often in fashion shoots, none of the models got a share of the profits despite their dominance and sexual power.)

Since the first moment of *Deep Throat* porno chic in the 1970s, the adult-film industry had been sending out a contradictory message for women and girls: that they could be most liberated while on their knees. By the aughts, as porn was being reclaimed as something fun, funny, loose—a casting-off of old sexual mores in order to celebrate our new, uninhibited, *millennial* freedom—very little had actually changed in terms of its power dynamics, its target audience, or the nature of its gaze. The same people who'd always had power and authority over how images of women were commodified and sold were simply repackaging an old product. And the more mainstream culture embraced porn's imagery, the more porn—to maintain its transgressive status—had to look out to the margins.

In his 2002 book *Striptease Culture*, the journalist and media scholar Brian McNair described the new wave of porno chic as not about porn per se but *representations* of it, investigations, pastiches that were being remade and transformed into "mainstream cultural artifact." Curious adults in creative industries were indeed playing with porn's material, cutting out and stitching together their own interpretations in the name of art. Often the process was as noteworthy as the product: In 2003, the journalists Victoria Coren and Charlie Skelton published *Once More with Feeling*, a book about their attempts to make a "different" kind of porn film in Amsterdam that layered hardcore tropes with intellectual detachment and jokey awkwardness. But for those of us who were teenagers not entirely versed in postmodern theory, we could be forgiven for seeing only this: In the early aughts, in any direction you looked, popular culture was constantly promoting and celebrating an "empowered" vision of sexuality that was wholeheartedly informed by male desire and male pleasure.

What's also become clear since then is that numerous women

did not come out from this moment unscathed. Several iconic aughts fashion brands have since been implicated in the predatory treatment of young models by powerful men: American Apparel, Abercrombie & Fitch, and Victoria's Secret. Terry Richardson, for his part, was unabashedly open, even flagrant, about all the ways in which he was abusing his power. In 2002, he told *Vice* about a shoot for the cult streetwear brand Supreme that "got a bit out of hand by the end. The woman producing the shoot got freaked out and had to leave. I think every person there fucked someone. It was intense." In 2005, he was sued for the first time by two models for invasion of privacy and emotional distress. In 2007, he shot the up-and-coming junior senator from Illinois, Barack Obama, the same year he told a magazine his advice for wannabe models: "It's not who you know, it's who you blow. I don't have a hole in my jeans for nothing." In 2010, he was confronted in public at Paris Fashion Week by the model Rie Rasmussen about his predatory behavior. In 2013, he directed the music videos for Miley Cyrus's "Wrecking Ball" and Lady Gaga and R. Kelly's "Do What U Want." (The latter, which supposedly featured Kelly hosting an "orgy" with Gaga's "anesthetized" body, was never released.)

When the magazine publisher Condé Nast finally ended its working relationship with Richardson in 2017—three years after well-publicized allegations by models sharing their experiences of being relentlessly harassed, manipulated, and coerced into sexual activity on shoots by him and his team—it was during a moment in which the #MeToo movement sparked reevaluations of the predation inherent in the fashion industry. But something else was happening in the aughts that was more complicated than one industry's abuses. Richardson's career ran parallel with a broader cultural fascination that would only intensify as the decade went on: the impulse to subject women—and men, but mostly women—to ruthless and often cruel exposure.

The roots of this era were established during the 1990s, when fashion's taste for transgression coalesced with a growing cultural interest in naked self-revelation. For the first time ever, people could disseminate images and videos of themselves online, to an unknowable audience. On television, people bared their most intimate secrets on daytime talk shows. And in fashion, the iconography of porn was being recontextualized into something that felt simultaneously more liberating and more modern—even if the reality turned out to be much the same as it had ever been.

TWO MAGAZINE PHOTO SHOOTS in particular captured the zeitgeist while anticipating what was ahead. The first was a 1990 cover shoot for *The Face* featuring a then-unknown sixteen-year-old from Croydon named Kate Moss. In photographs shot by Corinne Day, Moss grinned at the camera, crinkling her eyes and revealing jagged, uneven teeth; she puffed inelegantly on a cigarette; she ran naked out of the sea clutching a straw hat for modesty; she smiled at someone off camera, topless in a feather headdress and a string of love beads. The images were as much a repudiation of 1980s fashion, with its lacquered features and angular power wardrobes, as they were an assertion of new 1990s style: spontaneous, childish, imperfect. The tagline on the cover was "The 3rd Summer of Love," a nod to a euphoric rave culture that only sought pleasure and never wanted to grow up. The calamitous recession that began the month the cover came out would usher in a darker, more nihilist mood, but the image of Moss as a fragile young icon of 1990s femininity would stick, changing fashion's trajectory.

"We were just having fun," the shoot's stylist Melanie Ward remembered years later. "It was all very instinctual." (Day passed away in 2010.) There was no intention to present any kind of new movement, Ward said. Moss, interviewed in 2022 for the BBC radio show *Desert Island Discs*, remembered it differently, saying that Day bullied her into taking her top off and reduced her to tears. "I was really self-conscious about my body and she would say, 'If you don't take your top off, I'm not going to book you for *Elle*.' And I would cry. . . . But, you know, the pictures are amazing, so she got what she wanted and I suffered for them but, in the end, they did me the world of good. I mean, they did change my career." In 1992, Moss posed topless again for a Calvin Klein Jeans advertisement with the rapper-turned-actor Mark Wahlberg, which she said made her feel "vulnerable and scared. I think they played on my vulnerability. I was quite young and innocent. Calvin loved that."

It doesn't seem accidental that the early-1990s era of the

supermodel—strong, athletic, glamorous, unimaginably well-paid women—was followed so closely by the rise of the waif in the second half of the decade: frail, pallid, underage girls who didn't yet know how to negotiate or exert their power or assert their own boundaries. The iconic January 1990 *Vogue* cover by Peter Lindbergh featuring the jeans-clad Cindy Crawford, Christy Turlington, Naomi Campbell, Linda Evangelista, and Tatjana Patitz announced that the decade to come would be one of inclusive power and sisterhood. But the ideal didn't last. Fashion designers grew tired of dealing with the top models, who knew what they were worth and whose fame often overshadowed the clothes. Designers preferred girls. In her 2001 book *Fashion, Desire and Anxiety*, Rebecca Arnold quotes the booker Katie Ford observing late in the 1990s that "designers are looking for a very young look now. They want girls with a very straight shape—you don't have that in your 20s." The changing nature of desire was also an influence: During the AIDS epidemic, men were unabashed about being drawn to younger women with no sexual history. In 1992, the actress Drew Barrymore—seventeen at the time—posed naked for an *Interview* magazine spread shot by Bruce Weber. "In an age of creeping moral cowardice and paranoid image-control, our frightened culture and the movies that reflect it badly need a dose of fearlessness," the accompanying text declared, as though only the sexualization of underage girls could rescue America from intellectual and spiritual decline.

There are certain women who came up over and over again

in my research for this book, reappearing across different genres of culture and eras of history, embodying all the complexities and contradictions of performing womanhood in the public eye. Moss is one; Demi Moore is another. In 1991, Moore, pregnant with her second child with her husband, Bruce Willis, posed for a cover feature for *Vanity Fair*, shot by the photographer Annie Leibovitz. The editor of the magazine at the time, Tina Brown, had just had her own second child and wanted to capture Moore wearing a formfitting dress, flouting old norms that dictated pregnant women should only be photographed from the neck up. "I had been looking for a cover that would sort of turn the mood from the '80s right into the new '90s feeling of a slightly fresher era," Brown told CNBC in 2018.

When Leibovitz went to photograph Moore, she agreed to take a private picture of the actress nude, as a memento for Moore and Willis. But when Brown saw those photos, with Moore clasping her belly, radiating an unmistakable kind of maternal power, the editor couldn't let them go. Moore agreed to let the magazine use the photo, and the issue went to press, selling well over a million copies. Some retailers refused to sell it; others reportedly wrapped it in brown paper, like a porn magazine. The cover was extraordinary. It transformed the way pregnancy was portrayed in culture, destigmatizing women's bodies and encouraging a new kind of frankness regarding the physical state of gestating a child. Dozens of celebrities— Mariah Carey, Beyoncé, Britney Spears, Jessica Simpson, Serena Williams—later followed suit, with Williams in particular using coverage of her pregnancies to discuss the shocking mortality rate for Black women during childbirth and the discrepancies in medical care that they receive.

But Moore's cover also exemplified a shift that was coming in culture, as the 1990s leaned into confession, revelation, and self-exposure: a willingness to literally and figuratively bare it all in public. In 1990, the animal-rights organization People for the Ethical Treatment of Animals debuted a new campaign featuring nude celebrities under the tagline "I'd Rather Go Naked Than Wear Fur." *The Jerry Springer Show* debuted in 1991, compelling ordinary Americans to expose their most shameful secrets in order to get on television. In 1992, Sharon Stone uncrossed her legs in *Basic Instinct*. In 1994, Eva Herzigová posed for a series of eye-popping ads for Wonderbra, with captions such as "Hello Boys" and "Or Are You Just Pleased to See Me?" Shot by Ellen von Unwerth in black-and-white, the campaign capitalized on a new, vocally pro-sex faction in culture that was weary of "the puritanism and suffocating ideology of American feminism" and ready to embrace "the eternal values of beauty and pleasure," as Camille Paglia wrote in *The New York Times*.

Innovations in media helped capture the mood. Cameras were smaller, lighter, and more portable than they'd ever been and thus able to get into places they hadn't previously been able to access. In the mid-1990s, programming enthusiasts and extroverts began experimenting with a new mode of self-surveillant communication called "lifecasting." At the same time, technology was developing so rapidly that no one had the chance to build ethical frameworks to support it. When a tape of Pamela

Anderson making love with her husband was stolen in 1995 and then sold without her consent, the moment seemed to assert beyond doubt that the internet age would be postprivacy.

What happened to Anderson was emblematic of an ongoing negotiation in media over sexualized images of women. In their photo shoots, which captured iconic representations of 1990s femininity, Moss and Moore were both coaxed by photographers or editors to reveal more of themselves to the public than they'd intended. The theft and widespread sale of Anderson's tape—while much more obviously exploitative—also emphasized how little choice famous women had at that moment about what they were allowed to keep for themselves. Fashion, in its relentless pursuit of the novel, the edgy, the provocative, was pushing toward a heady new aesthetic of exposure.

ART HAD SEEN all this coming. From the 1960s onward, women artists had been parsing the unequal terms of the sexual revolution, using their own bodies as both subject and canvas. Madonna's 1992 book *Sex* understood itself as part of this tradition, while also anticipating the hypersexualized world of commercial self-presentation that was brewing. *Sex* was a graphic, high-concept coffee-table book of explicit content shot by the fashion photographer Steven Meisel and designed by Fabien Baron, a creative director for Calvin Klein. As Eminem would years later, Madonna created a persona to distance herself from the outrageous images depicted in *Sex*—an alter ego named Dita. "Everything you are about to see and read is fantasy, a dream, pretend," Madonna explains in the introduction. In images that pay homage to Robert Mapplethorpe, she poses in a nippleless black leather bra and thong, caressing her crotch and sucking on her own finger. In others, she goofs off, laughing and pulling faces as if to neutralize the tension of depicting herself bound to a chair, gagged, pulled tightly by her platinum-blonde hair.

Sex was novel mostly in the sense of who was photographed— one of the most famous women in popular music, a household name—and who was in charge: a woman. Considered through the lens of mainstream America, it was shocking. But within the context of the art world, it was simply part and parcel of an ongoing public discourse. If you consider Madonna a performance artist, as I do, with *Sex* she was placing herself in the lineage of artists such as Hannah Wilke, Joan Semmel, and Carolee Schneemann, who made work challenging art's sexualized depictions of women. In *Fuses* (1967), Schneemann filmed herself having sex with her partner and then attacked the film, cutting it, burning it, and painting directly over it to recontextualize it as a woman's creation. Semmel painted erotic portraits unmistakably framed from her viewpoint, looking down at her naked body during sex. Wilke posed topless in images she shot herself, covered in tiny vulvas shaped out of chewing gum. What all three artists sought to do was extricate them-

selves from the alienation of a lifetime of sexual imagery defined by and designed for men.

Sex, though less radically feminist in its intentions, was just as
preoccupied with power, as well as whether the exposed female
body is inherently dominant, vulnerable, or both. By the time it
appeared, artists were already experimenting with porn in ways
that Madonna, as a collector, would have been well aware of. In
1990, Jeff Koons began work on his *Made in Heaven* series, a
number of paintings, sculptures, and photographs that depicted
the artist having sex with his then-wife, the Italian porn star
Ilona Staller, aka Cicciolina. Presented in trite soft-focus, with
titles such as "Dirty Ejaculation" and "Ilona's Asshole," the
works seemed to represent the art world's commodification at
its most rampant. Looking back in 2010, the *New York Times*
critic Roberta Smith also wondered whether Koons, with minimal subtlety, was trying to reassert "white straight male privilege in an era when identity politics were ascendant."

The same year that *Sex* was published, the artist Cindy
Sherman—whom Madonna admires and has long compared
her chameleonic instincts to—debuted her series *Sex Pictures*.
The works, assembled out of pieces of anatomical female dolls
in sexually explicit and unnerving poses, were intended to comment on Koons's *Made in Heaven* series, which Sherman found
"puerile and sensationalistic," as she told *The New Yorker*. Her
photographs of disembodied orifices and dissected, sexualized
body parts seemed to implicate the viewer. If artists such as
Wilke were taking a risk in making work only a degree or two
removed from conventional pornography, Sherman was doing

the opposite: transforming the stylings of porn into something clearly grotesque and unnerving.

What Madonna was doing was different still, and because of her profile, it ultimately became much more influential over time. In presenting herself both as sexual subject and object, she was reclaiming some of the power that had been taken from her in the 1980s, when, while she was rehearsing for Live Aid, *Playboy* and *Penthouse* both announced they would publish nude photos of her taken when she was a teenager. The experience, her brother Christopher wrote, was liberating in that after the scandal, she had "nothing to lose anymore, nothing more to hide. . . . From now on, she is free to be as outrageous as she wants." As if to illustrate the postmodern concept of pastiche, Andy Warhol even turned the cover of the *New York Post* noting her defiance into a screen print: "Madonna on Nude Pix: So What!"

But it's also easy to see how *Sex* opened a Pandora's box of mainstream sexualized imagery that could not ever again be contained. The book was anarchic and perverse. It was also funny and irreverent. It proclaimed that sexuality for women was something to be celebrated, not stifled or shamed. But because of Madonna's extraordinary level of fame at the time of the book's publication, and how she fit within a stereotypically pornographic frame, the long-term impact was to license more and more sexual provocation in conventional media, reaching a tipping point during the aughts. The images in *Sex* were disruptive, but not enough. "Tragically, all that is transgressive and potentially empowering to feminist women and men about Madonna's work may be undermined by all that it contains that is reactionary and in no way unconventional or new," bell hooks wrote at the time. However radical *Sex* was intended to be, it could only be as subversive as its interpretation would allow.

And fashion, at least, was inclined to take the lesson of *Sex*'s breaking worldwide records for sales, especially when paired with the blockbuster success of Demi Moore's *Vanity Fair* cover. It was that much easier, post *Sex*, to argue that porn was art.

IN 1991, JEFFERSON HACK (the future partner of Kate Moss) and Rankin (the future photographer of Queen Elizabeth II and the *Down Under* vagina series) created *Dazed and Confused*, a zine that intended to promote an alternative to what its founders called a "synthetic leisure culture." Both were students at the time, at the London College of Printing. In the wake of the recession, real estate was cheap, and *Dazed* soon occupied an office in Soho below Corinne Day's apartment, smack in the middle of London's chaotic, hedonistic nightlife scene. Acid house and rave were the dominant aesthetic modes. Hack envisioned *Dazed* as pushing the boundaries of creative expression as far as they would go.

Along with *The Face* and *i-D*, two existing British magazines devoted to fashion and alternative culture, *Dazed and Confused* had an astonishing impact in the 1990s. For Generation X, obsessed with countercultural cred and disgusted by sellouts, it was an alt-chic bible. And for the fashion world writ large, *Dazed* was signaling where the rest of culture would soon follow. Rankin has said he saw *Dazed* as a "wolf in sheep's clothing"—a way to sneak conceptual art and disruptive ideas about culture into what looked like a straightforward style of publication. The magazine was noteworthy for publishing significant, groundbreaking images of trans models, older models, male models kissing, long before doing so was broadly acceptable in media.

Mainstream fashion magazines, terrified of being left behind, struggled to meet the moment. In 1993, British *Vogue* published a series of photographs shot by Day featuring Moss in a grimy London flat wearing lingerie, her posture hunched, the images defiantly unsexy and deglamorized for an underwear shoot. While some viewers interpreted them as calculated acts of rebellion—a middle finger to the industry and publication that commissioned them—others were unnerved by what they saw as the aestheticized exploitation of a teenager. One psychologist argued that the shoot bordered on child pornography. The issue was context: In an alternative magazine, few would have noticed, but in *Vogue*, the images signaled the normalization of an edgy, abrasive new style that rejoiced in going too far. Post-AIDS, against the backdrop of economic collapse, this mode of pictures reflected broader feelings of frailty and anxiety. More than ever before, fashion photography hovered in a space between advertising, social commentary, and contemporary art.

Sex was, inevitably, a theme: a way for photographers and editors to signal their transgressive credentials and for brands to gain mainstream exposure by offending the masses. Many photographers in this moment rejected the idea that they were working within the conventional realm of fashion advertising, seeing themselves instead as arbiters of cultural subversion. In 1994, Terry Richardson shot his first commercial campaign for the designer Katharine Hamnett, featuring upskirt images of models that revealed their pubic hair, something he later called "a happy accident." David LaChapelle's 1995 ad for Diesel featuring two sailors kissing was an open repudiation of the US military's "Don't ask, don't tell" policy on homosexuality. In an article for *Frieze*, Valerie Steele observed that Diesel's 1990s ads juxtaposed conventionally young and attractive models with banal, grotesque, or fetishistic scenes: adults in diapers, food play, even death. This kind of imagery, she noted, was "new to the media, having seldom been featured outside of pornography" and was presented with "an overarching tone of heavy-handed humour and sarcasm" that defied anyone to critique it.

By 1994, the fetish gear Madonna wore in *Sex* had also moved into fashion's mainstream. The September cover of *The Face*, shot by Ellen von Unwerth, featured the supermodel Nadja Auermann naked except for a rubber dog collar, heavy blue eyeliner, and shiny red lipstick. The image, as Arnold noted in *Fashion, Desire and Anxiety*, is perplexing because

Auermann exudes both "power as an emblem to eroticism" and her enslavement "to the poses and settings of the porn magazine." That same year, a *Mad Max*–inspired ad for Dunlop tires featured actors in rubber corsets and gimp masks. Magazines were also playing with concepts of power and vulnerability: The August 1995 cover of *Dazed and Confused*, shot by Rankin, featured a very young model in a striped dress lying on the floor sobbing, clutching her neck as if in pain. In 1997, the magazine ran a "scratch and see" panel over its Helena Christensen cover, teasing the opportunity to deface the model and reveal her breasts.

Images such as this one were presented as wry commentary on the exploitation that was rife within the fashion industry. For his *Hungry?* series in *Dazed*, Rankin photographed an underfed model, her too-big shirt pinned at the back with bulldog clips, ravaging a giant bar of chocolate. But something was getting lost in translation. At the same time, pornographic publications were rapidly adopting the style and design of highbrow glossies. By 2000, *The Face*'s "L'edition sexe," released in a pink plastic bag adorned with "XXX," was hard to distinguish from *Richardson*, an upmarket pornographic publication that *The Face* praised as a "beautifully shot fashion event sold in the Tate Modern, containing self-fisting yanks, wanking, and pissing Japanese teenagers."

Already, conventional media was taking note, capitalizing on the shifting boundaries of what brands could get away with regarding women. In 1995, the British publisher Felix Dennis had launched *Maxim*, a magazine that moved to the United States two years later and would eventually be published in sixteen editions across seventy-five countries. The magazine had bright, poppy visuals and the lowbrow simplicity of a frat house; it promised, on its cover, "Sex Sports Beer Gadgets Clothes Fitness." *Maxim* ranked female stars by hotness and joked ironically but insistently about sexual violence. Competitors soon followed suit: *Zoo*'s agony uncle once encouraged a reader to get over a breakup by cutting his ex's face, and *For Him Magazine* encouraged readers to calculate how much they were "paying" their girlfriends for sex. The ethos of *Maxim* also filtered into the nascent world of online media. In 2003, the *Gawker* founder Nick Denton launched *Fleshbot*, a sex-and-porn-oriented site that introduced itself by way of posting Paris Hilton's sex tape. Denton explained in an interview that he came from "the Felix Dennis school of publishing," where trashier meant better.

The flimsy boundaries delineating fashion, porn, art, and advertising had begun to collapse altogether. In 2003, Benetton announced a new exhibition at the KW Institute for Contemporary Art in Berlin of unpublished photographs shot by Terry Richardson for Sisley. In a press release, the company declared that "the meaning and artistic value of these photographs transcend their original function to become an expression of a manifest, transgressive sensitivity that is, however, so ironic that it enables the audience to overcome their immediate feeling of scandalized shock." One of the photos, of the model Josie Maran squirting milk directly from a cow's udder into her mouth, unmistakably staged to resemble a "money shot," was later included in *Terryworld*.

THROUGHOUT THE 1990S, porn's appropriation in certain cultural quarters enabled a new kind of genre that evaded definition. *Sofasosexy*, a 2002 exhibition by Rankin of photographs featuring porn actresses and models cavorting on a grubby orange couch, was described by its creator in one interview as "mucky pictures," "a piss-take, a real joke," and "just sex," as though anyone trying to find deeper meaning in it was entirely missing the point. *Naked London*, a 2000 book by the photographer Greg Friedler capturing "ordinary people first clothed, and then completely naked," seemed more like a documentary project, trying earnestly to find common ground among its exposed subjects rather than setting them up as postmodern punch lines. An unsettling 1999 photo spread by Richardson in *Dazed and Confused* that showed models including Eva Herzigová and Ivanka Trump hooked up to IVs in a medical ward was supposedly part of a campaign to raise awareness about giving blood, although it's hard not to read it now as emblematic of the way models are perceived: as human coat hangers, necessarily corporeal and vulnerable in nature but also absurdly interchangeable.

Fashion and art's experimentation with porn's motifs and

techniques was rapidly influencing mainstream culture, in ways that were heavily consumerist and stripped of irony. By 1999, porn had filtered all the way down from alternative media to the mall. The *Abercrombie & Fitch Quarterly*'s Christmas issue that year, titled "Naughty or Nice," featured nude photo spreads, mentions of oral sex and threesomes, and an interview with the porn actress Jenna Jameson, in which she was repeatedly harangued by the interviewer to let him touch her breasts. ("Do you ever get sore?" he asked her. "Absolutely!" she replied. "After my movie *Rocko*, I couldn't walk for two weeks.") The publication provoked outrage in the media, but the company's strategically sexual marketing to its teenage consumer base was sound: A 2000 *Time* story reported that sales had increased sixfold in just six years.

That year, R&B singer Sisqó's "Thong Song" peaked at number three on the *Billboard* charts, encapsulating how the G-string had been claimed by popular culture as a symbol of sexual power and freedom. Designers including Jean Paul Gaultier and Tom Ford (for Gucci) had already incorporated visible thong underwear in their 1997 spring/summer runway collections. By the early 2000s, the "whale tail," or the tiny strap of exposed underwear above a woman's low-cut clothing, had been modeled out in the world by Britney Spears, Christina Aguilera, and Paris Hilton. In 2001, the Victoria's Secret Fashion Show was televised for the first time, in a leering, strange broadcast on ABC in which the presenter Rupert Everett, at one point, rubbed his face up and down Heidi Klum's leg. The following year, Abercrombie & Fitch—whose consumer base was between the ages of thirteen and eighteen—started selling thongs imprinted with the words "Wink Wink" and "Eye Candy."

Visiting a 2024 retrospective of Rankin's work during the 1990s for *Dazed*, I was struck by how much of it appeared to directly influence or predict the style of the aughts. In one image, a woman's jean-clad backside was embroidered with the word "cheeky," long before pastel-colored Juicy Couture suits turned buttocks into walking billboards. In 1999, Rankin shot Kate Moss for a *Dazed* feature titled "Viva la Revolution," naked except for suspenders and stockings styled like a bandito's chaps. Three years later, David LaChapelle directed Christina Aguilera's "Dirrty," a wildly porn-inflected music video in which Aguilera (rebranded as "Xtina"), wearing chaps over red panties, writhed in a boxing ring while furries and heavily sweating men looked on.

While photographers in the 1990s had experimented with making art styled as though it were porn, a decade later, sex *was* culture. There was no need to pretend anyone was interested in anything else. After the release of *Striptease* and *Showgirls,* strip clubs were enjoying a renaissance, serving as the backdrop to countless music videos, and increasingly popular among women. At Sundance in 1999, two featured films included *American Pimp*, a documentary interviewing thirty different pimps about their careers, and *Sex: The Annabel Chong Story*, a portrait of the porn actress who attempted to set a world record by having sex 251 times in ten hours. The tendency toward self-exposure collided with a moment of porno chic in which memoirs about stripping and sex work felt suddenly ubiquitous: Tracy Quan's *Diary of a Manhattan Call Girl*, Belle de Jour's *The Intimate Adventures of a London Call Girl*, Michelle Tea's *Rent Girl*, Diablo Cody's *Candy Girl*. These works destigmatized sex work; they rarely glamorized it. They humanized and gave voice to the women who performed for everyone else's pleasure. But they also helped enshrine the idea that women's bodies were the ultimate millennial commodity.

What I remember most from this period was how little counterprogramming there was. Sexual objectification had been normalized and branded by a fashion industry that profited enormously in return. A 2000 ad for American Apparel was styled to look like a card advertising sex work, featuring amateurish shots of a young blonde woman posing awkwardly in a white thong and tank top. To many of us, underwear models and porn stars were the ultimate role models—avatars of commitment, liberation, and hustle. In 2003, when Snoop Dogg took two women wearing dog collars and leashes to the MTV Video Music Awards, few people protested. (A Getty caption simply noted that he was "observ[ing] the leash law" for New York City.)

Going back through the archives, I've come to think that what Ariel Levy called "raunch culture" in her 2005 book *Female Chauvinist Pigs*—a dominant cultural mode celebrating porn, sex, self-commodification, ironic sexism, and uninhibited self-exposure—started in fashion. It's an industry where the female body has long been sold, abused, and starved into submission, where men with power bully and manipulate and profit from the labor of girls with none. The sexual confusion of the 1990s, with its voyeurism and its fear of the future, created a space where it was all too easy to appropriate and commercialize female sexuality for profit, using pornography as both a look book and an instruction manual. But at the same time, porn was adapting to a world in which it was no longer on the margins. The more mainstream culture ripped off its imagery and its sexual excess, the more pornographers, to be able to stand out from the masses, had to go to extremes.

CHAPTER 3

Girls on Film

Sex Comedies from the
Multiplex to the Manosphere

To say that straight men are heterosexual is only to say that they engage in
sex (fucking) exclusively with (or upon or to) the other sex, i.e., women.
All or almost all of that which pertains to love, most straight men reserve
exclusively for other men. . . . Heterosexual male culture is homoerotic; it
is man-loving.

MARILYN FRYE (1983)

Cinema is a matter of what's in the frame and what's out.

MARTIN SCORSESE (2003)

Lately, having watched the 1999 comedy *American Pie*
more times than anyone over the age of eighteen should,
I keep coming back to Kevin. Caught within a movie
that rejoices in archetypes—nerd, jock, sex object, uptight
nag—Kevin (played by Thomas Ian Nicholas) is an odd anom-
aly, a dark-eyed, blandly handsome, weaselly absence of a character. He feels somehow off because *American Pie* is a gross-out
cringe comedy, but one with a surprisingly sweet heart. Jason

Biggs's Jim, suffering sexual humiliation after sexual humiliation, never sours or turns vengeful. Finch (Eddie Kaye Thomas) and Oz (Chris Klein) are redeemed from eccentric nerddom and jock-y cluelessness, respectively, by the movie's end. Stifler (Seann William Scott) is tortured for his sins with the Oedipal spectacle of his mother in flagrante with Finch.

So what's the matter with Kevin? He has no hobbies, no defining traits, no desires of note other than the one that consumes him: losing his virginity. Watch *American Pie* with Kevin front of mind and you'll start to notice his quiet cruelty, his pronounced lack of empathy. In his first scene, talking with his girlfriend Vicky (Tara Reid), with whom Kevin is trying with increasing desperation to have sex, the panic in his eyes when Vicky tells him she loves him is played for comedy. "Enough of this blow-job bullshit," he says to Jim later at a party, cavalierly bemoaning his status. "I've got to get laid already." He mocks Stifler for drinking the beer that Kevin recently ejaculated into, asking how the "pale ale" went down. After Jim accidentally broadcasts a video of himself bungling things with Nadia—twice—to the entire high school mailing list, Kevin callously greets his best friend as "minute man," prompting even beleaguered Jim to note that friends are supposed to be supportive.

And, crucially, it's Kevin who comes up with the device at the core of the movie—the pact among the four main characters to lose their virginity by prom or die trying. "It's gotta stay between us," he says, furtively, looking around Stifler's mom's oxblood-painted living room for anyone who might betray them. "Here's the deal. We all get laid before we graduate."

The others roll their eyes. They insist that this isn't a new idea, and it's hardly like they haven't been *trying*. Kevin persists, emphasizing that what they really need is accountability: "We'll be there to keep each other on track. Separately, we are flawed and vulnerable, but together we are the masters of our sexual destiny. . . . This is our very manhood at stake." He jumps up onto his chair, a paltry general leading his troops into battle. "This is our day. This is our time. And by God, we will not stand by and watch history condemn us into celibacy. We will make a stand. We will succeed. We will get *laid!*" The friends cheer triumphantly; the quest is on.

With its release, *American Pie* marked the beginning of a new golden age for what Hollywood dubiously calls the "teen sex comedy." Moviemaking tends to come in waves: an accidental hit, a wave of imitations that offer diminishing returns with each installment, a growing sense of exasperation among audiences, a new surprise hit, rinse and repeat. During the 1980s, the smash success of the debauched 1978 campus farce *National Lampoon's Animal House* inspired a string of exploitation-style comedies about teenagers and college students: *Meatballs, Fast Times at Ridgemont High, Porky's, The Last American Virgin, Revenge of the Nerds.* In 1984, *Hot Moves*—a comedy notable for its poster, in which four Lilliputian teenagers hang off the bottom half of a giant woman's red bikini—also featured friends making a pact to lose their virginities. Most of these works represented little more than a cash grab, a cynical attempt to capitalize on the consumer power of American teenagers, who were flush with pocket money and leisure time during the Reagan 1980s.

Sixteen Candles, also from 1984, signaled a sea change. The directorial debut from John Hughes, who'd previously written two National Lampoon follow-ups to *Animal House*, it centered the experience of Molly Ringwald's Sam and brought more emotional texture and drama to the genre. (It also featured the flagrantly racist parody Long Duk Dong and a scene in which Michael Schoeffling's Jake, the romantic hero, "lends" his passed-out girlfriend to another character to do whatever he wants with her.) What distinguished Hughes's movies from their predecessors was that they seemed at least to try to empathize with the turbulent inner lives of high schoolers. In 1985's *The Breakfast Club*, Ally Sheedy's Allison even gets a moment to skewer the precariousness of sexuality for girls: "If you say you haven't, you're a prude. If you say you have, you're a slut. It's a trap. You want to, but you can't, and when you do, you wish you didn't, right?" But by the late 1980s, particularly against the backdrop of AIDS, and in the wake of the box-office success of *When Harry Met Sally*, the teen sex comedy was all but abandoned for the more reliable formula of the will-they-won't-they adult romance. Collectively, our cultural imagination happily forgot about *Porky's* until 2018, when Brett Kavanaugh was nominated to the Supreme Court.

Knowing this, *American Pie* wore its anachronistic insecurities on its sleeve. When the script was being shipped around to studio readers, it bore the working label "Untitled Teenage Sex Comedy That Can Be Made for Under $10 Million That Most Readers Will Probably Hate but I Think You Will Love." Written by the twentysomething newcomer Adam Herz, who'd written a paper titled "Gross-Out Cinema" in college, the script updated the *Porky's* model for a late-1990s demographic. The tone is low (the aforementioned jizz beer, the opening interlude where Jim attempts to masturbate to a scrambled cable porn channel but is interrupted by his parents, the desecration of a homely apple pie), but the emotional intelligence is surprisingly high. The movie's moral compass is even honorable, if you squint the right way: The happiest character in the final scene is Oz, who gives up lacrosse glory for Heather (Mena Suvari) and declines to tell his friends whether he slept with her or not.

American Pie signaled the beginning of a new cultural fixation with adolescence: with the freedom, friendship, and misadventures it affords boys and with the sexual vulnerability it enforces on girls. I didn't find *American Pie* anything other than squirm-inducing when I watched it in 1999. Looking back, though, it appeared to connect intensely with the boys I knew, who were insistent on losing their virginities and often openly hostile to the girls whom they saw as thwarting them. Like Kevin, they seemed willing to scheme and emotionally blackmail and even bully their way toward sexual maturity. An endearing, absurd comedy, despite its best efforts, had helped affirm a culture of sexual entitlement in ways that would curdle and metastasize as the aughts went on.

In his book *American Pie: The Anatomy of Vulgar Teen Comedy*, Bill Osgerby notes how the movie differs from past generic predecessors, such as *Porky's* and *Animal House*, in that the characters have no institutional enemy, no tyrannical overlord to tear down. *"American Pie*'s young heroes . . . are not railing against social injustice or challenging corrupt authority figures," he writes. "Instead, they are on a more hedonistic quest for self-fulfillment via the heady thrills of sexual adventure and keg parties." I'd argue, though, that Jim, Oz, Finch, and especially Kevin do have a force that they're pitted against. The entire plot of *American Pie* is a quest to overcome male virginity, a state that the characters understand as pathetic at best and hierarchically unjust at worst. They are all involuntarily celibate. Sex is the goal, virginity the antagonist, and girls the gatekeepers—the ones who are standing in the way of the heroes' glorious and rightful destiny.

POPULAR CULTURE isn't an innocuous force; we don't go through adolescence—watching scenes and reading books and hearing jokes and listening to all kinds of dialogue—while wearing an invisible force field that bounces bad ideas away. We learn an awful lot of what we know from the stories we encounter. In the 1980s movies that Kevin and Brett Kavanaugh both grew up with, as the cultural critic Wesley Morris once summarized things, "girls got drunk, spied on, stuffed in car trunks and shopping carts, and laughed at." But during the 1990s, things got a little more complicated. The straightforward misogyny of *Porky's* and *Revenge of the Nerds* was replaced by filmmaking that saw girls as creatures with plenty of sexual agency of their own—maybe too much. The film historian Karina Longworth, on her podcast *You Must Remember This*, has analyzed in depth the trope of the 1990s Lolita: underage or teenage girls who were fetishized, revered, and feared on-screen in movies such as *Poison Ivy*, *Lolita*, *Wild Things*, and *The Crush*.

The influence of porn on these kinds of movies now feels undeniable, proffering barely legal cheerleaders, babysitters, stepdaughters, and schoolgirls, all fearless and too easily available. You can see its tropes start filtering into multiplexes throughout the 1990s and note the replacement of adult female sexuality with teenage "empowerment." In 1995, Alicia Silverstone, nineteen at the time, appeared in *The Babysitter*, a straight-to-video psychological thriller about three men—two teenagers, one adult—who are all sexually obsessed with the same girl. This was the year after Silverstone starred in three separate Aerosmith videos, one of which, "Crazy," features Silverstone and Liv Tyler—Steven Tyler's own daughter—playing Catholic schoolgirls who run away from school, shoplift from a gas station, flash the gawking attendant, enter "amateur night" at a strip club, and then collapse onto a bed with their cash prize. (In all three videos, Michael Musto wrote in a 1995 *Vanity Fair* profile, Silverstone played "a yearning, rebellious, mildly insouciant siren apparently designed to help usher young boys into puberty.")

Amy Heckerling's 1995 movie *Clueless*, in making Cher Horowitz's virginity part of its plot, only spelled out what other Silverstone products were implying: that teenage sexuality was the ultimate prize for any man worthy of claiming it. Movies of the 1990s thrilled at the gorgeously, inappropriately *young*, even if no lines were technically crossed: 1996's *Beautiful Girls* features a supposedly charming emotional relationship between the adult Timothy Hutton and a thirteen-year-old character played by Natalie Portman. In the 1990s, Longworth notes, *Esquire*'s annual "Women We Love" issue even featured a dubious sidebar, "Women We'd Be Willing to Wait For," featuring teenage stars—thirteen-year-old Kirsten Dunst, fifteen-year-old Christina Ricci—whom the magazine's editors couldn't help but be attracted to, even as they honorably pledged patience given the girls' tender ages. In 1997, as Adrian Lyne's adaptation of *Lolita* staged eroticized sex scenes between the characters of a fourteen-year-old girl and her forty-something stepfather, its star, the seventeen-year-old Dominique Swain, posed for the cover of *Esquire* to promote the movie, licking her finger in a denim playsuit.

But often, lines actually were crossed. *Kids*, Larry Clark's 1995 indie movie—purchased and distributed by Harvey Weinstein—has a six-minute opening scene featuring the "virgin surgeon" Telly cajoling a twelve-year-old girl into having sex with him, roughly brutalizing her while she begs him to stop, then laughing with his best friend afterward. *Kids*'s influence on 1990s film was profound. In oral histories and anniversary pieces, the people who made the movie always proudly claim that it could never be made today, as though subjecting prepubescent and teenage actors to prolonged rape scenes were something to be proud of, a hallmark of edgy cinematic fearlessness instead of creepy, callous disregard. ("Every dude was trying to bone Rosario on the movie," the screenwriter Harmony Korine told *Rolling Stone* in 2015 of the actress Rosario Dawson, who was fifteen at the time.) The opening scene of *Kids* is so intimately entwined with the performers, who kiss for several minutes, that you can see the beads of sweat on the twelve-year-old's face, the dull horror on her face when she realizes what she's "consented" to.

Kids was so shocking, so nihilistically, voyeuristically gloomy with regard to teenagers and sex, that everything that came after it felt safer by comparison. It was that much easier for Columbia Pictures to market *Wild Things*, an erotic thriller in which two Florida high schoolers, played by Neve Campbell and Denise Richards, celebrate pulling off a lucrative scam by having a threesome with their guidance counselor (Matt Dillon). It was simpler for Bernardo Bertolucci's 1996 *Stealing Beauty* to fixate on the question of who Lucy (Liv Tyler) will "give" her virginity to while the camera crawls over her body in a bathing suit—a question that the adults in the film debate and chew over at indecorous length. It was presumably also more defensible to have the movie's poster feature Tyler, naked and pouting, posed artfully in front of the rolling hills of Tuscany.

By the time *American Pie* came around, in 1999, it was cinematically commonplace to portray teenage girls as either scheming, hypersexual vixens or chaste, pluckable Madonnas. *Cruel Intentions*, released that summer, featured both, in the form of Sarah Michelle Gellar's Kathryn Merteuil—"You can put it *anywhere*," she tells her stepbrother, brandishing the prospect of anal sex as part of a sexual contract—and Reese Wither-spoon's Annette Hargrove, who volunteers at senior centers and once published an essay in *Seventeen* about saving herself for marriage. Movies during the 1990s tended to see girls either as exploiting their own sexuality for power or withholding it, also for power. In *Clueless*, Cher Horowitz fixates over the question of who to lose her virginity to—a decision much more complicated than one of desire. The movie was loosely adapted from Jane Austen's *Emma*, and the change in setting worked because the stakes of romantic attachment for an American girl in the 1990s were hardly less fraught than they would have been for an unmarried woman in the early 1800s: Cher sees her reputation, her social status, and her future as all being at stake.

Clueless, at least, gave Cher agency. What did girls want in the 1990s? The movies suggested: to be found desirable and to capitalize on that desire. *American Beauty*, which was released the same year as *American Pie*, positioned the character of Suvari's Angela as performing adult sexuality in a way that audiences could see through, even if Kevin Spacey's Lester couldn't. As Lester's porn-inflected fantasy, Angela flirts and poses and exudes mannered sexuality, even as Suvari is subtle enough as an actress to let us see how awkwardly it fits her. In scenes with Thora Birch's Jane, though, Angela is totally different: a tangle of goofy, bitchy energy, easily mockable and yet obviously vulnerable.

Voyeurism is a recurring theme in the movie, and for all its prurience, I'm grateful to *American Beauty* for how it shows Angela's performing eroticism for the male gaze in the way all teenage girls learn that they're supposed to do. The film allows us to see that her displays of sexuality are dishonest, far removed from what she might actually want if she were given the space to figure it out. That *American Beauty*, in fetishizing Angela as a teenage cheerleader for adult audiences, is also replicating the same trap it's smart enough to identify is a paradox I can't unwind. Teenage boys on film are simple in a way that does them a disservice. They want to get laid, as Kevin puts it, and they'll go to absurd, heroic lengths to do so. What girls want in movies is portrayed as being much more complicated, which both deters boys from trying to figure it out and turns sex into a power struggle where the terms can never be equal.

COMPREHENDING AND EXPRESSING sexuality, for girls, is complicated enough even without the additional concern of who else might be watching. The scene in *American Pie* that now seems the most indefensible begins when the boys are assembled in the library, marveling that Shannon Elizabeth's Nadia is coming over to Jim's house to study after ballet practice. "There's gonna be an Eastern European chick naked in your house, and you're not going to do anything about that?" Stifler asks, aghast. "What am I gonna do, huh? Broadcast her over the internet?" Jim replies. Kevin whips his head around from the next-door table, with urgency: "You can do that?" Jim knows enough to know that the idea is morally reprehensible, but he's shamed into it by Stiflerian logic: "Man, if you don't have the guts to photograph a naked chick in your house, how the hell are you gonna sleep with one?"

Jim sets up his webcam, quickly sends the link to a handful of contacts in his address book, invites Nadia into his room to change out of her ballet clothes, then sprints over to Kevin's house to watch her undress. "Now we're in business," Kevin says, as Nadia—a fantasy bombshell played by a twenty-five-year-old actress with long, tanned limbs and apparent breast implants—peels off first her shirt, then her shorts, then her bra. Instead of changing, she rifles through Jim's drawers, finds his stash of explicit magazines, and then starts masturbating, a scenario that makes no sense in any realm other than porn. The boys watching are beside themselves. "If you *ever* had a chance with Nadia, this is it," Kevin tells Jim. But before Jim can sprint back, Sherman alerts Kevin to the fact that Jim addressed the email wrong, meaning Nadia is currently being broadcast without her knowledge to everyone on their high school mailing list.

What happens next is set up as humiliating for Jim: Instead of triumphantly scoring with Nadia while his friends watch, he prematurely ejaculates, twice, witnessed by the entirety of his school community. Nadia, in fact, isn't seen again in person: An exchange student from the Czech Republic, she's immediately sent home in disgrace by her host family after the incident, bearing the brunt of the consequences despite having had no idea what was happening to her. Jim isn't disciplined by his school or even reprimanded. The implication in the movie is that his humiliation is punishment enough. After all, he didn't intend for so many people to see it. Only he and his friends were ever supposed to be watching.

The idea of virality, the awareness that something posted online or shared with one other person could spread all the way across the world, as irrepressible as knotweed or measles, hadn't quite coalesced in 1999. This was just two years after another bombshell, Pamela Anderson, had become the first celebrity to have footage of herself having sex disseminated on the internet without her consent, after a home video of her and her husband at the time, Tommy Lee, was stolen from a safe in their Malibu home. Now, more than a quarter of a century later, it's easy to see that what happened to Anderson was monstrous, a distinct kind of assault. But in the late 1990s, the rise of amateur porn as a genre, and the emergence of people willing to broadcast the intimate moments of their lives online, had made the boundaries between public and private sexuality seem hazy. When Anderson sued the company distributing and profiting from her tape, its lawyers told her that because she'd previously posed for *Playboy*, she had no right to claim she was being victimized.

This was how one of the most famous women in the world lost the right to a private sexual life. Is it surprising that men and boys interpreted for themselves a tacit right to take and share any images they chose? The message in *Porky's*, in *Screwballs*, and even in *American Pie* is that girls secretly *want* to be spied on—that becoming the object of someone's invasive gaze is affirmation of a distinct kind of value. *Girls Gone Wild* had debuted the same year as Pamela Anderson's stolen tape, selling videos in which college girls and often high schoolers willingly revealed their breasts, made out with each other, and performed stripteases on camera, all for the low, low compensation of branded merchandise and dubious street cred. The appeal of the franchise was that the girls caught on tape were so normal, *so familiar.* They could be anyone's lab partner, anyone's roommate's stuck-up ex. The objectification of one girl thus became the suggested discrediting of an entire generation: If these women were willing to show everything, could *anyone* complain if they were secretly being captured on camera? By 2005, "revenge porn" wasn't yet a recognized term, but the genre had its own website, exgfpics.com, which offered a space for lust cut with grievance and even hate.

When *American Pie* was released, the members of its creative team were quick to assert that their movie was more enlightened than most of its predecessors. Paul and Chris Weitz, the film's director and producer, even said they'd tried to watch *Porky's* as research but couldn't get through it, given so many, in their words, "terrifying instances of misogyny." Adam Herz, who wrote the screenplay, insisted that he "didn't want the girls to be your typical sex objects, the clichéd teen-comedy stereotypes. So I made sure that in whatever I wrote, I gave them as much credit, if not more, than the guys." In theory, this is a nice idea: Osgerby, in his book, notes that the female characters are given more depth than in standard teen sex comedies and are afforded space to consider sexuality for themselves. They're not two-dimensional objects, but nor are they models of self-actualization. Natasha Lyonne's Jessica, I'd argue, is the most truthful—the consummate example of a girl who's empowered herself by adopting a swaggering, chauvinist persona. "What do you expect him to drive to Cornell for?" she asks Vicky, when the latter is agonizing over whether to have sex with Kevin. "Milk and cookies?"

But *American Pie*, in trying to give its female characters agency over what happens in their sexual lives, also underscores that they are the gatekeepers. With the exception of Alyson Hannigan's Michelle, who's also revealed in the final act to be as callous and horny as Stifler, what the girls *want* is much less shaded than what they allow. The boys are the ones cajoling and wheedling and pleading for sex; the girls are the objects of resistance. The movie offers no insight into why that might be. There's no sense in the movie that any characters could be stigmatized or shamed for having sex; no fear of teen pregnancy; no shadow of disease or danger. This isn't to say that sex should have to be associated with any of these things. It's to note that in excluding them from its utopian narrative, *American Pie* makes the decision its female characters are reckoning with into an arbitrary one, which in turn makes it easier to blame them for withholding what the guys want—what they in fact *need* in order to complete their heroic, fraught journey from boy to man.

While the boys get to experience coming-of-age stories, the girls, having been imbued with all the sexual privilege and presumed experience, are allowed no such awakening of their own.

And so Nadia—humiliated, entrapped, intimately exposed to an entire town, sent away from the United States in disgrace—never gets to express to Jim what his actions meant to her. Instead, she's just presumed to have forgiven him and even returns to claim him in the sequel. She's less a real, authentic character than a prop, a pair, a punch line.

TO GIVE *AMERICAN PIE* credit for a moment, it's infinitely smarter, more thoughtful, more sensitive than the influx of teen comedies that came in its wake. As the Bush era unfurled, audiences delighted in movies with an adolescent mindset that rejected adulthood in favor of puerile antics. The worst, to my mind, is *Date Movie*, a 2006 parody of various rom-coms starring *American Pie*'s Alyson Hannigan and Jennifer Coolidge. Hannigan wears a fat suit in the opening scenes to play Julia Jones, a lonely single woman who notes in her diary that her weight is 389 pounds and her alcohol intake—in a dig at Hannigan's *American Pie* costar—is "Tara Reid status." Early in the movie, Julia leaves her apartment and dances joyfully in the street to Kelis's "Milkshake," her face exuberant, her energy radiant. It's a spectacle that the movie presents as wholly disgusting because Julia is fat: When she flashes her underwear at a construction worker, hoping to be catcalled, he takes out a nail gun and shoots himself in the head. When she dances by a fire truck, the firefighters turn the hose on her. When she dances down the street, men in button-downs flee from the sight of her, screaming.

Movies in the aughts *hated* women. Not all of them, and not all equally egregiously, but most. This was the decade of *Shallow Hal* and *Knocked Up*, *White Chicks* and *Bringing Down the House*. Women tended to be punch lines or footnotes or both. "Let's be honest," a studio executive told Tad Friend in a 2011 profile of Anna Faris in *The New Yorker*. "The decision to make movies is mostly made by men, and if men don't have to make movies about women they won't." In a decade dominated by franchises, genre films, sequels, prequels, and remakes, there was minimal interest in making products that were assumed to alienate 50 percent of cinemagoers even before the ink was dry on the contract. Teenagers were still a key demographic: By 2001, there were 31.6 million of them in America, and their discretionary spending was worth $172 billion a year, up 40 percent from 1998. And men, it was presumed, called the shots on what couples went to see on date nights. But more than ever, too, masculinity was in flux, with a new category, "emergent adulthood," describing twentysomethings who—while technically all grown up—still identified enough with adolescent humor, coming-of-age stories, and youth-oriented franchises to make those kinds of movies hugely profitable. Of the fifty highest-grossing films during the aughts, only two (*The Matrix Reloaded* and *The Passion of the Christ*) had a rating higher than PG-13.

Faris's career is a neat microcosm of what movies in the

aughts offered women. In 2000, alongside *American Pie*'s Shannon Elizabeth, Faris had her breakout role as Cindy in *Scary Movie*, a Wayans brothers product whose one selling point is that it exposes how homogeneously White teen movies had been up till that point (and would be long after). A parody of the teen slasher pics of the 1990s, *Scary Movie* took the puerile jokes and gross-out scenes of vulgar teen comedy and added a flagrantly misogynist edge. In the opening scene, Drew (Carmen Electra) is chased by a masked, knife-wielding killer who tears all her clothes off; after she runs through a series of sprinklers, stopping to adjust her cleavage, he attempts to stab her in the heart but, disgusted, pulls out her silicone implant instead. Brenda (Regina Hall), Cindy's best friend, goes to a movie and so exasperates the other filmgoers by talking on her cell phone that they collectively murder her, each stabbing her one by one until an elderly woman slits her throat. The scene is a nasty joke that relies on the audience's hating verbose Black women as much as the filmmakers apparently do. When Faris's Cindy is hooking up with her boyfriend and he goes to take off her thong, her pubic hair is so voluminous that it occupies the entire bottom half of the screen, requiring him to pull out a literal hedge trimmer and safety glasses to get to third base. After they have sex, he ejaculates with such force and volume that Cindy is propelled onto the ceiling, pinned and wriggling, like a bug being power-washed.

Somehow, Faris is luminously charming in the movie—and much funnier than she should be. "It was perfect casting," Keenen Ivory Wayans, the director, told Friend, "because Anna was new to the world, full of love and delight, but not sexually advanced." She could be sexualized, in other words, without seeming like a slut. *Scary Movie* grossed more than $275 million and spawned four more films in the franchise, three of which starred Faris. In 2002, she also appeared in *The Hot Chick*, a movie in which Rob Schneider's scuzzy small-bit criminal accidentally switches bodies with Rachel McAdams's high school cheerleader, mostly so Schneider can impersonate a vapid teenage girl and McAdams can have a pole-dancing scene in a fuchsia vinyl bikini. A year later, Faris was the single funniest person in *Lost in Translation*, playing an obnoxious actress. She took a tiny role in *Brokeback Mountain* to try to prove her dramatic chops, then was slapped on the ass by the director Ivan Reitman in 2006 while filming *My Super Ex-Girlfriend*, she revealed years later. "I hated being on that movie so much I was glad when it bombed," she said in the 2011 *New Yorker* profile. "These roles are destroying a generation of boys."

Of all the paler imitations of *American Pie*, none was interested in the way the original film considered negotiations of masculinity, homosocial relationships, or women. Instead, movies such as *Road Trip* (2000), *100 Girls* (2000), *Tomcats* (2001), *Sorority Boys* (2002), and *EuroTrip* (2004) mimicked the humor of bodily disgust, the voyeurism, the crass antics and borderline abusive treatment of women, gay people, trans people, anyone not White and male and wearing cargo shorts. And the celebration of juvenilia was so effective that it began filtering into movies aimed at adults, in what felt like a defensive retreat from maturity: *Old School* (Luke Wilson's cuckolded attorney establishes his own frat house), *Wedding Crashers* (Owen Wilson and Vince Vaughn use weddings to have sex with women in an emotionally vulnerable state), *Knocked Up* (Seth Rogen and his stoner crew are appalled when he gets an astonishingly beautiful and successful TV presenter pregnant), *17 Again* (Matthew Perry's sad-sack middle-aged man is whisked back into the Zac Efron–shaped body of his seventeen-year-old self).

This particular genre of films, occasionally categorized as the "bromance" or the "hommecom," was so successful during the aughts that it almost obliterated the romantic comedy altogether, edging out the one category of picture that—often but not always—understood that women had value and offered actresses leading roles. During the rom-com's golden age in the late 1980s and early 1990s, movies portrayed women as fully realized, flawed human beings whose experiences were centered and whose certainty that they were worthy of love was affirmed by the plot. But bromances, as Beatriz Oria wrote in 2022, pushed "women to the margins in one of the few women-centric genres in Hollywood," while featuring "male characters perpetually stuck in adolescence whose romantic relationships rarely seem as fulfilling as their homosocial bonds." Women, even when technically playing the romantic other to their man-child leads, tended to be stereotyped as shrill, sexless nags or trampy, adulterous harpies. In 2008, after Katherine Heigl told *Vanity Fair* that she considered the treatment of women in *Knocked Up* to be "a little sexist," she was condemned by Rogen and the movie's director, Judd Apatow, for not playing ball.

For women to gain access to such a male-dominated sphere,

they had to be crafty. In the mid-2000s, frustrated with the roles she was getting, Faris came up with the idea for *The House Bunny*, the story of a Playboy Playmate who's evicted from the mansion when she turns twenty-seven—"fifty-nine in bunny years"—and finds a job working as a house mother for a sorority. Faris and the film's cowriters, Karen McCullah and Kirsten Smith, pitched the movie nineteen times, selling it finally to Adam Sandler's Happy Madison production company after Faris showed up, in Smith's words, "in a miniskirt, there ten minutes ahead of time." The movie looks a lot like a raunchy teen comedy—Faris teeters around in furry mules and a pink balconette bra, and transforms her slovenly, tomboyish charges (including a young Emma Stone) into knockout babes—but offers sly metacommentary on Hollywood tropes and all the things women have to do to be accepted as fully human. In 2010, Stone starred in the slyly subversive *Easy A*, a *Scarlet Letter* update that skewered the double standard for teenage girls.

By 2011, a generalized anxiety about women, raunch culture, and sexuality surfaced in *What's Your Number*, a genial comedy directed by Mark Mylod (later of Emmy-winning *Succession* fame). Faris stars as Ally, a thirtysomething woman who's terrorized by a magazine article claiming that 96 percent of women who have more than twenty sexual partners in their lifetime never get married. Intent on settling down, Ally decides to track down all nineteen of her former lovers in the hope that one of them might be marriage material. The movie was a flop (critics compared it unfavorably to *Bridesmaids*, released a few months earlier), but Faris is winning, and *What's Your*

Number has a distinct thesis underneath the pratfalls. Ally's exes, generally, are awful: commitment-phobic, creepy, power abusers, obsessed with puppets. For years she's been running around, trying her best, openheartedly doing her utmost to connect with people. Is it possible, the movie wonders, that she's not actually the problem?

IF ANNA FARIS'S career can be understood to represent what women (or at least, White women) experienced in the aughts, the creative trajectory of the director Todd Phillips offers a darker encapsulation regarding men. After starting out as a documentary filmmaker in the late 1990s—profiling the scatological punk artist GG Allin, fraternity culture, and Phish— Phillips's first comedy was the 2000 movie *Road Trip*, starring Breckin Meyer and *American Pie*'s Seann William Scott as college students on a mission to retrieve an incriminating sex tape. Phillips's second, *Old School*, helped usher in the age of the adult frat comedy. Next came a cinematic remake of *Starsky and Hutch*, where women appear only to strip in front of the speechless detectives in a locker room or have a threesome with Hutch. Phillips's 2006 movie *School for Scoundrels* remade a 1960s British film into a sour comedy about a manipulative professor who teaches alpha masculinity to insecure softies. In 2009, he debuted *The Hangover*, a movie about a Vegas bachelor party gone wrong that grossed almost half a billion dollars on a $35 million budget. "The one-liners on my movies sound really retarded," Phillips told *The New York Times* that year, in a piece that noted how he'd made cinemas a safe space for "countless more regressive male comedies."

Two *Hangover* sequels followed, and then 2016's *War Dogs*, an erratic but topical adaptation of a true story about two incompetent arms dealers. But in 2019, Phillips had the critical and commercial hit of his career with *Joker*, a stand-alone, 1980s-set narrative based on the DC Comics character about a lonely outcast and aspiring clown who becomes a murderer with a cult following. The movie came about in part, Phillips told *Vanity Fair*, because he was finding it increasingly difficult to make comedies amid a more enlightened Hollywood mood and was tired of being critiqued by "30 million people on Twitter." Liberally cribbed from Scorsese movies, *Joker* told the story of Arthur Fleck, an outcast with a neurological condition that induces outbursts of uncontrollable laughter. Over the course of the movie, Arthur is beaten up, preyed upon, bullied, and publicly humiliated when he attempts to perform his stand-up routine. When budget cuts deprive him of both his therapist and his medication, he unravels, shooting a talk-show host on live TV in an act that's as much about performance as it is violence.

I found *Joker*, the first time I watched it, to be an enthralling portrait of disintegration, a man and a society breaking down in tandem, spiraling into horror. In *IndieWire*, David Ehrlich agreed, but also found it "incendiary, confused, and potentially toxic," a movie "about a homicidal narcissist who feels entitled to the world's attention." That sense of entitlement, to me, is what makes *Joker* such a potent, disturbing work and such a fascinating locus in the arc of Phillips's career. For two decades, Phillips had been making movies that seemed to coalesce with perceptions of White masculinity writ large: fratty antics, disgruntled self-pity, midlife ennui. *Joker* was something infinitely darker: toxic insecurity calcifying into brutal, theatrical, nihilist spectacle. It was easily the most artful and agitating thing Phillips had ever made. And it was all the more troubling for how it connected with reality in 2019, one year after a self-described incel drove a rented van into a crowd in Toronto, killing eleven people, five years after the son of a film director killed six people in Isla Vista in an intentionally political act, and seven years after a mass shooter killed twelve people at a midnight screening of *The Dark Knight Rises*, a movie featuring the Joker.

At the beginning of this chapter, I referred to Kevin and his friends as "involuntarily celibate." There's a difference, though, between the unhappy virgin, a long-standing movie-comedy trope, and the incel, a twenty-first-century term associated with virulent misogyny, sexual entitlement, and even acts of terrorist violence. The term *incel*, as the philosopher Amia Srinivasan writes in her 2021 book *The Right to Sex*, can "be applied to both men and women, but in practice it picks out not sexless men in general, but a certain kind of sexless man: the kind who is convinced he is owed sex, and is enraged by the women who deprive him of it." In 2014, after Elliot Rodger went on his murder spree in Isla Vista, the *Washington Post* film critic Ann Hornaday published a column arguing that the "outsized frat-boy fantasies" that had dominated the last decade in film were at least partly at fault for a woman-hating culture that Rodger represented. "If our cinematic grammar is one of violence, sexual conquest and macho swagger—thanks to male studio executives who green-light projects according to their own pathetic predilections—no one should be surprised when those impulses take luridly literal form in the culture at large," she wrote.

Hornaday was immediately excoriated by the actor Seth Rogen and the director Judd Apatow for citing their movie *Neighbors*, with Apatow accusing her of using "tragedy to promote herself with idiotic thoughts." The critic responded that she had intended not to single out any one director or movie as being in any way responsible for Rodger's horrific acts but rather to parse whether Rodger's specific resentments could have been informed by the filmmaking culture in which he grew up. And with regard to that idea, the 137-page manifesto Rodger left behind does seem strikingly informed by what a lifetime of visual storytelling told him about sex and power. The document, which takes the form of a chronological biography narrating his path to what he calls his "Day of Retribution," is studded throughout with details about movies Rodger loved as a child, the particular kinds of fantasy stories he was drawn to, the video games he took comfort in, and the images that shaped—and possibly warped—his psyche and sexuality.

At the age of eleven, he writes, a friend whom he'd met in a chat room sent him pornographic images, crystallizing his early ideas about which kinds of women are objects of desire. He recounts watching *Jurassic Park*, *Star Wars*, and *The Lord of the Rings*, and then the "traumatizing" time he sees an older teenager watching hardcore porn at an internet café. He decides to move to Isla Vista after watching the Santa Barbara–set movie *Alpha Dog*, which he writes "depicted lots of good looking young people enjoying pleasurable sex lives . . . I had the desperate hope that if I moved to that town I would be able to live that life too." He delights in the first season of *Game of Thrones*. He buys a gun. "Who's the alpha male now, bitches?" he thinks to himself. In his epilogue, after laying out the plan for his attack, he concludes that "the ultimate evil behind sexuality is the human female. They are the main instigators of sex. They control which men get it and which men don't."

He was by no means alone in feeling this way. Comedies had long presented sex as something girls had to be tricked or cajoled into agreeing to—a byproduct of sidelining adult female sexual choice in favor of fetishized teenage seduction or acquiescence. In an interview, the producer Chris Moore once said that what appealed to him about *American Pie* was this exact same quality: "The girls ultimately decide who has sex in the movie." This is a lot of power to give to a teenage girl, and yet without it, girls have no choice at all. (In the 2009 comedy *Observe and Report*, Seth Rogen's character has sex with Anna Faris's character while she's passed out after taking pills and drinking excessively, a fact that is supposedly neutralized by a moment when she briefly wakes up to chide him for stopping.) Obviously, no one movie is responsible for acts of misogynist violence. *American Pie*, it's easy to forget, was released just a couple of months after Columbine. People tried with some insistence at the time to connect that atrocity to popular culture and were rightfully shut down.

And yet, in the ten years since the Isla Vista killings, the incel community has often defined its ideology by drawing directly from movies: from the frustrated masculine disaffection of *Fight Club*, from the "red pill" architecture of *The Matrix*, from *Taxi Driver*, the same portrait of Travis Bickle's psychotic alienation that Phillips drew from with *Joker*. Meanwhile, a 2021 study by the British Government Equalities Office on the relationship between porn use and violence toward women also found that TV shows and movies were highly cited by frontline workers dealing with offenders as "narratives that contributed to systemic gender inequality and sexual expectations." And a 2021 study conducted by two researchers in the United Kingdom found that the language used in incel forums is often identical to the language used in mainstream pornography, with both routinely employed to dehumanize, degrade, and sexually humiliate women. (The old standards of "bitch," "cunt," and "whore" still apply, but so do neologisms such as "meathole," "foid," and "roastie," the latter of which is used to refer to a woman who's had so many sexual partners that her labia supposedly resemble roast beef.)

Watching *Game of Thrones*, Elliot Rodger would have seen countless scenes of sexual violence and sadism; the lesson for Daenerys in the first few episodes is that the man she's been sold to will rape her less violently if she can try to be more of a willing participant in her own assault. From 2000s movies and porn alike, Rodger could have internalized that the only attractive women are large-breasted, hairless, thin, and White. Picking virtually any comedy from 1999 to the year he murdered six people, he could have buffeted his conviction that sex is something all young men are entitled to, a heroic path to manhood that affirms someone's value while negating, almost entirely, what women choose or desire. Not to mention that the movies he watched almost universally twisted any kind of male need for love and connection into the more comic and less stigmatized desire to get laid. It's impossible to argue that any of these cultural works was responsible for what he chose to do. But it would also be myopic not to consider the footnotes that Rodger himself gave us. "I'm twenty-two years old and still a virgin, never even kissed a girl," he says in a video he uploaded to YouTube before his attack. "College is the time when everyone experiences those things such as sex and fun and pleasure. In those years I've had to rot in loneliness; it's not fair."

The researcher Shannan Palma has analyzed to what extent the tenets of incel entitlement seem drawn from what she calls "fairy-tale logic," or "a mode of magical thinking typified by the belief that certain functions, fulfilled correctly and in the right order, lead to predictable outcomes." Stories—from *Beauty and the Beast* to *Knocked Up*—have long affirmed the idea that undesirable men can be redeemed by beautiful women. (*Beauty and the Beast*, Maria Tatar has argued, was originally written to prepare young French girls for arranged marriages to wealthy older men, and the feeling that they might have been dispatched by their families to share their lives with a monster.) This no more indicts the Grimm brothers for incel beliefs than it does Judd Apatow, who told *The New York Times* in 2007 that there was a "nerd's fantasy" embedded in many of his films: the wish that "somebody would take the time to get to know us, and love us, warts and all." It does, though, point to the stickiness with which stories take root inside our minds. Especially when there's no counternarrative.

Incel mythology, with its "chads" and "stacys," is at least as ridden with archetypes and moralistic projection as any children's story. And the resentment incels feel seems to be based on what they see as feminism's fundamental perversion of the way things ought to be: the "refusal" of women to play their proper roles in redeeming men and offering them a happy ending. "The potential for *violence*," Palma writes, "crystallizes in fairy-tale logic when the only way to move one's story forward is to punish the villain." If the hero's curse, as seen in *American Pie*, is unwanted virginity, then who is the villain who cursed him? Inevitably: a teenage girl.

CHAPTER 4

Girl Fight

Regression and Representation in the Early Years of Reality Television

Television is our culture's principal mode of knowing about itself.
Therefore—and this is the critical point—how television stages the world
becomes the model for how the world is properly to be staged.

NEIL POSTMAN (1985)

Visibility is a trap.

MICHEL FOUCAULT (1975)

During the late 1990s, two women named Jennifer seemed to intuit precisely where the next decade of popular culture would lead. One was the actress Jennifer Lopez, who launched her music career in 1999 with a single, "If You Had My Love," and an accompanying video that reads now as strikingly prophetic. This was a couple of months before the Dutch producer John de Mol would debut a new reality-television show called *Big Brother*, a year before fifty-one million people in the United States would watch the season finale of *Survivor*, and twenty-five years before Lopez would turn her romantic life into a metafictional musical dramedy titled *This Is Me . . . Now*. The video for "If You Had My Love" features the actor Adam Rodriguez, who sits in front of his computer to do an internet search. Spiraling down a dial-up rabbit hole of fragmented code and buzzing sound, he arrives at Lopez's website, a dystopian series of all-white rooms constantly monitored by cameras. When Rodriguez's character clicks on one box, he can watch Lopez dance in a white bikini in her living room. Click on another, and he—and everyone else with one eye on the video stream—can watch her shower.

The recent history of technology is written on women's bodies. Not quite a year later, Lopez would wear a vivid-green jungle-print Versace dress to the Grammy Awards, cut so spectacularly low that it became the most popular search query Google had seen to date. In response, developers created Google Images, a whole new online visual infrastructure. When Jawed Karim, Chad Hurley, and Steve Chen founded YouTube in 2005, it was because Karim had been searching for videos of Janet Jackson's wardrobe malfunction at the Super Bowl and couldn't easily find one. Before any of this, "If You Had My Love" anticipated a digital landscape where artists could fully capitalize on the extent to which we want to watch them.

But the video also seemed to be alluding to another Jennifer, the first woman to allow the internet unfiltered, unmediated access to her life. In 1996, a nineteen-year-old student at Dickinson College named Jennifer Ringley bought a webcam that she connected to a computer in her dorm room. Ringley was, in her words, a "computer nerd," and she wanted to see if she could write a programming script that would take pictures in real time and upload them to her website. The script worked, and Ringley began to post: regular, unposed black-and-white images that published first every fifteen minutes, and then every three. The banality of the pictures seemed to be, for her, the point: She sat at her computer, she ate, she talked on the phone, she slept. "I think the camera would be a lot less interesting if I paid that much attention to it," Ringley told Ira Glass on a 1997 episode of *This American Life,* by which time her "Jennicam" was getting upward of half a million hits a day. "It would be more of a staged show. And you can go see a staged show anywhere."

Ringley seemed to see her project as part internet experiment, part performance artwork. She wasn't shy about doing the things most college students do—showering, changing clothes, even having sex—on camera, but nor did she have an exhibitionist's impulse to be watched doing any of these things. She simply wanted to broadcast a version of her life online that was truly, radically authentic. Being constantly surveilled, for her, wasn't threatening; the internet was still so new that it felt less like a morass and more like a springboard toward infinite possibilities for connection. When Ringley was away from her camera, or when it was turned off or broken, she felt sad, she told Glass, as though she were "completely alone."

Even in 1997, before Ringley was interviewed on *The Late Show with David Letterman,* before she amassed a following of several million daily visitors to her site, there were clues as to where the information age was heading. The majority of visitors to her site, she said on *This American Life*, were men. At that point, she was receiving more than seven hundred emails every day, only ten or so of which were from women. Many of those emails were soliciting personal items in exchange for money— private photos or clippings from her hair. When she agreed to meet up with people who contacted her, usually they ended with what she described politely as "improper passes," underscoring the extent to which she was being seen as a sexual object. Often, people seemed interested in Jennicam less for its humdrum snapshots of everyday life and more for the long-odds hope that Ringley would do something salacious while they watched her. The first time she invited someone over who wasn't so alarmed by the camera that they fled, so many flocked to her site to watch that they crashed the server and ended up seeing nothing.

Ringley's intentions weren't to actively court what the film theorist Laura Mulvey termed "the male gaze," and she wasn't deterred by the camera from doing anything that she felt like doing. She was laying her life bare online to try something new, brokering a parasocial intimacy with the people watching her. But what the majority of them wanted to see—and what even well-meaning interpreters such as Glass and Letterman wanted to talk about—was nudity and sex, the most fascinating contours of private life turned into public spectacle.

By 2000, when Brooke A. Knight surveyed the new terrain of cam artists, or "camgirls," as they were inevitably called, what he found was that the majority of subjects and producers were women, who all seemed to "understand, participate in, and profit from the specular economy." Plenty were more overtly sexual than Ringley, actively soliciting money for images. What made cam artists "troubling and captivating," Simon Firth wrote in *Salon*, "is that, instead of giving us something we already know, they are pioneering both a new erotics and a new kind of performance—one that could be called the art of the publicly lived private life." The typical dynamic between voyeur and subject was being disrupted by the fact that the camgirls *wanted* to be looked at, within the security and comfort of their own domestic spaces. "This will replace television," David Letterman predicted in his interview with Ringley, and he was at least partly right.

What Ringley was pioneering—"lifecasting," it was called at the time—wasn't quite reality television. (*The Real World* had launched in 1992, while an intensely intimate documentary about Madonna, *Truth or Dare*, had broken box-office records a year earlier.) Lifecasting was closer to the dominant visual art of the 2020s: the meticulous, regular presentation of an online self. By now, most of us are astute curators of ourselves as seen by strangers. We craft and pose and filter and edit as seasoned veterans. But the most interesting thing to me about revisiting the practice that began with Jennicam, and that persists today across TV and the internet, is seeing all the ways in which womanhood has been tailored into something narrow and even archaic, by a media culture that has trained us to surveil ourselves and adjust things accordingly. No matter how authentic anyone perceives herself to be, there is still something about the scrutiny of others that influences the ways in which we behave, for good and for bad.

The aughts were a decade in which women were more visible in public life than ever before, and yet still mediated by the limited ways in which audiences wanted to see them. The rewards could be unimaginable; the blowback could be fatal. In 2000, Ringley found herself at the center of a media storm when she slept with a man who was engaged to someone else, in her apartment, captured by her camera. The parasocial relationship her followers had built with her over the years was destabilized by the revelation that she was, in fact, human.

"Jenni, how could you?" the *Washington Post*'s Libby Copeland wrote. "You redheaded little minx! You amoral man-trapper! Stealing your friend's fiancé and making love to him in front of thousands!" The cheating party later moved in with Ringley, who in 2014 told a podcast that she felt obliged to continue the relationship much longer than she actually wanted to, for fear of how breaking it up would be perceived. For years, she'd labored to show her online audience only her most authentic self. But the pressure of needing to win back the approval she'd lost from her fans left her, for the first time, performing for the cameras.

At the very end of 2003, after more than seven years of broadcasting her life online, Ringley shut down her site. There were complications with PayPal, which had imposed regulations against the nudity that Jennicam occasionally revealed. But Ringley also felt that her project had come to a natural end.

(For her, not for the rest of us—MySpace had launched earlier that year, providing a brand-new platform for the curated public self.) For almost all her adult life, she had shared her "reality" with anyone who wanted to watch. As she retreated into a determinedly offline existence, the cultural fascination with seeing people perform their lives for entertainment was soaring. It would influence how women looked, how they related to one another, how they ate and spent money and defined their ambitions and raised their children. All because there was something so thrilling about seeing the imperfect dynamics of real life transformed, by cameras, into media spectacle. "Oh, Jenni, you are so very bad," Copeland wrote in her *Washington Post* piece. "We cannot stop watching."

FROM ITS VERY EARLIEST DAYS, reality television as a genre has been defined by two almost chaotically oppositional impulses: a desire to examine humans through a sociological lens and the more crucial imperative to make money. Ringley, on her website, once described Jennicam as a "virtual human zoo," a way to put our behavior under the same scrutiny that nature documentaries give to animals. Craig Gilbert, who's credited with creating the first reality show in the early 1970s, PBS's *An American Family*, had previously made a documentary about the anthropologist Margaret Mead, who herself proclaimed *An*

American Family to be "as new and significant as the invention of drama or the novel." For seven months, Gilbert's crew filmed the Loud family, a husband and wife with five children living in an upscale home in Santa Barbara. The footage was edited into twelve hour-long episodes that captured the breakdown of Bill and Pat Loud's marriage and the revelation that Lance Loud, the couple's eldest son, was gay. The Louds became celebrities in a blink; Lance, an Andy Warhol fan, told *Time* magazine that the show had affirmed "the middle-class dream that you can become famous for being just who you are."

But even then, the question of authenticity loomed large. Viewers wondered whether Gilbert had artificially "instigated drama and . . . overstepped boundaries," as a 2011 *New York Times* analysis put it. "They picked four negative shots for every one of the other," Bill Loud griped soon after the show aired. Audiences, though, relished the spectacle. Throughout the next few decades, producers tweaked the format in less ambitious ways, with game shows and documentaries such as NBC's *Real People*. But around the end of the 1980s, two things happened that made reality more attractive as a format. The 1988 Writers Guild of America strike, the longest in the union's history at 153 days, led to scheduling holes that spurred the development of the Fox shows *Cops* and *America's Most Wanted*. And the emergence of nonlinear editing systems made it simpler, and cheaper, to whittle down hours of video footage into a more enticing package. MTV's *The Real World* honored the curious underpinnings of the genre—what happens when people forced into close confines with each other stop being polite and start getting real?—while attempting to mitigate the fact that licensing music videos was expensive, and that MTV, until that point, had neither drawn big ratings nor made big money. The arrest of O. J. Simpson in 1994 after a televised car chase, and his trial for murder over eleven months in 1995, meanwhile crystallized the concept of true crime as riveting, real-time TV drama.

The first reality shows to fully capture the public imagination were the ones that gratified our voyeuristic impulses. Coming out of the tabloid-and-talk-show 1990s, where the secrets of people's inner lives had dominated the decade, we were now suddenly being given the ability to see even more, all the time. I can still remember, in astonishing detail, the first season of *Big Brother* in the United Kingdom. The show debuted in the summer, and there was something surreal and immersive about feeling the sticky heat of the season while watching the castmates swelter in bikinis in their monitored garden. The format, based on a Dutch series that had premiered the year before, was so new that most contestants—while presumably aware that they were being watched and acting accordingly—hadn't yet finessed the art of turning themselves into TV characters. Their interactions *felt* honest. For the first time in British television, you could watch a twenty-four-hour live stream of the house online, an emulation of Jennicam that was similarly dull in practice while touting the same perpetual possibility of stunning revelation.

Big Brother, like *The Real World*, presented itself as an experiment, an analysis of human psychology under pressure that was self-aware about its slightly sadistic leanings—the constant scrutiny, the isolation from the real world, the imposition of changing circumstances intended to put stress on the contestants and create drama. The show wanted people to break, and often they did. I recently rewatched a canonical scene from the seventh British season featuring Nikki Grahame, a gorgeous, brittle twenty-four-year-old who went into the house in the full *Playboy* attire of a pink silk corset, bunny ears, and black suspenders and then proceeded to unravel on camera at a frantic clip. In a monologue now enshrined as the "Who Is SHE?" speech, more emotive and venomous than anything from *Richard III*, Grahame erupts in fury over the contestant who's just nominated her for eviction. During her time in the house, she frequently complained about being cold, which gave her a reputation as a diva. But Grahame had also been severely afflicted since childhood with anorexia, a disease that killed her in 2021. In a televised tribute aired that year, the *Big Brother* presenter Dermot O'Leary noted, with striking candor, that Grahame embodied all the qualities of the best kind of reality-show star: She was authentic, fallible, kind, empathetic, and fragile.

It was hard, watching contestants such as Grahame, not to have the distinct feeling that you were seeing something you shouldn't—the curious but loaded sensation Ringley evoked with her "human zoo" analogy of watching animals move dejectedly around an enclosure that's nothing like their natural habitat. Zoo animals and reality-TV contestants alike are both habitually bored; deprived of stimuli, they loll around, fight, or peacock for attention. During the first British season of *Big*

Brother, a sociologist made a formal written complaint to the show's network, Channel 4, about the psychologists consulted during production, arguing that *Big Brother* was a "game show, not a serious attempt to explore human nature" and that it was placing participants under such extreme stress that they could potentially suffer long-term damage. At this point, his theory was hypothetical, but the winner of the first-ever Dutch series later stated that he'd suffered multiple breakdowns after his time on the series. Like *The Real World*, *Big Brother* was frequently promoted as a social experiment. But above all else, it was a television show, relying on advertisers to turn a profit and requiring moments of human effusion and conflict to draw viewers to watch all those ads in turn.

There was a novel aspect to the show that proved even more compelling. Once a week, anyone watching at home was given the power to decide which contestant put up for elimination was voted out of the house. We were all, in our ways, practicing the ancient Roman judgment of *pollice verso*, pointing a thumbs-up or thumbs-down to adjudicate which housemate had won the public's favor that week and which had failed to do so. This simple participatory component of both *Big Brother* and *Survivor* would go on to be incorporated into many of the biggest reality shows of the twenty-first century, transforming the ways in which audiences related to television. When, in the summer of 2000, the lifecaster and cam artist Ana Voog uploaded a picture of herself watching American *Big Brother*, the image captured the layers of surveillance and interactivity that were beginning to form in modern life. We could broadcast ourselves to be watched while watching others in turn. The boundaries between reality and "reality" were breaking down. And for women, in particular, presenting ourselves to be seen was rife with the same old-world dynamics with a new twist. We would soon be able to assess in real time how the world wanted to view us—and adjust ourselves instantly in response.

IN HER 2022 BOOK *True Story: What Reality TV Says About Us*, the sociologist Danielle J. Lindemann explains why reality shows, which are overwhelmingly watched by women, have catered virtually since their inception to a straight-White-male worldview. Research suggests, she writes, "that women are socialized to perceive *themselves* through this gaze, and to internalize female objectification."

But in the early 2000s, the question of what kind of femininity women were supposed to perform was highly polarizing. Reality television, more than any other genre of entertainment in that moment, was defined by the collision of 1990s voyeurism with post-AIDS traditionalism. In 1996, Demi Moore became the highest-paid actress in Hollywood for her role in *Striptease*; to promote the movie, she stripped down to a padded bra and G-string on *Letterman*, gyrating her hips so sinuously that the host was momentarily struck dumb. Money and sex were becoming intricately entangled in the public imagination, just as women were emerging as a powerful financial demographic in their own right. At the same time, a movement imbued with nostalgia was encouraging women to quit their jobs and retreat to the safety of their homes. "My mother was convinced the center of the world was 36 Maplewood Drive," a voice sighed in a radio spot for *Good Housekeeping*'s "New Traditionalist" campaign. "Her idea of a wonderful time was Sunday dinner. She bought UNICEF cards, but what really mattered were the Girl Scouts. And she felt, no matter what, there was always enough love to go around. . . . I'm beginning to think my mother really knew what she was doing."

If this kind of weaponized nostalgia feels familiar, it should. It was inherent to virtually every aspect of the feminism backlash of the 1980s and 1990s. In 1995, a self-help tsunami of a book titled, innocently, *The Rules* advised women who wanted to get married to look to 1950s feminine mores for guidance: Don't pay for anything, play hard to get, be pleasant and charming, never mention marriage, try generally to act like a bewildered cartoon fawn or a genie in a 1960s sitcom. By 2000, the journalist and food writer Nigella Lawson had condensed the New Traditionalism into a cookbook for modern women that welcomed them back into the kitchen. "At times we don't want to feel like a postmodern, post-feminist overstretched woman," she wrote in the preface, "but a domestic goddess, trailing nutmeggy fumes of baking pie in our languorous wake."

This was the particular moment when reality TV emerged as a media powerhouse, as women were being encouraged to embrace their femininity both as passive, glowing housewives and frenetic, dehumanized sex objects. Sitcoms of the 1980s and 1990s had celebrated women who worked (*Murphy Brown, Living Single*) and who raised children as single mothers (*Kate & Allie, Grace Under Fire*). But by 2000, the number of working mothers was starting to decline. Even Moore, who'd been derisively nicknamed "Gimme Moore" by the media for her supposed bargaining power, stepped back from her career in 1996 to raise her daughters on a ranch in Idaho. In this moment, reality television had a vested interest in reminding women of their rightful place: either disempowered in the domestic sphere or performing sexuality for ratings. Or, better yet, both.

From the earliest days of the genre, the idea of the female body being a hot-button commodity was baked into the format. When Fox, in the wake of the 1988 writers' strike, proved that documentary-style clip shows such as *Cops* could be unexpected hits, HBO soon countered with *Real Sex*, a voyeuristic peek into the lives of strippers, phone-sex operators, porn directors, and exhibitionist couples looking for an audience. The show, according to HBO's head of documentary programming, Sheila Nevins, was a direct response to cultural fears regarding sexuality that had been stoked by the AIDS crisis. Showing sex, she said, had become "much more important because of all the terror that surrounds it." The first episode of *Real Sex* was watched by 2.8 million people, more viewers than had watched any HBO documentary besides *The Making of the Sports Illustrated 25th Anniversary Swimsuit Issue*. (Whose own success perhaps suggests why Nevins thought *Real Sex* would work.)

The series went on to run for thirty-three episodes over

nineteen years, introducing cable viewers to polyamory, BDSM, and gender fluidity long before such concepts were in the mainstream. Directed by Patti Kaplan—who would later lead HBO's *Cathouse*, a series that took viewers literally inside the bedrooms at a Nevada brothel—*Real Sex* had a defiantly sex-positive attitude, profiling legendary feminist filmmakers and porn stars including Candida Royalle, Annie Sprinkle, and Jeff Koons's ex-wife, Cicciolina. (In the United Kingdom, the similarly long-running *Eurotrash* offered the same magazine-style format of outlandish eroticism, with a heightened sense of the absurd.) Made by a mostly female crew, it was unapologetic about sexual equality. "I think now women are much clearer about what they deserve," Kaplan told *Vulture* in 2013. "The show opened up the door." No one involved saw it as porn: People who were desperate to order it on video to watch on demand were disappointed by HBO's insistence that it was *not that kind of product*. And yet what *Real Sex* revealed was that reality TV could draw huge ratings by showing sex or even teasing it, just as Ringley's hookup had crashed her servers.

In the United Kingdom, the remit that nonfiction programming should be educational as well as entertaining meant that early reality shows consisted of more documentaries and lifestyle shows and fewer of the spaghetti-on-the-wall ratings ploys that would later come to define network television. In the United States, the idea that reality TV was a bold new frontier of entertainment meant that it was also a minefield of edgy, sometimes questionable experimentation. The producers behind HBO shows such as *Real Sex*, *Cathouse*, and *G-String*

Divas insisted that they were portraying empowered subjects pursuing sex for both money and pleasure, while their series were ultimately doing the same thing: indulging people's desire to see sex on-screen while maximizing profits. But on network TV, thanks to the impulses of certain producers with space to fill, what was emerging was a crude new genre that insistently presented women as being up for sale.

Before he created *Who Wants to Marry a Multi-Millionaire?* in 2000, Mike Darnell was a five-foot-tall, ninety-three-pound "shock-doc" producer known for products such as *Alien Autopsy: Fact or Fiction?* and a show that once featured the removal of a woman's record-breaking tumor. Darnell met Mike Fleiss, an ambitious up-and-comer whose second cousin was the infamous Hollywood madam Heidi Fleiss, when the latter pitched him a show focused on catching people doing awful things on tape. Darnell was trying to find Fox's answer to *Who Wants to Be a Millionaire?*, an imported British show presented by Regis Philbin that was pulling in up to thirty million viewers per episode on ABC. Darnell's brain wave, finally, was the same concept with an astonishingly regressive twist: the New Traditionalism on steroids. Fifty beautiful women would compete, pageant-style, to marry a wealthy man on live television whom none of them had ever seen. It was Fleiss who suggested the pageant setup. "Mike and I knew this show was going to be a crazy public-relations nightmare," he later gleefully told *Vanity Fair*. "We knew that the National Organization for Women would hate us. That this would be the most controversial show ever!"

The live, two-hour special aired on February 15, 2000, the

day after Valentine's Day. The show was shot in Las Vegas, where an infinite number of regrettable marriages had preceded it. The host, Jay Thomas, laid out the concept: None of the fifty women had seen the prospective bachelor, Rick Rockwell, and none would, given that they were only assumed to be interested in his wealth. Rockwell would, however, get to survey the women and choose from a veritable harem of accountants, TV reporters, doctoral students, and engineers. The lucky bride's "gifts," donated by Fox, included a brand-new car and a three-carat diamond ring. The women varied in age from nineteen to forty-three; some in the initial round wore business attire, as though they were heading to a job interview. As the final ten were selected on looks alone, their smiles seemed visibly strained, as though the reality of what they'd signed up for were beginning to sink in.

The media critic Jennifer L. Pozner, in her book *Reality Bites Back: The Troubling Truth About Guilty Pleasure TV*, describes the reality genre as the "most vivid example of a pop cultural backlash against women's rights and social progress." Watching grainy YouTube footage of this particular product, I find it hard to argue. The women competing for the prize of a wealthy husband they'd never seen were Ivy League grads, executives, academics—all reduced to parading themselves for purchase like prize livestock at the country fair. *Who Wants to Marry a Multi-Millionaire?*, by my read, was the beginning of reality's determination to view twenty-first-century women through a nineteenth-century frame: Jane Austen heroines who, deprived of agency or power of their own, could only compete to claim status and self-betterment through their looks, their alliances, and their rivalries.

Fleiss was right—the show proved to be controversial. But this was largely because, shortly after the special aired, it was revealed that Rockwell's ex-fiancée had imposed a restraining order on him, accusing him of beating her up and threatening to kill her. (Rockwell denied the allegations.) The "winner," Darva Conger, an emergency-room nurse, promptly had her marriage annulled by a Nevada judge within weeks of the live televised wedding. Later that year, she posed for *Playboy*, a magazine whose long-standing association with reality TV was formalized in 2005 with the E! show *The Girls Next Door*, a series documenting Hugh Hefner's relationship with his stable of blonde girlfriends. Fleiss, after the briefest of periods in TV purgatory, returned with ABC's *The Bachelor* in 2002, a show that, in one of the producer's words, used "smoke and mirrors" to apply a romantic gloss to *Who Wants to Marry a Multi-Millionaire?*'s cynical setup. The women still compete against each other for an eligible man, only this time under the guise of doing so for love, not money—a tweak so significant that, in 2025, *The Bachelor* is still on air.

Who Wants to Marry a Multi-Millionaire? enshrined what would become one of reality TV's most enduring principles: the idea that a woman's value corresponds to her success in catering to the desires of others. "I was always told to be a cook in the kitchen, a lady in the parlor, and a whore in the bedroom," Melissa Gorga explained on *The Real Housewives of New Jersey*. Patti Stanger, on *Millionaire Matchmaker*, asserted that what her male clients reliably wanted in a partner was "Madonna in the bedroom, Martha Stewart in the kitchen, and Mary Poppins in the nursery." In the first episode of HBO's *Cathouse*, a sex worker tells the camera: "Everybody does it. We're just smart enough to get paid for it." Out of eleven female contestants from the 2006 season of the British *Big Brother*, four posed topless after leaving the show. In many ways, this was a pragmatic choice—why not capitalize on a moment of fame that might otherwise be fleeting? But it also underscores all the ways in which women on television were being set up as objects, to be looked at, scorned, sexualized, and emulated—often all at the exact same time. For the last twenty-five years, the women our culture has loathed the most have unfailingly been the same ones we can't stop watching.

IN 2007, THE SOCIOLOGIST Rosalind Gill theorized that postfeminism was less an ideology than a "sensibility." Its identifying features included the obsessive monitoring of one's own and other women's bodies, a preoccupation with self-discipline and self-surveillance, a makeover paradigm, an emphasis on individual gratification over collective effort, a belief in gender essentialism (the understanding that men and women are intrinsically and naturally different), and a preference among women to present themselves as active sexual subjects rather than passive objects. Bridget Jones—counting calories, agonizing over the choice between a lacy thong and a pair of control-top granny panties, and never managing to actually read *Backlash*—is the archetypal postfeminist. But the qualities of postfeminism are also all the defining characteristics of reality TV. This was a medium that, during the aughts, watched women, weighed them, waxed them, cut them open, groomed them to be more feminine, trained them to be more ladylike, exposed all their secrets, and built them vast business empires based on persuading other women to do all these things too. And the paradox of reality is that because the genre was dismissed as trash—as so many cultural products aimed at women are—few were scrutinizing the values and norms it was atomizing out to millions of female viewers.

In the early aughts, in the United States, the only mandate for reality-TV producers was to make shows that people would watch. Networks went all in on novelty, emboldened by the fact that they could sell just as many or more ads for a reality series that cost a quarter of what it took to make a scripted drama. Both Fleiss and Darnell, a *Vanity Fair* profile from 2003 noted, "have revolutionized television by laying off conventional sitcom, drama, and newsmagazine writers, directors, and producers and turning the tube over to the great unwatched horde of ordinary people, who will, it seems, do absolutely anything to get on television, and who usually deliver the goods once the cameras are on them."

In practice, this revolution often resulted in shows that embodied the swaggering bravado of the second Bush presidency, where men were cowboys, women were feminine to a fault, and the specter of the Ugly American loomed large in the background. On UPN's 2001 show *Chains of Love*, contestants were physically tethered to four potential romantic partners for four days and nights. On Mike Fleiss's 2003 ABC show *Are You Hot?*, members of the public stripped in order to be assessed by a panel of judges including the soap actor Lorenzo Lamas, who used a laser pointer he called a "flaw finder" to identify parts of people's bodies that offended him. ("A poorly executed softcore porn special that thinks it's a genuine beauty contest," *Variety* lamented.) In a story for *Entertainment Weekly* promoting the show, Fleiss posed crouched down on his knees between a woman's parted legs, peering up at her crotch, unintentionally mirroring the cover of 2 Live Crew's *As Nasty As They Wanna Be*. He was battling with ABC, he said, "to allow the contestants to wear thongs, because that's what women wear."

Individually, these shows were often trivial, schlocky garbage, deceptively edited and manipulatively filmed. Collectively, they were disseminating a message about women that was all the more emphatic for how familiar it felt: We were slutty, gold digging, uptight, hysterical, untrustworthy, nasty. (Defending *The Bachelor* in 2002, Fleiss—sounding for all the world like a pimp touting for trade—told *The New York Times*, "If you met 25 women in the singles scene, I can guarantee that some would have sexually transmitted diseases. Not on our show. We test for that. Clean is clean.") Mike Darnell's 2003 show *Joe Millionaire* inverted the format of *The Bachelor* by having a group of women compete for the affections of a wealthy man who was revealed in the finale to be just an ordinary working joe. Almost thirty-five million people tuned in for the finale, in hope of seeing a supposedly materialistic woman get her dramatic and very public comeuppance.

For women of color, reality television was even more fraught. In the early days of reality TV, Pozner writes, "broadcast networks kept their casts predominantly white, and the presence of people of color was marked by marginalization, tokenism, and typecasting." *The Bachelor* didn't have a Black man in the leading role for almost *two decades*, until the death of George Floyd prompted a nationwide reckoning with structural racism in America. Its sister show *The Bachelorette* had featured a Black female lead for the first time in 2017, spurring one of the male contestants to declare himself "ready to go Black, and I'm never going to go back." In 2023, Fleiss announced that he was leaving the show he'd created, amid reports that he was being investigated by ABC after allegations of racial discrimination by multiple employees. (In 2019, he'd been accused of domestic violence by his pregnant wife, a former Miss America, who claimed that he'd also ordered her to get an abortion; Fleiss denied all allegations and the couple have since reconciled.)

But as reality television began to expand its lens beyond American Whiteness in the second half of the aughts, its yen for grabby, inflammatory fare and its distinct lack of scruples often led to shows that typecast and fetishized women of color. If you were White, and had the requisite porcelain smile and bouncy barrel curls, you could be on *The Bachelor*, competing for roses, a proposal, and a sponcon diamond as big as a blueberry. If you were Black or Latina, you'd likely be relegated to VH1 or MTV, on *Flavor of Love, Charm School,* or *A Shot of Love with Tila Tequila*—shows where women of color were dehumanized and, in the case of *Flavor of Love,* given new names and identities in order to join Flavor Flav's gynaeceum. On *The Bachelor,* Chris Harrison told contestants that they were competing for the chance to find the great love of their life, a fairy-tale narrative enhanced by the fact the show aired on Disney-owned ABC. On *Charm School,* Mo'Nique told the assembled women that there were seven bathrooms in their house and so on no account should anyone take it upon themselves to shit on the floor.

The filmmaker Justin Simien, in his 2014 book *Dear White People,* made a case for reality television as "the new blackface," arguing that shows such as *Flavor of Love, I Love New York, Bad Girls Club,* and *The Apprentice* affirmed racist cultural stereotypes about Black women's being promiscuous, aggressive, and superficial. What was worse, Simien added, was how addictive he and his friends found these shows—how irresistible they were and how insidious. "This is an issue," he wrote, "not only because it's often the way some white people learn about black people, but also because it's the way some black people learn about themselves." In a 2016 assessment of *Love & Hip Hop: Atlanta,* a series about women in the music industry, the communications professor Melvin Williams argued that the show displayed clear evidence that Black women were also falling under the influence of postfeminist ideals: getting plastic surgery to better perform femininity within the sphere of hip-hop, shrewdly capitalizing on sex tapes, and identifying their physical attractiveness as "a key source of identity, power, and self-pleasure."

Visibility, on reality television, presents a paradox: Is it better for women to be seen on television as a stereotype or not seen at all? The media theorist Racquel J. Gates has argued that *Flavor of Love* is in fact "best understood as a satire of *The Bachelor* and white heteronormativity" and that shows such as *Love & Hip Hop: Atlanta* give Black women space to reject conventional respectability politics, particularly with regard to their identities as wives and mothers. In a media ecosystem where women are often shamed for their parenting and typecast as wives rather than introduced in their own right as individuals, the women of *Love & Hip Hop*, Gates writes, deal "a blow against the larger operations of patriarchy that all mothers feel to different extents." They demand to be seen as real women with multiple facets to their lives and personalities, in a TV genre that has long required its female characters to be as one-dimensional as they come.

Looking back from the context of the 2020s, though, I think it's also undeniable that so many of our most dispiriting contemporary trends were first disseminated to mainstream audiences on reality television. The early 2000s were the moment when the stickiest archetypes for women in the new millennium were being set. The Duggar family, whose ever-growing fundamentalist Christian family was documented in granular detail on TLC, seems pivotal to the tradwife movement, while also anticipating the disproportionate influence of evangelicals on

American politics and reproductive freedom. *The Bachelor*, the *Housewives* franchise, and the TV debut of a mediagenic Calabasas family later in the decade would go on to cement the idea that a meaningful life for twenty-first-century women revolved around grooming, power struggles, and the procurement of wealth. If reality TV during the first half of the aughts was about getting people to watch, its next act would be conspiring to come up with all the glorious things it could sell us.

WHEN *THE ANNA NICOLE SHOW* debuted on E! in 2002, the series managed to accomplish a trifecta of reality-TV ambitions all at once. It featured a blonde former *Playboy* model who'd married a billionaire who was six decades older; it peeped into the chaotic "real" life of an American celebrity; and it was a car crash in slow motion. The show's tag line was "It's not supposed to be funny, it just is." Smith, who by this point had gained weight since her modeling days and was heavily addicted to opioids, slurred and slouched her way through a series of setups. She went house hunting, picking out snacks from strangers' fridges; she got tattooed; she visited a strip club, groping the woman giving her a lap dance; she made her son and her Svengali-like lawyer participate in an eating contest at an Italian restaurant. In scripted clips between scenes, Smith was coherent enough to play up her reputation for the cameras, bolstering the suggestion that the show was a comedy. But as the cameras followed her around, she was barely functioning, heavily sedated and minimally comprehensible. In an interview with *Time* to promote the series, Smith reported that the E! producers kept giving her Red Bulls to perk her up, at one point cracking open what she said was her seventh of the day. In the interview, as on the show, she was sloppily chaotic, with moments of startling lucidity: "Everybody I know has made money from me and thrown me away," she said.

If reality television in the aughts was playing up preconceived notions about women in society, it was also doing something else at the same time that was more interesting and arguably more enduring. Shows such as *Anna Nicole* and *The Osbournes* had started chipping away at the boundaries between celebrities and ordinary people. At the time, this felt almost democratic. But in retrospect, the genre was also preparing viewers for a future in which they'd be expected to monitor themselves, broadcast the most significant details of their lives to audiences of varying sizes, and groom themselves accordingly. To watch normal women exposing themselves to constant surveillance and becoming celebrities in the process, and to see lower-tier stars ascending in status by opening up their lives for the cameras, asserted that being *seen* was enough to be powerful.

The already-famous quickly grasped the format's potential. In January 2003, a random assortment of stars (MC Hammer, Corey Feldman, Gabrielle Carteris) agreed to move into a Hollywood mansion together for a WB show called *The Surreal Life*. A month later, a pretransition Caitlyn Jenner was one of ten famous people dropped into a deliberately spartan jungle camp for ABC's *I'm a Celebrity . . . Get Me Out of Here!*, a tepid remake of a popular British franchise. Later that summer, the peachy pop star Jessica Simpson and her stolid new husband, Nick Lachey, exposed their marital life in *Newlyweds: Nick and Jessica*. Simpson is a fascinating case study for fame in her era; her father, Joe, a Baptist minister, had given her a purity ring when she was twelve and had steered her career away from the more overt sexuality of her peers' careers while seemingly remaining fixated on her undeniable desirability. "She's got double-Ds!" he once remarked, explaining the difficulty in selling her to a Christian market. "You can't cover those suckers up."

Simpson's marriage, though, opened new avenues of commercial possibility. The unspoken tease of *Newlyweds* was that viewers might get to see what happens after a woman is deflowered—the TV equivalent of an eighteenth-century nobleman hanging the sheets up for public view after his wedding night. "Jessica can stand up here in this white wedding dress because a long time ago, she committed her purity to God," the minister marrying her said, in scenes from the first few minutes of the show. In a 2004 profile for *Blender* titled "Queen of the Boob Tube," Joe Simpson said: "She waited for marriage, and now she's happily married and having sex every day. Now she's going crazy. And that's cool."

The series did what it was supposed to, in that it reinvigorated Simpson's music career and made her a bona fide star. But it also presented her as an archetype that was becoming increasingly popular in 2000s media—the dumb blonde. Like Anna Nicole Smith, Simpson was prone to speaking in nonsensical sound bites and messing up simple tasks: wondering out loud whether tuna was "chicken or fish" and appearing not to understand how to work a washing machine. You could forgive a twenty-three-year-old raised on the punishing work schedule of the child performer for any of this, but in the realm of reality TV, Simpson was seen as failing at the most fundamental of all roles: wifehood. (Lachey, who seemed to do nothing domestic during their relationship apart from watch sports and criticize his wife, received a rumored $12 million divorce settlement when the marriage broke down because Simpson, by that point, was the family's main earner.)

At the end of 2003, Fox debuted a similar new show that was already notorious, by virtue of real-life events surrounding one of its stars. *The Simple Life* featured the heiress Paris Hilton and the Hollywood scion Nicole Richie playing what Hilton described in her 2023 memoir as incapable "characters" dropped into fish-out-of-water scenarios in heartland America. A few weeks before the show was set to premiere, a sex tape featuring nineteen-year-old Hilton with her then-boyfriend, Rick Salomon, leaked online. Plenty presumed that the star had distributed it herself to promote her show, something that Hilton has said she was horrified by. "Buzz was off the chain because— *comedy gold*—it was too easy," she writes. "The potential for blond jokes, the opportunity for self-righteousness, the degradation of someone living a posh life. It was like an X-rated version of *America's Funniest Home Videos*." And this, in fact, was exactly it: Even in 2003, the presumption that what we were being sold as "reality" was fake made the excavation of "real" celebrity videos seem even more valuable. Reality television offered a voyeuristic peek into the lives of the rich and famous, but it was sanitized at best and completely staged at its most spurious; meanwhile, here was actual unfiltered footage of Hilton doing things that were never intended for public view. With this context collapse in mind, it's a little easier to understand how so many people relished watching what Hilton has likened to revenge porn.

The author and sociologist Joshua Gamson has concluded that the most crucial recent shift in celebrity culture has been its "decisive turn toward the ordinary." No genre has instigated this adjustment more effectively than reality TV has, with its stars humbled down to the strata of civilians, and its normal people raised up into the pantheon of celebrities. So it was inevitable that the next iteration of reality television would focus on the in-betweeners: wealthy women and teenagers who could be branded and monetized as stars, but without all the costly apparatus of cultural work that had previously been required. By 2004, MTV had long since switched out expensive music videos for cheaper reality programming that hooked young viewers. In 2004, *Laguna Beach: The Real Orange County*, capitalized on the success of Fox's hit drama *The O.C.* but at a fraction of the cost. It was shot with the polished production values of a network drama, as opposed to the shaky vérité-style steadicam of most reality shows. And more than any other show to date, it confused all the categories of entertainment production, turning ordinary high schoolers into bona fide stars who seemed almost just like us.

Now it felt truer than ever that the only difference between an ordinary person and a multimillionaire permanently covering *Us Weekly* was exposure. "The celebrity industry certainly doesn't need its celebrities to be extraordinary," Gamson writes. "What the celebrity industry does require of its humans is that they live, whether glamorously or not, for the camera." But I'd argue that glamour is, in fact, a crucial part of the bargain. The women who become most famous on reality television are the ones who agree to meet its standards: feminine to a fault, impeccably groomed and tweaked and tucked, walking advertisements for infinite products. The next era of reality television would embody this in spectacular fashion, turning from retrograde characters to uber-feminine, Frankensteined constructions of twenty-first-century womanhood, uncanny to behold and impossible to look away from.

CHAPTER 5

Beautiful Girl

The Goldmine of Impossible Expectations

Only one standard of female beauty is sanctioned: the girl.

SUSAN SONTAG (1972)

Beauty isn't actually what you look like; beauty is the preferences
that reproduce the existing social order.

TRESSIE McMILLAN COTTOM (2019)

In 1964, an episode of *The Twilight Zone* imagined life in a near-future, around the year 2000, where every nineteen-year-old would undertake a mandated ritual called "the Transformation." Science, Rod Serling explains in his introduction to "Number 12 Looks Just Like You," has developed the means of giving every individual the face and body of their dreams; the process requires them to choose from a number of stock models, which their physicality is then surgically altered to match. Marilyn, an eighteen-year-old approaching her own Transformation, is resisting the process, perplexing her family and friends. "Most girls your age are thrilled to death when it's time to pick a pattern," trills her mother, a svelte, symmetrical blonde in the leotarded body of a twentysomething. Afterward, she reassures her daughter, "You'll be *beautiful*."

The moral, when it comes, lands with the subtlety of a cartoon anvil: The Transformation was originally designed to eliminate conflict, illness, and inequality but has ended up wiping out empathy and free thought. Once changed, humans glide around like serene automatons, identical, blissed-out, and compliant. In the final scene, Marilyn gazes rapturously at her new reflection in the mirror, stunned by the smallness of her waist, the bounce of her hair. "Improbable? Perhaps," Serling says sonorously. "But in an age of plastic surgery, bodybuilding, and an infinity of cosmetics, let us hesitate to say impossible."

I thought of Marilyn while watching a 2004 episode of *The Swan*, a Fox reality show that ran for two seasons and is occasionally revisited now in retrospectives condemning it as one of the most monstrous television series ever made. *The Swan* took women who were desperately, dysmorphically unhappy with the way they looked—"ugly ducklings," in the show's twee parlance—removed them from their homes and families for several months, and subjected them to as many as a dozen cosmetic surgeries: breast implants, liposuction, facial sculpting, rhinoplasties, dental veneers, brow lifts, fillers. While undergoing all these procedures, the women were cut off from mirrors, which set up a grand reveal at the end of each episode where they saw themselves for the first time. "I feel beautiful now," one contestant, Marsha Meddleburg, said in season two, touching her nose and her hips with exactly the same reverent, ecstatic disbelief as Marilyn's. "I believe in myself. . . . I don't know who the old Marsha is anymore."

When we talk about body image during the aughts now, we tend to lament a revival of what's referred to as "noughties fatphobia" or "2000s diet culture," terms that don't capture the totality of what was happening. In 2004, the year Marsha appeared on *The Swan*, approximately two dozen reality-TV makeover shows aired on American television, as the gender-studies professor Brenda Weber notes in her book *Makeover TV: Selfhood, Citizenship, Celebrity*. Five years later, the number had ballooned to more than 250, putting people's faces, bodies, houses, kids, and even cars through a process of total metamorphosis. The mode of the decade was self-improvement; the aesthetic was tanned, toned, homogenized beauty, a plasticized kind of perfection made all the more desirable because it could be purchased. Anybody's body—*anybody*—could be refashioned as a status symbol, an emblem of conspicuous, shop-till-you-drop consumption. More than ever before, people's exteriors were understood to reflect their inner identities, both of which seemed malleable and endlessly improvable. Cosmetic surgeries were widely touted and understood to be fixes for the imperfect self, with reality shows in particular hammering home the message that becoming skinny, hot, and sexy would totally change a person's life.

The first wave of reality series compelled us to watch. The second wanted us to imagine ourselves through the camera's unforgiving lens, and its shows had a vested interest in selling us things that might improve the picture. Late in the decade, a family emerged that had a particular genius both for capturing our imaginations and monetizing our fascination. Revisiting dozens of works for this chapter, I kept thinking about a quote from the art critic John Berger's 1972 collection *Ways of Seeing*, about images in advertising. "The spectator-buyer is meant to envy herself as she will become if she buys the product," he writes. "She is meant to imagine herself transformed by the product into an object of envy for others, an envy which will then justify her loving herself. One could put this another way: the publicity image steals her love of herself as she is, and offers it back to her for the price of the product."

By 2009, 12.5 million cosmetic procedures were performed per year in the United States, up 69 percent from the beginning of the decade. The use of Botox, a relatively novel technology, had increased by 509 percent; buttock lifts were up by 132 percent; lower-body lifts by an astonishing 4,184 percent. "Doctors have sold us on the notion that surgery is no longer an issue as crass as mere cutting and suturing; it is merely part of the journey toward enhancement, the beauty outside ultimately reflecting the beauty within," Alex Kuczynski wrote in her 2006 book *Beauty Junkies*. Cosmetic work, she argued, is "the embodiment of that American Dream, the success story of getting eyeballs on one's self, of self-transformation."

So it made sense that reality television, with its roving, perpetual gaze, was the perfect showcase for an ideology of extreme self-modification. The word "transformation," which conveyed sinister undertones on *The Twilight Zone*, was suddenly ubiquitous both on makeover shows and across the self-help industry, which by the aughts was a cultural phenomenon all on its own. In 2006, when I was floundering after college and my father was dying of cancer, my mother signed me up for an intensive three-day self-improvement seminar involving motivational lectures and confession, the culmination of which was a public event in which we revealed our "transformed" selves onstage. The feeling was intoxicating—not just the optimism of identifying as a shiny, new person with limitless potential but also the rapturous applause from the other people in the room, the group hugs, the *validation*. Who doesn't want to be seen by the world as the best possible version of themselves? What could be so bad about wanting to be made anew?

There is, though, something fundamentally destabilizing about a process of total self-overhaul, whether it's physical or psychological. The women on *The Swan*, deprived of mirrors for several months, found themselves so altered after dozens of procedures that their own children sometimes couldn't recognize them. This was particularly ironic because the idea for the show came to its creator, the former Telemundo president Nely Galán, when she was recovering from having her first child and feeling particularly alienated from her own body. "I felt ugly, I felt fat," she told the journalists Sirin Kale and Pandora Sykes for an episode of their podcast, *Unreal*. "And so I went to a fat-farm place, and it was like this luxurious spa. . . . It was all about exercising and eating well and doing holistic things, and I thought to myself, the only thing that would make this a perfect experience was if I could go to a surgeon and have a breast lift after breastfeeding a kid for a year. And I thought, *Oh my God, that's a TV show*."

The Swan was initially intended for the Latino market, where cosmetic procedures were more normalized at the time. (Brazil, Mexico, Argentina, and Colombia have among the highest rates of plastic surgery worldwide, and Brazilian citizens are assumed to have a "right to beauty" that's directly associated with job prospects, social mobility, and happiness—not to mention Whiteness.) But when the show became too expensive for Telemundo, Galán pitched it to Mike Darnell at Fox, where the pair landed on a pageant setup: The contestants would compete with each other to have the winner crowned, finally, "The Swan." This was what distinguished the series from ABC's *Extreme Makeover*, which had debuted in 2002 with a similar premise, and from countless other plastic-surgery shows airing in the same moment. It was astonishingly cruel: Even after undergoing grueling medical procedures, being subjected to restrictive diets and isolated from their families, most of the women would still, in the end, have their physical selves found lacking by an arbitrary panel of judges.

We're taught as children about inner beauty—about the magic of difference, about there being no one way to look or feel beautiful. I grew up watching "We All Sing with the Same Voice" on *Sesame Street*, an ode to kids of different ethnicities from different cultures all singing together; I read to my children now from *We're Different, We're the Same*, a picture book with the same ethos. But what makeover shows relentlessly emphasized during the aughts was the idea that there *was* only one way for women to look: intensely feminine, straight, sexy, middle-class, and White, or at least with any visible signs of difference chiseled into submission.

Not to mention that one's physical self, in this era, was widely understood to be not just a representation of one's inner character but also the predominant source of a woman's social and economic value. "When you look beautiful, that's how you make money," a contestant from MTV's *I Want a Famous Face* told Anderson Cooper in an interview. "Doesn't everybody want to make money?" I was working in restaurants at this time to save for graduate school, navigating a pattern of disordered eating that offered, during my father's illness, the illusion of control. And it was unmistakable: The more weight I lost, the smaller the clothes I wore, the more tips I received in return. Being skinny seemed to bring blessings from the universe, even if none of them was happiness.

The message reality shows were propagating was the same one I had internalized as a teenager in 1999—the understanding, as Susan J. Douglas has put it, "that it is precisely through women's calculated deployment of their faces, bodies, attire, and sexuality that they gain and enjoy true power." Reality television's earliest iterations taught us about the financial rewards of self-exposure; now, the genre was preaching a kind of prosperity gospel of the body, the idea that self-reinvention could be lucrative too. The winner of *The Swan* received a smorgasbord of prizes, including $50,000, a modeling contract, a 2004 Jaguar, and a $10,000 "transformation scholarship" for the self-help coach Tony Robbins's "Mastery University." For becoming the public face of the questionable weight-loss product TrimSpa in 2003, Anna Nicole Smith was reportedly paid half a million dollars a year. By 2009, when Jessica Simpson was fat-shamed for wearing what were deemed unflattering "mom jeans" to perform at a Florida chili cook-off, the *Daily Beast* ran a piece suggesting that it would be easy for her to sign an endorsement deal and turn "fat cow into cash cow."

Reiterating all the same messages at the same time was porn, a booming industry in the early 2000s whose financial model hadn't yet been disrupted by the internet. The media-studies professor Elizabeth Atwood Gailey has written about the similarities between violent pornography and the ways in which extreme-makeover shows "depict female bodies as they are probed, painted, suctioned, carved with surgical instruments, and stuffed with foreign objects." Porn also set the physical standard that all female bodies were supposed to aspire to. In a 2004 essay for the *London Review of Books*, the writer Hilary Mantel noted that the ideal woman of the era had "breasts like an inflatable doll, no hips at all, and the tidy, hairless labia of an unviolated six-year-old." Such a form, it's worth noting, can't actually be humanly attained. It has to be purchased.

What else were we supposed to take away from this moment other than the idea that only spending vast sums of money on changing how we looked could validate us? MTV's *I Want a Famous Face*, which debuted in 2004, featured people so in thrall to celebrities such as Carmen Electra and Pamela Anderson that they underwent multiple cosmetic procedures to remodel their own faces as theirs, partly in tribute, partly in aspiration. Celebrity seemed so tantalizingly close, as though by playing the part you could manifest it into existence. (The self-help book *The Secret*, which encouraged doing exactly that, was published in 2006.) By the end of *The Swan*, as Brenda Weber writes, the contestants "have learned to pose, turning their bodies in ways to be fully seen and admired . . . saturated in signifiers that denote celebrity." When Heidi Montag, the plucked-from-obscurity star of *Laguna Beach* and *The Hills*, underwent her own Swan-like transformation in 2010, at the age of twenty-three, undergoing ten cosmetic procedures in a single day, the moment felt like an inversion of reality hierarchy. Here was a star subjecting herself to the same punishing rituals as those of ordinary mortals to try to further her career. Montag's TV scenes were often set up, even scripted, but her physical reinvention was totally authentic in its prostration to artifice.

By 2013, the idea that beauty could be bought had been wholly accepted, all over the world. That year, a short list of twenty finalists for a beauty pageant in South Korea—which recently claimed the highest rates of cosmetic surgery per capita in the world—went viral when all the women appeared to look identical, with the same almond eyes, neat white teeth, sculpted noses, and heart-shaped faces. "Plastic surgery means many kinds of beauty queens, but only one kind of face," Dodai Stewart concluded in *Jezebel*. *The Twilight Zone*'s vision of identikit, cookie-cutter beauty had finally come to pass.

IN HER 2004 BOOK *Appetites: Why Women Want,* the writer Caroline Knapp unpacks how cultural messaging teaches women to suppress any and every form of hunger: for food, for sex, for power. "The underlying questions of appetite, after all, are formidable—What would satisfy?" she writes. "How much do you need, and of what? What are the true passions, the real hungers behind the ostensible goals of beauty or slenderness?" Naomi Wolf, in her canonical 1990 book *The Beauty Myth*, makes a similar argument. The power of what women really want is so forceful, so potentially iconoclastic, she argues, that the only way to control it is to distract us with self-loathing, and the lifelong project of disciplined self-maintenance.

It's only with Wolf and Knapp in mind that I can really wrap my head around the tenor of 2000s diet culture—hypothesizing that it was as cruel as it was, as vicious and prejudiced and uncompromising, because it was weaponizing shame in a way that would neutralize women's ambitions and agency, as well as protect patriarchal power. Every magazine I read during my teens and twenties, every TV show featuring a doe-eyed teenage star with visible clavicles, seemed to contain the same message: *shrink*. In the United Kingdom, the weekly gossip magazine *Heat* had a feature known as the "circle of shame" to identify celebrities' errant cellulite dimples, sweat patches, or tummy bulges. In the United States, the gossip sites *TMZ* and *Perez Hilton* delighted in pictures of stars caught in unflattering poses, the more humiliating the better. Any deviation in the public female body from porcelain smoothness, any sign of visible human corporeality, exposed a person to ridicule and disgust. Interpreted all together, it's enough to turn you into a conspiracy theorist, which is, unfortunately, what happened to Wolf.

It's impossible to overstate how fixated the media was during the early 2000s on the particulars of women's bodies. Fashion, caught somewhere between heroin and porno chic, was valorizing clothes that offered nowhere to hide: low-rise jeans cut all the way down to the pubic bone (a riff on Alexander McQueen's "bumster" trousers from the mid-1990s), corset and handkerchief tops, dresses with cutouts so expansive that the term "nip slip" was in perpetual rotation in the tabloids. None of this would have been remarkable, except for the license magazines seemed to take in response to obsess over the physicality of young stars. "Lindsay Lohan has been eighteen for just under a week when she tells me her breasts are real," Mark Binelli wrote in *Rolling Stone* in 2004, for a story accompanying a cover image with the words *"Hot, Ready, and Legal!"* "I did not ask (gentlemen never do), though my reporting (discreet visual fact checking, a goodbye hug) seems to confirm her statement."

The proliferation of celebrity pictures in magazines such as *Us Weekly* and *In Touch Weekly* gave us unprecedented visual access to stars, but also new power—in a moment when celebrity could be claimed just by looking the part, it was easier to judge those who were failing to keep up their end of the bargain. Tabloids often had doctors on speed dial, ready to put a number on a particular star's body in any given week. Covers that focused on weight loss or weight gain, a former *In Touch Weekly* reporter told *Slate* in 2022, sold especially well. The phrases "postbaby body" and "scary skinny" entered the modern lexicon, blasted out next to unflattering pictures of women who couldn't win. "I owe Renée Zellweger an apology," Kate Betts wrote in *The New York Times* in 2002, noting that she'd pulled a photo from the cover of *Harper's Bazaar* the previous year simply because Zellweger was "too fat" in photographs after gaining weight for *Bridget Jones's Diary*. (When Zellweger promptly lost the weight in record time, she was labeled "shockingly gaunt" by the *Daily Mail*.)

Often, women were publicly shamed for internalizing the same toxic standards that had been weaponized against them. In interviews promoting the first season of *The Simple Life*, Nicole Richie said, "People would ask me how I felt about being a voluptuous woman," even though she was undeniably petite at the time. After she lost weight, she was interviewed by Howard Stern in 2005, who raved about how hot she looked and asserted that he'd rather "do her than Paris" with her new body. Stern also tricked her into standing on a scale for part of the interview, then announced to listeners what she weighed. Two years later, Richie was excoriated when an email invitation she sent to a Memorial Day barbecue went viral: "Let's glorify this day in your sluttiest tops and your tightest pair of Tsubi jeans, even though we have no clue what Memorial Day really means!! There will be a scale at the front door. No girls over 100 pounds allowed in. Start starving yourself now. See you all then!!!"

The jokily savage tenor of this moment, paired with images of concave hips and jutting chest bones, has been impossible to forget. I had a particular fascination at the time with diet books, which exploded in popularity around 2003: Atkins, South Beach, *French Women Don't Get Fat*. As the decade went on, cult publications went from offering tough love to doling out actual verbal abuse. In 2005, a former modeling agent and model teamed up to publish *Skinny Bitch,* whose unique selling point was the idea that humiliation gets results. "Are you sick and tired of being fat? Good," the book begins, before launching into a punishing invective of taunts: Its readers are "gross," not being skinny is revolting, eating animal fat leads to "lumpy shit all over your ass, thighs, sides, arms, and stomach." "You need to exercise, you lazy shit," the authors write early on. A disclaimer: "We have some fat, gross body parts, too," chapter 12 confesses. "We're women."

What's remarkable to me rereading *Skinny Bitch* now is how well its voice mimics what the body-acceptance activist Katie Sturino calls "a self-shit-talking spiral." "Don't be a fat pig anymore," the writers state. "You know what you have to do, now do it." Beyond eliminating animal products, the advice in the book encourages what we might now interpret as disordered eating: reading the labels of absolutely everything you consume, fasting for between twenty-four hours and *ten days* depending on "how light, clean, and healthy you want to get." Despite all this, *Skinny Bitch*'s dedication is to the self-help icons Tony Robbins and Wayne Dyer, and ends with a proclamation of "Namaste." The diet advice, it turns out, is veganism, transformed into a cult weight-loss bible thanks to what its publisher described as "a crystal-clear message" of weaponized self-hatred. *Skinny Bitch* ended with an exhortation to readers to practice "affirmations," saying things like, "Every day in every way my ass is getting smaller," while going about their daily routines. It's a reminder of how the fatphobia of the aughts had a distinctly New Age undertone, combined with some good old-fashioned *can-do-ism*: If you were "fat," or "ugly," you just weren't trying hard enough.

Skinny Bitch did moderately well until 2007, when the former Spice Girl Victoria Beckham was photographed carrying it in Los Angeles; after that, it rocketed onto the bestseller charts in both the United States and Britain. Celebrities have sold us on the promise of diets since Oprah Winfrey pulled a wagon bearing sixty-seven pounds of animal fat onstage in 1988, representing the weight she'd managed to lose on a regime of meal-replacement shakes. Beyoncé, after stating that she'd lost weight for her 2006 role in *Dreamgirls* following the Master Cleanse, indirectly prompted a spike in women subsisting on lemon juice, maple syrup, and cayenne pepper. Sarah Jessica Parker and Kate Hudson supposedly preferred the Hamptons Diet, a basic low-carb plan with a gimmicky emphasis on macadamia nuts. And yet the constant parade of new fad diets, one after another after another, would seem to be evidence of their collective failure.

During the 2010s, the body-positivity movement occurred in response to a decade of cruel, ritualized self-hatred. What had started with Dove's Campaign for Real Beauty in 2004 gained momentum as more scientific evidence emerged that diets simply did not work. In 2016, the plus-sized model Ashley Graham appeared on the cover of *Sports Illustrated*'s swimsuit issue, the same year that Mattel began selling Barbies with different body types and skin colors. A 2023 study found that young women exposed to body-positive posts on Facebook over a two-week period reported having an improved sense of self-image and were less inclined to compare their bodies to those of others. But the exploding popularity of weight-loss drugs such as Ozempic and Mounjaro around the same time shifted the goalposts yet again. Once again, celebrity bodies were shrinking in front of our eyes, and once again, the product responsible for their newfound leanness was for sale.

FAT-SHAMING WAS PAR for the course on reality television during the aughts, of a piece with a consumer boom in diet and workout manuals, fitness videos, and ultra-processed branded snacks. When *The Biggest Loser* premiered in 2004 on NBC, it did so with an opening montage of isolated body parts jiggling, accompanied by a chorus of voices condemning the things the contestants most hated about themselves. "These 12 people have one thing in common," a voice-over explains. "They're *fat.*" (The word "fat" is delivered with emphatic, disgusted relish.) The series was *built* on shame: exposing contestants' bodies in minimal clothing at an introductory weigh-in, confronting them about their regrettable choices, punishing them in gym sessions designed to make them vomit, cry, suffer. At the end of the first season, Ryan Benson was crowned the show's winner, having lost 122 pounds, or 37 percent of his body weight. He had, as he confessed to *The New York Times* in 2009, also deprived his body of food and water to the point where he was urinating blood, a possible indicator of kidney damage.

This was a cultural moment of abject cruelty disguised as tough love. *The Biggest Loser* taunted its contestants with imagery and language meant to remind them of their gluttony: During elimination rounds, everyone assembled around an oversized dining table in a room in which serving dishes of food were displayed behind glass walls, just out of reach. When each person revealed which contestant they'd voted to eliminate that week, they pulled that name from beneath an empty silver platter. "It's time to cut the fat," the host, Caroline Rhea, asserted. On *America's Next Top Model*, which had premiered a year earlier, weight was no less of an obsession: Ten women, each one vying for the prize of a modeling contract, were measured and weighed by a trainer at the beginning of the series, with the implication being that they'd whittle themselves down with his help. "She has a little more insulation than me," Elyse (114 pounds) said of Robin (165 pounds, the designated "plus-size" contestant) during the first photo shoot. "You've gotta watch the thighs," Janice Dickinson, one of the judges, told Ebony (131 pounds). "You've gotta watch that big booty thing. You've gotta really watch the diet and exercise." (I should note that the two women most explicitly body-shamed here were both Black; Paulini, a contestant on *Australian Idol* in 2003 who was famously advised by a judge to "choose more appropriate clothes or shed some pounds," was Fijian Australian.)

America's Next Top Model became a reality-TV phenomenon,

running for twenty-four seasons. In the beginning, possibly thanks to its shoestring budget, the show was broadly representative of what trying to make it as a model actually required: the elimination of the body's fat and hair (the girls all received bikini waxes in the first episode), the tiny loft apartment shared with too many other women, the strange "assignments" (such as when the final four models went to Paris and were charged with charming men they'd never met at lunch while wearing couture). Walking through the city to a go-see, Adrianne—the eventual winner of the first season—was groped by a man she asked for directions, an assault that deeply affected her. And yet, when she missed one of her four casting calls that day as a result, she was reprimanded by the judges for being unreliable. The show's ethos of plain talk and tough love for its stable of young women was best embodied by Tyra Banks herself, whom the critic Ann Powers once compared to Ayn Rand for her ferocious, uncompromising commitment to *earning* success. When the corporeal form of your body is the only thing standing between you and material wealth, why be sentimental about what happens to it?

Every episode of *America's Next Top Model* was titled after a particular contestant, who was stripped of her name and reduced to a storyline: "The Girl Who Deals with a Pervert," "The Girl Who Is a Visual Orgasm," "The Girl Who Hates Her Hair." The insinuation was that the women on the show were every one of us as much as themselves—avatars to sell us CoverGirl makeup and Lee Jeans and Smartwater. And as the decade went on, we civilians began experiencing a little of the same scrutiny. The newfound ubiquity of digital cameras, and the birth of MySpace in 2003 and Facebook in 2004, meant that we were suddenly being bombarded with unflattering pictures of ourselves and each other: exposed, sweaty, disheveled, shameful.

Shame, on *America's Next Top Model* and *The Biggest Loser*, wasn't intended to be cruel for mere cruelty's sake. It was portrayed on both shows as a necessary process, a kind of cleansing ritual that revealed who was weak and who was fully committed to the project of capitalist self-perfectibility. As *America's Next Top Model* went on, E. Alex Jung observed in a retrospective, the series "tried to excise the inherent subjectivity of assessing physical beauty by arguing that it's a skill that can be honed." All the better to encourage us to buy the diet books, the workout videos, the magazines that revealed celebrities failing—just like us!—at the project of themselves. Diet culture, Wolf writes in *The Beauty Myth*, promises "the American dream come true: One can re-create oneself 'better' in a brave new world." Or, as a 2007 *Ladies' Home Journal* cover celebrating Kirstie Alley's weight loss blared, the product perpetually on sale is "You—Only Better!"

SOME QUICK CONTEXT about the state of things in 2006, before a handful of people changed the landscape of visible womanhood forever. In this moment, housing prices in America had more than doubled over the eight years prior. *Desperate Housewives* was one of the most-watched shows in the country. And *Queer Eye for the Straight Guy* had only recently spearheaded Bravo's evolution from a performing-arts showcase that turned into a softcore porn channel at night. All these elements influenced *The Real Housewives of Orange County*, a show pitching itself unabashedly as a voyeuristic peek into the lives of the rich and fabulous. "Life is different in a gated community," a husky female voice says, by way of introduction. "The land here is a million an acre. The average price of a house is a million eight to two two." The camera pans over Rolls-Royces, diamonds, men playing golf on manicured greens against a flat blue sky. It's instantly clear, as it should be, that this is a show about money—having it, spending it, transforming it through elaborate rituals into the visible markers of status and consumption. "This isn't just a place to live," a different voice elucidates. "It's a lifestyle."

What's striking now, watching almost twenty years later, is how *ordinary* the women on the show look—how rumpled and frowsy and recognizably human compared with the glowed-up, pillow-faced, slightly alien Housewives of the current era. Jeana Keough, a former Playboy Playmate turned real estate agent, sports uneven bangs and silver jewelry, like any mom you'd run into shopping at T.J. Maxx. Still, in his 2021 book *The Housewives*, the writer Brian Moylan notes how, in one promotional photo used for the premiere, all five women on the show are wearing Sky Tops, inexpensive, colorful halter necks popular at the time in California for how they showcased gravity-proof cleavage. ("85 percent of the women around here have had breast implants," Kimberly Bryant explains in her first scene.) The women are well-preserved, definitely, but not yet fully pickled in the bedazzled reality-TV aesthetic: *bigger, brighter, tighter.*

Against a cultural backdrop that fetishized youth—"It's Totally Raining Teens!" as that *Vanity Fair* cover from 2003 blasted—the Housewives were unusual. *Desperate Housewives* aside, women in their age bracket, late thirties and forties, weren't exactly prominent in popular culture at the time. ("There are only three ages for women in Hollywood," as Goldie Hawn rants in the 1996 movie *The First Wives Club.* "Babe, district attorney, and *Driving Miss Daisy.*") The interest in the women of Orange County wasn't related to their beauty, necessarily, or their family dynamics or their alcohol-lubricated shenanigans. It was about how they presented themselves. "On reality TV, women in particular bear the onus of displaying themselves—hair, face, breasts, and accessories—as spectacularized works in progress," the media-studies professor Misha Kavka wrote in 2014. She labels the particular art form the Housewives excel at as "flaunting," a peacocking performance of hyperfemininity, emotional excess, and wealth.

In the *Housewives* universe, the art of personal upkeep has come to be known as "glam." Erika Jayne Girardi, a fifty-three-year-old cast member on *The Real Housewives of Beverly Hills* with the taut, uncanny face of an AI-generated image, spends $40,000 per month on glam, she confirmed in a 2024 reunion episode presided over by the franchise's trickster god, Andy Cohen. In Carole Radziwill's first season of *The Real Housewives of New York*, she wrote in a 2020 essay for *Allure*, she styled her own hair and did her own makeup. Five seasons later, glam teams had been fully incorporated into her life on camera, with Bravo often picking up the check if it could film the procedures involved: "Botox injections to smooth our foreheads, chemical peels to tighten our skin, lasers to reduce ass fat." Usually, Moylan observes, after a season of watching themselves on television, the women are able to assess themselves physically and make adjustments: a new haircut here, a nip-tuck there—all part of the postfeminism self-surveillance playbook. "Glam," Louis Staples wrote in *The Cut* in 2022, "is now embedded in *Housewives* as a narrative device."

This is because cosmetic work, in reality-TV land, is really *work*, a kind of labor that both embodies and enables money. It's glam more than anything else that signifies how the women on the shows transform from real people into TV celebrities, and the promise is that for us watching at home, too, such enhanced status can be bought. In 2022, a *Bustle* writer calculated that there were fifty-two separate beauty brands that had emerged out of the show, among them Karen Huger's perfume, Candiace Dillard's wig collection, Kim Zolciak's skincare line, and Jen Shah's eyelash collection (the last one doomed by Shah's conviction for fraud via a telemarketing scheme). The Housewives, by way of their evolving presence on our screens, normalize what the academic Sandra Bartky called the disciplinary project of the feminine body. And then they sell to us the instruments for our own upkeep, an ouroboros of image, consumption, and profit.

This is, it has to be said, what celebrities have done forever; the Housewives just happen to be exceptionally good at it and especially appealing to women with disposable income. I should note here that I'm as susceptible to the lure of beauty products as anyone and that the unboxing of a new store-fresh product usually provides the biggest thrill I've gotten since I had my children. There are plenty of reasons why we love to watch these beautiful, constantly upgraded, perpetually bedazzled women. In good times, they represent the optimism of the perfected self; in bad, they offer wanton escapism. When *The Real Housewives of Atlanta* debuted in 2008 smack in the middle of the Great Recession, a *New York Times* review noted that its lavish shopping sprees and vulgar displays of wealth could end up being a cursed time capsule of a prodigal decade. Ultimately, though, the unfettered consumption the franchise celebrated was just too beguiling.

What's most interesting about beauty on reality television is that although upkeep is imperative, there's no one way to do it, and there are often gradations between shows and franchises that reflect class, race, and social status in the real world. *The Real Housewives of Potomac* has led to heightened discussions of colorism—the preferential treatment of lighter-skinned women—on the show and in America writ large. On the British shows *Love Island* and *The Only Way Is Essex*, as Anita Bhagwandas writes in her 2023 book *Ugly*, cast members often present themselves with hypervisible signs of grooming—blinding white porcelain veneers, ostentatious fake tans, arachnid eyelashes—that turn self-maintenance into conspicuous consumption. And shows such as *What Not to Wear* in both the United States and the United Kingdom routinely employed bitchy, elitist insults to encourage working-class women to elevate their self-presentation, usually by spending money they don't have.

But beauty on reality television is also unfailingly gendered. Series such as the *Housewives* franchise, *The Girls Next Door*, and *Jersey Shore*, Kavka writes, "foreground women whose visibility . . . seems to consist of little more than their ability to flaunt a codified hyper-feminine attractiveness." Femininity is as much a prize to be flaunted as is wealth; the implication is that the two are inextricably linked. In a 2023 essay for *The New York Review of Books*, Anna Shechtman argued that the Housewives from the very beginning exhibited all the tropes of drag culture: "women aging in high definition, negotiating their value after their childbearing years, compensating for youth with ornament, competing for attention from an audience that is prone to look away." Reality-television stars use their very appearances as a kind of self-protection that repels criticism, demands visibility, and exorcises shame.

On reality television, exterior womanhood is *work*, which is perhaps why, paradoxically, trans women have been more visible and more welcome within the genre than virtually anywhere else in popular culture. The labor they've put in, and the totality of the makeovers they've endured in order to become fully themselves, represent, in this realm, the ultimate badge of honor. (When Caitlyn Jenner first revealed her gender-affirmed self on the cover of *Vanity Fair*, she was wearing that most loaded symbol of feminine comportment: a corset.) Before Laverne Cox became famous for her role as Sophia Burset on *Orange Is the New Black*, she was a contestant on *I Want to Work for Diddy* in 2008; she later cohosted a 2010 show called *TRANSform Me*, on VH1, where three trans stylists gave a makeover to a fashion-challenged cisgender woman. Isis King was the first trans contestant on *America's Next Top Model* in 2008, and elements of both her transition and the transphobia some of her fellow contestants displayed toward her were featured on the show. *RuPaul's Drag Race* premiered in 2009, a show that, despite having questionable attitudes to trans women early on, proved definitively, as Danielle J. Lindemann writes, "that gender can be *performed*." Reality television has offered thoughtful, sensitive portraits of transition in *Becoming Chaz, I Am Jazz*, and *I Am Cait* that bely the genre's slipshod, dehumanizing origins.

This wasn't always the case. In 2004, a British reality show called *There's Something About Miriam* took six men to Ibiza to compete for the affections of a twenty-one-year-old model named Miriam Rivera and a £10,000 cash prize. The twist was that Rivera was transgender, something she revealed in the finale while the five runners-up linked arms and snickered in the background. The series had made clear to viewers that Rivera still had a penis, making the suspenseful element of the show the question of how the winner, Tom, would react. Would he accept her as she was, having gotten to know her? Or would he erupt in transphobic rage? In the end, he did neither, although he and the other contestants did sue the production company for conspiracy to commit defamation, sexual assault, and personal injury.

Later that year, the cruelty of how Miriam was exploited was thrown into sharper definition when Nadia Almada, a trans woman, won the fifth British season of *Big Brother*, having become popular among viewers for her chain-smoking, her ribald antics, and her machine-gun laugh. When she exited the house, she was cheered robustly by the crowd, with one fan holding a sign that read NADIA—SHE IS ALL WOMAN. Her visibility on her own terms had transformed British awareness regarding trans people, and proven that reality viewers were perhaps more empathetic and forward-thinking than producers had ever given them credit for.

VISIBILITY IN MASS MEDIA can be revolutionary; it can also be an ambush. Around the turn of the millennium, one of the paradoxes of the way fashion magazines and imagery fetishized underweight White beauty while excluding women of color was that young Black girls typically scored higher on self-esteem assessments and had much more positive attitudes toward their bodies than did their White peers. "White girls," the scholar and writer Imani Perry wrote in 2003, "are inundated with images of beauty that are impossible for most to attain: sheets of blond hair, waif-thin bodies, large breasts, no cellulite, small but round features, high cheekbones. Over the years, black women have been relatively absent from public images of beauty, an exclusion that may have saved black girls from aspiring to impossible ideals." But, Perry argued, "with the recent explosion of objectified and highly idealized images of black women in music videos, it is quite possible that the body images and even self-esteem of black girls will begin to drop."

To some extent, it was already happening. Between 2003 and 2004, as the culture critic and academic Aisha Durham has noted, there was a fivefold increase in butt augmentations in both the United States and the United Kingdom, with many women taking images of Jennifer Lopez and Beyoncé to their appointments. (In 2001, Beyoncé wrote the song "Bootylicious" after being criticized for gaining weight, offering up an island of body positivity in the fatphobic ocean of the decade.) A profound shift in what was regarded as the bodily ideal for women was underway. "In this moment, a particular brand of whiteness is disrupted," Durham noted. "Both ideal beauty *and* sexual desirability are mapped onto the curvaceous, ethnically marked female body."

All of which is to say that when a new E! reality show called *Keeping Up with the Kardashians* debuted in late 2007, there were a number of historical factors that had primed female viewers in particular to be enthralled by this Calabasas family. The name "Kardashian" was familiar to anyone alive during the 1990s; O. J. Simpson was Kim Kardashian's godfather. Jennifer Lopez's celebrity had led to a rising cultural fascination with lavish, undulating female forms. Aspiration was the watch-word of the decade. Celebrity-gossip magazines and websites had endless space to fill, while the aggression of paparazzi pho-tographers had started to spook A-list stars, who refused to en-gage, leaving a void.

Kim Kardashian was well-positioned to try to emulate Paris Hilton's trajectory. She'd worked for Hilton as a stylist before *Keeping Up* premiered, had been widely photographed with her, and had even appeared on *The Simple Life*, including one scene where she "helped" Hilton give her Chihuahua a pregnancy test. In March 2007, Vivid Entertainment released a sex tape Kardashian had filmed with her then-boyfriend, the R&B singer Ray J, in 2003, titled *Kim Kardashian, Superstar*. The branding was curious—at the time of the movie's release, Ray J was the more famous of the pair, and Kim was a relative no-body, leading to speculation that Kardashian and her manager-mother, Kris Jenner, had colluded together to release the tape to raise Kardashian's profile. (The *Girls Gone Wild* founder Joe Francis—a Kardashian family friend who'd previously dated Kim's sister, Kourtney—stated in a 2023 documentary series, *House of Kardashian*, that he helped broker the deal. The Kar-dashian family has vociferously denied these claims.)

Whatever the tape's origins, *Keeping Up with the Kardashians* instantly became, upon its premiere, the most-watched show on Sunday nights for women aged eighteen to thirty-four, a coveted advertising demographic. And in the almost two de-cades since, the women it featured have upended the way people think about beauty, influence, bodies, and wealth. The criticism and disdain the family has drawn have been caustic—I started working at *The Atlantic* in 2014, and on the rare occasion I'd write something about the family or the show, I'd receive a flood of irate messages for lowering the tone of a storied American publication by covering what readers deemed to be trash. By now, though, it's inarguable that Kim Kardashian is one of the most powerful women in the world, as well as the most famous. When she posed for the cover of *Paper* magazine in 2014, in a spread of photographs by Jean-Paul Goude that exposed her oiled buttocks while seemingly referencing a history of racist imagery exploiting Black women's bodies, the story made up nearly 1 percent of all internet traffic in the United States that day. In the introduction to *True Story*, Lindemann writes that more of her sociology students can name the entire Kardashian clan than can list the members of the US Supreme Court.

In large part, this is because of how, from the very beginning, the Kardashians gratified our collective desire to *watch*. The family dynamic of the show—with its sibling rivalries, births and deaths, and all-out fights—followed in the anthropological footsteps of *An American Family*, albeit with less earnest intentions and more product placement. The Kardashians were close enough to celebrity to seem bathed in its aura—and rich enough to satisfy a prurient desire to see wealth up close—but "normal" enough to feel accessible, at least at first. And the series cannily turned the objectification of its female stars into a kind of agency: The women of the family were the nexus, with a pretransition Caitlyn and a young Rob relegated to subplot status, often as figures of emasculated fun. ("Bruce is going through menopause," Kourtney says dryly in one episode, referring to Jenner.)

Sex was also embedded in the show, not as an intimate element but as a mechanism through which both fame and fortune can be won. In the first episode, Kim buys her mother and stepfather a stripper pole for their wedding anniversary, prompting freckled nine-year-old Kylie to demonstrate her own moves with unnerving aplomb, bending over, biting her finger in an imitation of seduction, and then spinning around the pole in a pair of five-inch silver stilettos. Later, in a scene set up for the cameras, Kris "hires" a nanny for her two youngest daughters who turns out to be the porn actress Bree Olson. When Kim, Kourtney, and Khloe fly to Mexico to shoot an ad for *Girls Gone Wild* swimwear—with Joe Francis memorably calling Kris to offer her the gig while he's in prison for racketeering—Kendall and Kylie Jenner are left under the charge of their brother, Brody, whose "manager" films Kylie while she pretends to flash him. "You girls are a little crazy, but you know what, I'm gonna start managing you," he says. "Put this like on YouTube or something." In the very next episode, Kris encourages Kim to pose for *Playboy*, saying, "I think it would be an awesome experience . . . and on top of that, it's a ton of money."

Keeping Up with the Kardashians, Maria Pramaggiore and Diane Negra wrote in 2014, "may act as an infomercial for beauty products, clothing, and Kardashian spinoffs, but mainly it sells Kardashian women as sexualized signifiers of social status and high net worth." The family has been critiqued from the very beginning for being famous for no good reason, and yet these women's defining skill, I'd argue, is salesmanship. The Kardashian-Jenners are the original influencers, performing consumption to encourage infinitely more of it. Their constantly changing faces and bodies present the human form as a perfectible project, ready to be molded and painted and tucked in any way that will encourage engagement and sell products. Just as the show has charted the family's economic evolution—from living in a luxurious but chintzy bungalow in the first season to occupying various minimalist temples of obscene wealth—it's revealed how all five sisters have changed from recognizably human to monolithic, uncannily contoured, shrunken, and plumped to the same template.

Their relationship with beauty has been more enduring than any of their individual relationships, and no less complicated. As women with Armenian heritage and the kind of olive coloring that's often labeled, vexedly, as "exotic," Kim and her sisters are both White and ethnically ambiguous. (The persistent rumors that Khloe Kardashian is secretly O. J. Simpson's love child point to just how ambiguous.) Before Kim became famous, the beauty standards of the aughts were largely defined by the kinds of physiques that could carry off what Rosalind Gill has called "midriff advertising": low-slung hipster jeans and ten inches of taut, tanned stomach. Nicole Richie's physical diminishment between seasons of *The Simple Life* led to her elevation in status from Paris's sassy sidekick to size-double-zero aughts fashion emblem, a frail, childlike figure whose accessories were so big they threatened to topple her.

Kim, though, was curvy, with a pronounced backside. "She's got a little junk in the trunk," Kris Jenner states, by way of introducing Kim to America in the first-ever episode of *Keeping Up*. Hilton, who seemed irritated by her competitor's expeditious rise, compared Kim's butt in 2008 to "cottage cheese inside a big trash bag," an expressive but inaccurate description. Kim's figure seemed to represent abundance and excess; in that sense, it was a better avatar for the prerecession 2000s than all the jutting hip bones and ribs usually seen on red carpets. By 2010, Jay Leno was joking that the American economy was "so bad even Kim Kardashian is losing her ass." Some critics have deduced that the family's gaudy celebration of wealth and extravagance is what made them so popular as a foil to the temperance of the Great Recession.

Kim's physique was what distinguished her from every other reality star on E!, but the ways in which it was received as a novelty pointed to how Black women were still being sidelined and ignored by swaths of popular culture. Her *Paper* cover, which presented her backside as a kind of fascinating curiosity, trafficked in the same kind of imagery that had been used to fetishize Black women's bodies in the past, from Sarah Baartman to Grace Jones. Being White, Kardashian could capitalize on culture's condescending gaze without being exploited by it. Since then, her self-adornment has mimicked Black aesthetics—

the journalist Wanna Thompson coined the term "blackfishing" to describe the art of doing exactly that—on multiple occasions, with her in one instance appearing in *Vogue* with what seemed to be darkened skin and a braided updo.

Still, the more famous Kim became, the more her and her sisters' faces and bodies became, through astonishingly persistent self-exposure and salesmanship, the defining model for twenty-first-century beauty. While the Kardashians are often touted for helping to replace skinny chic with a more substantial ideal, the products they've sold over the years have been archaic and cruel: "flat-tummy tea" (laxatives) to reduce "bloating"; "waist trainers" (corsets) to compress a woman's waist to better emphasize the chest and butt; shapewear (from a line initially called "Kimono" until it prompted cries of yet more cultural appropriation) to tuck and compress the female body into a more disciplined, streamlined form.

The launch of Instagram in 2010 has been inextricable from the Kardashian-Jenners' takeoff as living billboards, exposing them to an enormous new audience. And their influence has been easy to measure. After an episode of *Keeping Up with the Kardashians* aired in which a now teenage Kylie finally confessed to having had lip fillers, searches for the procedure jumped 3,233 percent in the United States. The fastest-growing cosmetic surgery in the world is the Brazilian butt lift, a hugely painful redistribution of one's own fat into one's backside, which some researchers have estimated kills one in every 3,000 patients. In 2021, there were 61,387 in the United States alone.

Between 2010 and 2021, according to *Allure*, cosmetic procedures performed on people of color increased by 70 percent, compared with 12 percent for White people.

But in Kardashian-land, the body is endlessly malleable. In 2023, fans noticed that the women of the family were getting smaller, more angular, less convex. In order to fit into a dress once worn by Marilyn Monroe for the Met Gala, Kim reportedly lost twenty-one pounds, sparking rumors that she and Khloe Kardashian were taking Ozempic. Around the same time, the model Angela White (formerly known as Blac Chyna), who'd once had a relationship and a child—and a short-lived reality show—with Rob Kardashian, announced that she was having her breast implants removed, her dermal fillers dissolved, and seven rounds of illegal butt injections extracted. "I was so young, I just wanted that body, 'cause I saw everybody, you know, my crew, getting it. And I wanted to be with the 'it girls,'" White told ABC News. Her evolution has been revealed and charted in detail—where else?—on Instagram.

Regardless of dimensions, the Kardashian look is still ubiquitous, and it shows no signs of fatigue. In 2019, the writer Jia Tolentino described "the gradual emergence, among professionally beautiful women, of a single, cyborgian face," and no one seems to have pioneered its uncanny lifelessness more effectively than the Kardashians. The visage Tolentino described as "Instagram face" seems to belie age, background, and ethnicity; it erases individuality and imperfection in favor of a singular painted symmetry. Any features can now be contoured to fit Eurocentric beauty ideals, with makeup, with Facetune, and—eventually—with a scalpel. No one is totally immune. Even tweens with enough natural collagen to make a Housewife weep are now begging for antiaging products, comparing their own living faces with the immaculate masks of Instagram and TikTok, and seeing only fallible features in need of a fix.

CHAPTER 6

Final Girl

Extreme Sex, Art, and Violence in Post-9/11 America

> Flesh comes to us out of history; so does the repression and taboo that governs our experience of flesh. . . . Sexuality, in short, is never expressed in a vacuum.
>
> ANGELA CARTER (1978)

> Porn does not inform, or debate, or persuade. Porn trains.
>
> AMIA SRINIVASAN (2021)

The first half of Eli Roth's 2005 movie *Hostel* could be spliced into virtually any fratty sex comedy from its decade: Two American friends, Paxton and Josh, arrive in Amsterdam, ready to smoke, drink, and fuck around. Their offbeat new Icelandic friend, Óli, is the first to score, texting them a picture of himself jubilantly banging a faceless blonde in a nightclub bathroom. At a brothel in the red-light district, Paxton is repulsed by a woman dancing in one window—"I hope bestiality is legal in Amsterdam because that girl's a fucking hog," he jeers—but is placated by a sexier one. Josh, the most sensitive of the group, wanders through the establishment, nervously watching the silhouetted figures of strangers behind various closed doors. Hearing a woman shriek repeatedly, he opens the door, convinced someone is hurting her, only to find that she's actually the aggressor, a leather-clad dominatrix flogging a customer.

The twist, of course, comes after the group is convinced by a friendly-seeming stoner stranger to go to Slovakia on their quest to find the hottest, easiest girls on the Continent. The hostel he directs the guys to turns out to be not a Playboy-meets–Peace Corps fantasy but a hellhole where unwitting tourists are auctioned off to be tortured by paying customers with a predilection for extreme brutality and death. "There is a place where all your darkest, sickest fantasies are possible," the trailer for the movie boasts (a little presumptively). "Where you can experience anything you desire." Sex and sadism are so intimately entwined in *Hostel* that the film critic David Edelstein coined a new term for the genre it spearheaded: "torture porn." Not quite midway through the movie, Josh wakes up in a fetid basement, chained to a chair, his head covered with a hood. An avuncular-seeming man in a leather apron then proceeds to penetrate his leg with a power drill, which we see in tight close-up, the blood spurting out against the cold metal—a gruesome, gory money shot.

The film historian Linda Williams once wrote that there are three distinct categories of movies that elicit strong bodily reactions: melodrama (to make viewers cry), pornography (to turn them on), and horror (to induce visceral disgust and terror).

She calls these the "body genres," excessive and critically derided forms of entertainment that their fans nevertheless consume with relish. Torture porn is arguably a combination of all three. Its lurid, feverish scenarios, wanton sex, and disturbing violence made it one of the defining cultural genres of the aughts, reflecting anxieties about a decade marked by war and disaffection. During the 1950s, fears of a nuclear holocaust played out in movies such as *The Blob* and *The Incredible Shrinking Man*; in the 1970s and 1980s, widespread concern about violent crime and serial killers inspired a spate of slasher movies. Torture porn, morally ambiguous and often nihilist to an extreme, seemed to exemplify the post-9/11 era, with its jarring violence and impulsive thirst for vengeance.

Hostel, in a sign of . . . something, was produced by Mike Fleiss, the creator of *The Bachelor*, and executive produced by Quentin Tarantino, an auteur of highly stylized, provocative brutality. Roth, the writer-director, was the son of a psychoanalyst and a painter who once hired a magician to pretend to cut their son in half with a chainsaw at his own birthday party. He often gave shifting reads of his own movie. In one interview, he described *Hostel* as very much a reflection "of my disgust with the Iraq War and the Al-Qaeda beheadings . . . about capitalism gone awry and American imperialism," but in a featurette discussing the sequel, he explained that audiences just "want to see people getting fucked up—bad!" To promote *Hostel 2*, he posed nude for a photo titled "Eli Roth has the biggest dick in Hollywood," complete with a monstrous prosthetic penis covering his own genitalia. The sequel's poster, banned in the

United States but revealed at New York Comic Con, also featured the actress Bijou Phillips, naked, holding her own severed head. (*Hostel*'s provocations started a trend: In 2007, a poster campaign for the movie *Captivity*, featuring images of a terrorized Elisha Cuthbert alongside the caption "Abduction. Confinement. Torture. Termination" and drew so many complaints for seeming to delight in the degradation of a woman that it was quickly withdrawn from public view. A producer for the movie later defended the film's plot as being about "empowerment.")

It was obvious that the *Hostel* movies were intended to shock. What was less clear was whether Roth had any other kind of agenda he was working with. But torture porn was part of a larger thematic trend playing out across moviemaking, from European film festivals to the San Fernando Valley. As arthouse directors in the late 1990s began experimenting with explicit sexual imagery, in movies such as Catherine Breillat's *Romance* and Lars von Trier's *The Idiots*, the porn industry was responding with its own shift in direction. Pornography is by nature transgressive—if its aesthetics and values are fully integrated into mainstream culture, it loses its reason to exist, its unique selling point. In the new millennium, as fashion photographers displayed their own ejaculate in Manhattan art galleries and serious filmmakers put real sex on-screen, porn had only one direction to pursue. "The new element," Martin Amis wrote for *The Guardian* in 2001, reporting from Los Angeles on the movies of porn director John Stagliano, "is violence."

Sadistic horror movies, usually as crassly commercial as they were unerotic, didn't qualify as either art or porn. But they represented something distinct that was manifesting across different forms of media in the aughts: a taste for cruel, dehumanizing extremity. The "shockumentary" specials that Mike Darnell produced for Fox at the end of the 1990s about record-breaking tumors and vicious animal attacks reflected audiences' appetites for lurid excess. In 1995, after the porn actress Annabel Chong had sex 251 times in a single ten-hour period, she went on—where else?—*The Jerry Springer Show* to discuss her experience, while audience members gasped and cringed at the spectacle. Chong's feat of endurance, the reality special *Who Wants to Marry a Multi-Millionaire?*, and the 2002 Gaspar Noé film *Irréversible*—which included a nine-minute anal rape scene featuring the actress Monica Bellucci—were all arguably extensions of the same idea: testing the limits of what men could do to women for entertainment while cameras rolled.

Torture porn is not porn—it's not made to produce arousal or pleasure. But it does, in much the same way as a lot of porn does, reduce human beings to pieces of flesh and meat, to be manhandled, skewered, and dissected while we watch. The gender politics of *Hostel* and its sequels are vexing: In the first movie, the male characters are reduced to the historically feminine archetype of victims, being gruesomely abused in sexualized games by other men who've paid for the pleasure. In the second movie, the American tourists are female, as is one of the "customers," who luxuriates underneath the gushing blood of a younger woman she's slicing into ribbons. Writing for *Cinéaste*, Christopher Sharrett concluded that "the triumphant woman of *Hostel: Part II* is little more than another instance of the female constructed as male, internalizing fully the values of the predatory, dominant society the film pretends to critique." Every time Roth seems to be subverting a dubious tradition in movies—the casual misogyny of aughts-era sex comedies or the idea that torture can be a moral imperative—he replicates that tradition at the same time or even *wallows* in it. In his movies, as in the extreme porn that came out of the 1990s, violent excess and degradation were key. With sex and brutality no longer off-limits on-screen, these were the commodities that people would still reliably pay good money to see.

IN 2000, THE FILMMAKER and writer Stephen Walker was commissioned to make a documentary about a young British woman who was heading to Los Angeles to try to establish her career in porn. Felicity, twenty-five years old when Walker started filming her, is in many ways an ideal subject: sweet, chatty, frank, clear about what she will and won't do to be cast. Her agent, Richard—a dismal, cigar-chomping villain whom she rebukes for repeatedly propositioning her—takes her through the list of potential scenes, compensated on a sliding scale in terms of what's considered least extreme (blow-job scenes, girl-on-girl) to most (interracial porn, which Felicity seems surprised to learn is both better paying and more taboo than sadomasochism or having anal sex with multiple men at the same time).

She won't participate in gang bangs, and she won't do double anal, which she knows would physically damage her. "I'm not abusing myself on this trip," she says.

Richard, who nevertheless wants a maximal payout for Felicity's three-week tour, steamrolls past all her boundaries and takes her to watch a scene where ten men are having sex with one woman in a boxing ring. All Walker can shoot are the discarded tissues on the floor and Felicity's stricken face as she begins to comprehend what she's signed up for. Later, she cries after calling her daughter and kisses her picture. Richard then takes her to meet Max Hardcore, a producer notorious for abusing women with gynecological instruments, dressing them up as children, choking them with his penis to the point of blackout, spitting saliva and phlegm in their mouths, and inserting Sharpie markers into their rectums, with which he has them write, "I am a little fuck hole." Marcos, Max's cameraman, tells Felicity that he likes the girls to look "young." The movies, he adds, are about "how far we can take it."

The scene that follows is nightmarish, all the more depraved because it's real and because Walker, by this point, has truly humanized his subject in a way antithetical to porn, capturing her ambition, her troubled childhood, and her desire to make a better life for her daughter. Max's house is the stuff of horror movies: vast, quiet, smelling strongly of cleaning fluid. Felicity is clearly scared. When Max finally arrives, he's quiet, faux-solicitous, and intensely sinister, stalking around her soundlessly like a predator. He puts some lube on his hands, unzips his pants, and penetrates Felicity with his penis by way of greeting: "This is how we check out your qualifications, miss," he says, while she seems to disassociate. Later, after Max chokes her during oral sex to the point where she becomes hysterical and then bullies and berates her into filming more extreme scenes, Walker intervenes, stops filming, and removes Felicity from the house. He later revealed that she sobbed in the car all the way home. She was terrified, she said, that Max was going to kill her.

The documentary that Walker ended up making conveys something substantially different from how porn was broadly portrayed in British popular culture at the time, in series such as *Sex and Shopping*, *Eurotrash*, and *Boogie Nights in Suburbia*. The vibe of 2000s porno chic was cheerful sleaze rather than outright abuse. Some saw *Hardcore* at the time as a necessary corrective, given how unflinchingly it depicts the psychological dismantling of a young woman in front of our eyes. "A typical Max Hardcore scene looks like a rape," wrote Evan Wright, a former editor at *Hustler*, in 2000, describing Hardcore's movies as "psychodramas of rage directed at feminine beauty." The sadistic degradation of women in his scenes is the entire point. Max has a small penis, Richard tells Felicity, as if to make working with him seem more appealing. You don't have to be a Freudian to interpret that in the ways in which he abuses his subjects—or did, since he died in 2023—inserting specula into their vaginas and stretching out well past the point of pain, seems to be overcompensating for something.

The type of porn that Max Hardcore made over several decades is often called "gonzo porn" in the industry, a genre that mimics amateur porn for how it dispenses with narrative to focus on action and tries to immerse the viewer within the scene. Gonzo, David Foster Wallace wrote in 1998, is "more or less a cross between an MTV documentary and the Hell panel from Bosch's *Garden of Earthly Delights*." During the golden age of porn, around the mid-2000s, actors were stars, budgets could rival those of indie movies (the 2008 film *Pirates II: Stagnetti's Revenge*, featuring Jesse Jane and Sasha Grey, cost $8 million to make), and movies followed basic narrative structures. But humming along in the background at the same time was a darker, absurd iteration of the medium, more "real" and more explicitly interested in crossing lines. One director Richard takes Felicity to meet claims proudly that he runs "the best company in porn." When Walker asks him what that means, he explains, "We've got the filthiest, nastiest sex, we don't use rubbers, it's all anal." The people who buy Max Hardcore films, one actress tells Walker, "are the people who are very near the edge."

In his 2001 dispatch from the Valley, Martin Amis interviewed the director John Stagliano, whose Evil Angel studio was instrumental in mainstreaming what had up until then been understood as extreme acts: choking, spitting, slapping, abuse. The Italian porn actor Rocco Siffredi, whose "rough" style incorporated many of these hallmarks along with a fetishistic dedication to anal sex, developed a cult following for his collaborations with Evil Angel. "I was the first to shoot Rocco," Stagliano told Amis. "Together we evolved toward rougher stuff. He started to spit on girls. A strong male-dominant thing, with women being pushed to their limit. It looks like violence but it's not. I mean, pleasure and pain are the same thing, right? Rocco is driven by the market. What makes it in today's marketplace is reality." By 1997, Evil Angel was the most profitable studio in the porn industry, selling about half a million videos in the previous year.

In the real world, porn's mores were filtering out into broader culture. A 2005 story for *The Guardian* analyzed the misogyny rampant in men's magazines at the time, noting a *For Him Magazine* feature that encouraged readers to calculate what their girlfriends were being "paid" for sex, by way of flowers, drinks, cinema tickets, and other expenses, comparing price points to "a Cambodian whore," "a Cypriot tart," and "a Cuban showgirl." A 2011 study from the *British Journal of Psychology* found that many young men weren't able to distinguish between derogatory quotes about women taken from men's magazines and quotes from convicted rapists. In stand-up footage from 2006, the comedian Russell Brand jokes about liking "them blow jobs, right, where it goes in their neck a little bit . . . them blow jobs when mascara runs a little bit." In 2023, as allegations emerged that Brand had harassed and assaulted multiple women during the aughts, one woman stated that he had choked her with his penis when she was sixteen years old—a technique referred to as "cockgagging" in porn—to the point where she had to punch him to get him to stop before she suffocated.

"We have a saying around here," Max Hardcore tells Felicity while he's penetrating her. "We're not happy until you're not happy." John Stagliano put it slightly differently to Amis in *The Guardian* in 2001: "Pussies are bullshit." Both filmmakers main-

tained that the violence itself wasn't real, but performers sometimes said otherwise. In a 2000 issue of *Adult Video News*, the
performer Regan Starr described her account of filming an extreme scene for the director known as Khan Tusion: "I got the
shit kicked out of me," she said. "I was told before the video—
and they said this very proudly, mind you—that in this line
most of the girls start crying because they're hurting so bad. . . .
I couldn't breathe. I was being hit and choked. I was really
upset, and they didn't stop. They kept filming. You can hear
me say, 'Turn the fucking camera off,' and they kept going." In
2022, Khan Tusion—sometimes referred to as "the Freddie
Krueger of porn," whose movies have titles including *Piss Mops*
and *Meat Holes*—was revealed by the *Daily Beast* to be a wealthy
property developer and Democratic donor named Mark
Handel. He was not, by his own account, making these kinds of
movies for money. He was doing it for pleasure.

WITHIN PORN, extremity was a selling point. But in European art-house movies of the aughts, it was becoming a
movement, experimental in style, nihilist in tone, and characteristically riddled with Gallic ennui. Writing in *Artforum* in
2004, the critic James Quandt labeled what he was seeing in
cinema "the new French Extremity." In the movies of filmmakers including Lars von Trier, Gaspar Noé, and François Ozon,

he wrote, "images and subjects once the provenance of splatter films, exploitation flicks, and porn—gang rapes, bashings and slashings and blindings, hard-ons and vulvas, cannibalism, sadomasochism and incest, fucking and fisting, sluices of cum and gore—proliferate." Quandt struggled to identify exactly what was behind this particular development in film, but he noted that some of its most interesting practitioners were women: Claire Denis, whose 2001 erotic-horror film *Trouble Every Day* starred Béatrice Dalle as a woman who seduces and then eats unwitting men, and Marina de Van, whose 2002 directorial debut *In My Skin* presented a woman who develops a fixation with gouging and cutting her own body. *Baise-Moi*, a ferocious, sexually explicit crime thriller directed by the writer Virginie Despentes and the former porn actress Coralie Trinh Thi, charted the murderous, thrill-seeking road trip of two friends after one of them is gang-raped.

All three movies seem animated by anger, but also hunger—by desires that had not and were not being met in a world where sex was oriented around male power. "The point is not to be shocking," Despentes once said, "but to change the shape of things." In her 1999 movie *Romance*, Breillat presented a young teacher, Marie, who's driven almost to madness when her boyfriend, Paul, refuses to have sex with her. The movie's color palette is unsubtle: Marie and Paul live in a stark white apartment so sterile that it resembles an operating theater; their clothes and underwear are white. Paul, a model, seems to crave a monklike serenity, disciplined and calm. He offers Marie no reason for why he won't sleep with her, which is precisely what disturbs her. "You despise me because I'm a woman," she suggests. "I disgust you." He doesn't correct her.

Furious, Marie leaves their bed and goes to a bar, where she meets Paolo (who's played, in an audacious piece of casting, by the porn actor Rocco Siffredi). Later, she sleeps with him in what appear to be unsimulated, explicit scenes. Marie tells Paolo, somewhat unconvincingly, that what she craves is her own degradation: "I want to be a hole, a pit. The more it gapes, the more obscene it is, the more it's me, my intimate part, the more I surrender. I disappear in proportion to the cock taking me." At the same time, Marie explores bondage and sadomasochism with her boss, Robert, who tells her he's had more than ten thousand lovers, because he understands that women simply want to be talked to. When a stranger mutters an obscene request to Marie in the street one day, she agrees to grant it in the stairwell of her apartment building, only for him to anally rape her by force and then taunt her with her own violation. Marie wonders whether nymphomania simply means "destroying yourself because you choose the man who doesn't love you." Maybe, she thinks, "I really want to meet Jack the Ripper. He'd certainly dissect a woman like me."

Romance is enthralling until this scene, which implies through monologue, with considerable provocation, that Marie has enjoyed her own rape, even as her body language tells an utterly different story. "I'm a feminist," Breillat has said, "but not in my films." At seventeen years old, the director published a novel that was banned in France for young readers because of its explicit content; in her twenties, she had a brief role in Bernardo

Bertolucci's *Last Tango in Paris*, one of the most galvanizing and controversial explorations of sex in film history. Her debut movie, 1976's *A Real Young Girl*, is about a fourteen-year-old's strange, violent fantasies, presenting explicit sexuality in a way that fully defies male pleasure. *Romance* is similarly charged. Breillat stages what she seems to understand as stereotypical male ideals—a woman desperate for sex, a woman bound and gagged—and renders them in ways that make them both psychologically explosive and wholly unsexy. The film professor and author Maria San Filippo has suggested reading her films as "simultaneously feminist performance art and an (auto) critique of pornography," works in which Breillat chooses to recreate and work within a culture of female subjugation in order to point out how hollow and absurd porn's tropes and imagery are.

Her casting of Siffredi seems ultraloaded on this front. In *Romance*, he's a graceful actor, a sympathetically human foil to Paul's perplexing, ascetic blankness. When Paolo and Marie have sex—"Caroline seemed to be frightened of me and was crying," Siffredi told *The Sunday Times*, as speculation mounted in the media about how "real" the movie's scenes were—he offers to penetrate her anally, which she declines, as though Breillat is giving an explicit nod to Siffredi's reputation and career. The director later cast him again in *Anatomy of Hell*, a movie based on her 2001 book *Pornocracy*, in which a woman pays a gay man to stare at her naked for four whole days, culminating in a deeply unsettling climax. Breillat's project, the author Chris Kraus wrote in an introduction to *Pornocracy*, "has been to exhume the unspeakable 'horror' of hetero-female identity and look at it, coolly." What Breillat sees, Kraus argues, is "that we are still powerfully shaped by the fundamentalist fear and loathing of all things female . . . and this vestigial hatred just might explain the lingering absence of women in public culture." In one scene in *Anatomy of Hell*, the man paints lipstick around the woman's vagina and later rapes her with the handle of a rake—both expressions of immature, ferocious loathing, coincidentally or not, that proliferate in the pornography of Max Hardcore.

The question of whether or not someone can replicate abusive imagery in order to explore what it means—without falling into its trap—is the question of Breillat's work, but also of sex itself. How can women define sexuality for themselves in a culture constructed so robustly out of male desire and even outright male hatred for women? Porn, the feminist filmmaker Erika Lust has argued, is essentially a discourse about what people want from sex where only one male voice is speaking. Breillat's characters often seem to have internalized their own abjection, to be fundamentally dissatisfied because what they crave is debasement—which, in its way, is just another iteration of the conditioned impulse to give men what *they* want. And in this sense, she's playing into a long-standing national tradition. The most celebrated literary narrative of female desire in France during the twentieth century was *The Story of O*, a 1954 novel about a Parisian fashion photographer who's indoctrinated into willing sexual servitude by her lover and subsequently branded, tagged, and passed around like a sexualized piece of livestock. The book's moral is that happiness lies in slavery; the author, Anne Desclos, revealed forty years after publication that she'd written it as a dare for her married lover, whom she worried was losing interest in her. Her goal wasn't the confident expression of her own desires, but self-abnegation so profound that it would render her irreplaceable.

In 2001, the French art critic Catherine Millet shocked the literary establishment when she published a memoir, *The Sexual Life of Catherine M.*, in which she revealed that for most of her life she'd thrilled in offering herself up at orgies, at parties, and in public parks to anyone she happened to meet, sometimes thirty men at a time, relishing her reduction to "a choice piece of merchandise." (Breillat, for what it's worth, stages a fantasy scene just like this in *Romance*, in which women, hidden from view from the waist up, are penetrated by multiple men they can't see—bifurcated into people at the top and objects at the bottom.) Millet's account, boastful and yet detached, rarely mentions pleasure; the thrill for her, she says in the beginning, seems to be in accumulation and submission—in being the most prolific, most willing, most objectified object she can be. One of the most cherished memories from all her carnal adventures, she notes, is when a male friend writes in his diary that she "deserves the highest praise for her calmness and availability in every situation." She's thrilled to be seen as the perennial fantasy of an emotionally uncomplicated, sexually available woman.

In *Female Chauvinist Pigs*, Ariel Levy argues that sexuality in the aughts was so defined by a kind of conformist, "liberated" exhibitionism that many women found themselves completely detached from their own desires. What's worth noting, though, is that movies made by male filmmakers in this movement don't seem animated by pleasure either. In Michael Haneke's 2001 movie *The Piano Teacher*, Isabelle Huppert plays a professor at a music conservatory whose emotional and sexual repression leads her to a disturbing masochistic relationship with a student. Patrice Chéreau's 2001 film *Intimacy* stars Mark Rylance and Kerry Fox as lovers who meet weekly in a filthy studio apartment for sweaty, urgent, joyless sex. Their encounters, strikingly explicit and rendered with a clinical realism, are steeped in shame and regret, and yet each cannot give the other up.

In the beginning of the movie, the camera pans over Rylance's sleeping body with a clinical eye, assessing the pouchy skin, the body hair, the vulnerable, deglamorized kind of physicality you typically only see when you're on deeply close terms with someone. "Most people will find *Intimacy*'s graphic display of sex and nudity neither beautifully erotic nor excitingly pornographic," Alan A. Stone wrote in the *Boston Review* shortly after the movie was released. "But it is as real as Chéreau means it to be, and real sex can be disturbing." The movie studies postmodern sexual compulsion, Stone argued, the kind that "offers no liberation, but only repetition and the search for new aphrodisiac rituals, new partners, and new experiences . . . isolating people rather than connecting them." Its title is ironic: Rylance's character, Jay, craves real intimacy and connection with someone more than anything, but cannot have it.

The writer Alexandra Kleeman has suggested that sex, on-screen, presents an ongoing puzzle, because it "cannot be separated from the malignancy of the social structures that surround it." Amid a broader discussion of desire, equity, and consent that emerged in the years following #MeToo, authors including Nona Willis Aronowitz and Katherine Angel have tried to unpack what "good" sex might require or mean now. How can we untangle what we want from what we've only ever seen on-screen? Where does indoctrination end and exploration begin?

But in the new digital age of the aughts, as interpreted by auteur filmmakers, sex was both shockingly explicit and deeply sad, mired in melancholy and isolation that would come to seem prophetic. The desire to make sex appear *real* on-screen—in the movies of Breillat, Chéreau, Despentes and Trinh Thi, Vincent Gallo, Lars von Trier—seems to be to shock us out of complacency, out of the comfort of assuming that art is just art, and to realize what it's telling us about our own lives. It's the female filmmakers, though, who grapple with the most difficult truth of all: that contemporary sexuality has been shaped and informed by a million cultural products and experiences long before any one movie begins. And that for women, true satisfaction might require a drastic reappraisal and redistribution of power.

IN 2004, there came a story that defined in stark visual form how obscene the sexualized abuse of power could be. First, *The*

New Yorker obtained a fifty-three-page secret report on a US military prison in Iraq called Abu Ghraib that revealed multiple instances of "sadistic, blatant, and wanton criminal abuses" at the prison, as well as acts of sexual assault and abuse. The CBS series *60 Minutes* then received photographic evidence of some of the worst incidents—the forcible sexual humiliation of Iraqi prisoners, who were stripped, chained and hooded, made to masturbate, piled into pyramids made of human bodies, and posed as if they were giving oral sex to other prisoners. In one photo, the former specialist Charles Graner kneels over the body of a detainee who's been tortured to death, smiling and giving a thumbs-up for the camera. With his black-framed glasses, mustache, and teeth-baring grin, Graner bears an uncanny resemblance to the photographer Terry Richardson.

It was Richardson, in fact, who identified what genre the photographs belonged to. He saw the images from Abu Ghraib not as evidence of horrific sexualized abuse, but as personal snapshots documenting adventures. "I know most people have collections of this kind of material, even in the fashion industry," he said in the introduction to *Terryworld*. "You look at the images from Iraq, with that 20-year-old girl making prisoners masturbate for the camera. It comes from porn." This was, he argued, the new normal: people with cameras, documenting their sexual activity, collecting the evidence and displaying it to friends, no matter what kind of cruelty it revealed. It was a millennial impulse everyone seemed to have internalized—in the art world, on college campuses, in the military. The mode of the moment was "ironic" X-rated performance, edgy and detached.

(A 2010 ad for American Apparel in France even arranged female models on top of one another as a "pyramide humaine," completing the imitative circle.)

In *The Porning of America*, Kevin M. Scott and Carmine Sarracino argue that by 2008, porn had "so thoroughly been absorbed into every aspect of our everyday lives—language, fashion, advertisements, movies, the Internet, music, magazines, television, video games—that it has almost ceased to exist as something separate from mainstream culture." Contemporary porn by the aughts was its own kind of audiovisual lingua franca, whose tropes and stylistic habits were recognized by almost everyone. At Abu Ghraib, the soldiers engaging in the torture and abuse of prisoners weren't explicitly trying to make porn—it was just how they had internalized expressions of dominance and power. Conditions at the prison for the soldiers were reportedly chaotic, aggressive, and wildly sexualized, with widespread nudity. "The stories that have surfaced suggest a mix of teen sex comedy, porn movie plot, and horror movie," Scott and Sarracino wrote. They likened one instance of an army captain secretly photographing female subordinates while they showered to "a scene straight out of *Porky's*." One prisoner was given the nickname "Ron Jeremy," after the hirsute, portly porn legend.

What the soldiers ended up capturing on camera, though, was also torture porn, ideologically and aesthetically aligned with movies that often seemed to present a revenge defense for acts of extreme humiliation and violence. Taboos are willfully flouted: In one photo, a cowering prisoner is smeared with human excrement; in another, a man whose hands are behind his head is threatened with two dogs. Both men are naked. The female soldier Lynndie England points and grins at a male prisoner being forced to masturbate while she watches; Megan Ambuhl injects a man in the leg with an unknown substance. The violation of the prisoners' bodies is the text, but the violation of their religious beliefs and dignity as Muslims is the subtext. The sexual humiliation of detainees, the feminist scholar Laura Sjoberg argued, was intended to signal "the victory of hegemonic American manliness over subordinated Iraqi masculinities."

In *Hostel*, Óli casually photographs himself having sex with a stranger in a bathroom, sharing the image for proof. Later, to persuade the tourists to visit the murder-hostel, Alexei shows them photographs of himself having group sex with multiple blondes. "The pictures taken by American soldiers in Abu Ghraib," Susan Sontag wrote in 2004, "reflect a shift in the use made of pictures—less objects to be saved than messages to be disseminated, circulated." England and Graner reportedly recorded themselves having rough, sadomasochistic sex—reorienting things to make themselves the object, although with the very obvious difference that they willingly participated in what they were doing. (England argued that she was coerced by Graner into taking many of the photos with prisoners and that she did whatever he told her to because she didn't want to lose him.) In 2005, reporters learned that some soldiers in Iraq were posting pictures of Iraqi corpses and body parts on a website called Nowthatsfuckedup.com in exchange for free access to the site, which also hosted porn—sex, death, and atrocities all commingling together on the same jaunty forum.

Sontag argued that most of the Abu Ghraib pictures "seem part of a larger confluence of torture and pornography: a young woman leading a naked man around on a leash is classic dominatrix imagery. And you wonder how much of the sexual tortures inflicted on the inmates of Abu Ghraib was inspired by the vast repertory of pornographic imagery available on the Internet—and which ordinary people, by sending out Webcasts of themselves, try to emulate." It was, she concluded, all part of a culture in which self-debasement had become a popular spectacle: "Secrets of private life that, formerly, you would have given nearly anything to conceal, you now clamor to be invited on a television show to reveal. What is illustrated by these photographs is as much the culture of shamelessness as the reigning admiration for unapologetic brutality." Not long after the Abu Ghraib photos emerged, in fact, some porn sites began to copy them, with new websites titled Sex in War and Iraq Babes capitalizing on an audience who relished the degradation: images replicating images replicating images, all trading in the currency of sex and the commoditizing of body horror.

By the time *Hostel* was released in 2006, its portrayal of Americans drawing premium prices as auction items to be tortured to death felt politically loaded by the context of Abu Ghraib and ongoing interrogations of American power. The first half of the movie presents Paxton and Josh as stereotypical douchebros on tour, riding roughshod all over Europe in search of sex, drugs, and stupidity. It almost feels self-aware, as though

Roth is reminding audiences, *This is how the world really sees us*. But in the second half, after sensitive and ethical Josh is murdered, Paxton instantly becomes the film's vengeful hero, shooting and stabbing his way to safety. His are the kind of values it takes to really triumph over evil, *Hostel* insinuates—a message that most American filmgoers found inherently familiar and much easier to digest.

WHILE AUTEURS WERE RENDERING sex on film with joyless shrugs, and horror directors were crafting scenes so bloody and *jouissant* that they felt sexual, porn was itself evolving. "The looks of actresses and styles of pornography change and shift every few years, along with the tastes of viewers," a *Los Angeles Magazine* profile of a new teenage star named Sasha Grey explained in 2006. "Sasha is not blond and endowed like [Jenna] Jameson. But with her pale, adolescent looks and a penchant for extreme hardcore scenes, she is a girl of the moment."

Porn's new "It Girl" had appeared in 2006, when, shooting her first-ever sex scene with Rocco Siffredi shortly after her eighteenth birthday, she unexpectedly asked him to punch her in the stomach. Youth has historically been a prized asset in the industry, where careers tend to last just a few years at best. But Grey—slender, dark-eyed, angsty, and eager for scenes so rough they made even her agent raise an eyebrow—was a sign of porn's new status quo in other directions. "As far as I'm concerned, Suicide Girl types with black hair and tattoos are the new blondes with bolt-on tits," she told *Rolling Stone* in 2009. "Those women look the same, and they're idiots." Her interviewer, Vanessa Grigoriadis, described Grey envisioning herself "as a performance-art Camille Paglia," someone who was "exploring the outer edges of pornography" in rebellious, slightly trollish style. Watching a scene in which Grey choked herself to orgasm using a black necktie, Grigoriadis noted, "Her performances are calibrated to destabilize, and they succeed at that goal."

Raised in Sacramento, Grey saw her first porn clip at the age of eleven. Jameson, who was previously the biggest adult-film star in the world, had famously defined her career on her own terms, refusing to do anal scenes or double penetration. By the early 2000s, she'd evolved from a humble performer into a global brand, selling sex toys and lingerie but also action figures and homewares. Grey, by contrast, arrived on the scene ready to unsettle people with the nature of what she enjoyed. The things she'd do, she told *Los Angeles Magazine*, included, "slapping, peeing, spit, vomit." Even electrocution. It wasn't just that she sensed the industry's shift toward extreme content and wanted to succeed, although she did. Erudite and endlessly curious—her MySpace page mentioned Yeats, Baudrillard, and Nietzsche—she seemed to see pain as a wild artistic adventure, like a millennial, gender-flipped Marquis de Sade.

Grey's affect on-screen was somehow one of both controlled,

detached hauteur and total, unrestrained release. And her philosophy, she told *Rolling Stone*, was one of female liberation—she wanted girls who watched her scenes to realize that "it's OK to be a slut." The tension of her particular stardom was in how well her particular sexual tastes happened to suit a moment in which violent, misogynistic treatment of women during sex was becoming mainstreamed. In large part, this was because of how easily accessible extreme porn became during the second half of the aughts, when three free tube sites—PornHub, RedTube, and YouPorn—were established that together would lead to the consolidation of sex online. Porn no longer had to be paid for; virtually anything you wanted to see was contained within the same platform: fetish clips and rape scenes posted alongside revenge porn and nostalgic fragments of Jenna Jameson. By 2013, sites under the PornHub umbrella were estimated to be drawing one billion visitors a month.

One 2010 study of more than three hundred popular pornographic scenes found that 88 percent contained some kind of physical aggression, typically spanking, gagging, or slapping, with force overwhelmingly being meted out against women by men. Inevitably, these kinds of behaviors filtered out, leading to demonstrable changes in how people were having sex in their own lives. A 2019 study found that 38 percent of British women under forty reported having experienced unwanted slapping, choking, gagging, or spitting during sex. The emphasis here should be on the word "unwanted": Every adult should be free to have sex however they want with whoever consents to join them. I'm not interested in kink-shaming, and I'm not remotely opposed to porn. I'm curious, rather, about how culture conditions desire, and what it means that the impulse to inflict violence on women is often blindly sanctioned in a sexual context in ways it would never be otherwise. "As heartbreaking as it is to think of sorority girls trapped in dorm rooms with boyfriends who expect them to act like Grey," Grigoriadis wrote in *Rolling Stone*, "it's just as sad to think of Grey as a repressed office drone who has to live out her fantasies in secret on Craigslist over the weekend. Someone is going to lose here, and it's not Grey."

But nor was the actress, nor anyone else in porn, totally immune from the forces that were destabilizing the industry and the rest of the economy. In 2009, the director Steven Soderbergh cast Grey in his low-budget indie movie *The Girlfriend Experience*, playing a high-end call girl, Chelsea, who offers clients a more intimate kind of service tailored to their emotional needs as much as their sexual desires. The movie takes place against the backdrop of the financial crisis, as Chelsea's wealthy clients fret about their plummeting portfolios and how much they're about to lose. Chelsea keeps meticulous notes about what she wears and what she does with each date: a Michael Kors dress and La Perla lingerie for dinner and a movie screening of *Man on Wire*; a Kiki de Montparnasse corset for lunch at Nobu. Some clients don't even want to have sex; they just want someone to talk to. "I'm feeling kind of stressed out," one tells her. "I should probably see a shrink, but it seems like a lot more fun to see you."

Grey is fascinatingly inscrutable in the role—she has a smoldering, sleepy-eyed presence on-screen, but in a slightly alien kind of way, eating, laughing, fucking, and scrutinizing herself without any discernible signs of pleasure. The movie, ultimately, is much less interested in sex than in money, and in anticipating the ways in which everyone will have to commoditize themselves in the future. Chelsea is a product for sale, but so is her boyfriend, a personal trainer, and so are her clients, screenwriters and investors and producers, and so is the journalist who interviews her for a story and the web producer helping her to improve her Google ranking. Chelsea, in fact, ends up feeling like the avatar for an entire generation of millennial job seekers being forced to learn how to hustle—how to market and orient themselves and perform intricate kinds of emotional labor in order to stay above water.

The Girlfriend Experience was prophetic in other ways too. The end of what had felt to many performers like an artistic and commercial golden age for the industry was now here, as porn's business model was upended by file sharing, piracy, and the total domination of a handful of free sites. A *New York* report from the 2011 Adult Video Awards in Las Vegas described an industry in rapid freefall, with some companies' profits having declined by as much as 80 percent. For their careers to survive, many performers would later find themselves pivoting to cam work and personally commissioned videos, before the 2016 launch of OnlyFans and the inevitable rise of artificially generated scenes would transform the marketplace yet again. Contemporary performances of sex would come to rely on the same emotional component as Chelsea's "girlfriend experience"—workers giving clients something they intimately needed that they couldn't get for free elsewhere.

One irony of the marketplace-driven sex economy was that the consumer suddenly had a lot more influence over what porn looked like. Where mainstream pornography had presented a cookie-cutter array of mostly toned White bodies, platforms such as OnlyFans allowed for more diversity of desire. A 2023 survey of celebrities making the most money on the platform found that many were in their fifties: the *Wild Things* and *Real Housewives* star Denise Richards, the *Sopranos* actress Drea de Matteo, *Scary Movie*'s Carmen Electra, *Baywatch*'s Donna D'Errico. Where Hollywood had long excised women in midlife from sexual roles, OnlyFans proved that plenty of people still found them extraordinarily desirable. "Everything changes," one of Chelsea's financier clients tells her in *The Girlfriend Experience*. This much was clear by 2010: Neither porn nor sex would be the same again.

CHAPTER 7

Gossip Girls

The Degradation of Women and Fame in Twenty-First-Century Media

As modern industrial societies change and as women themselves offer resistance to patriarchy, older forms of domination are eroded. But new forms arise, spread, and become consolidated.

SANDRA BARTKY (1982)

How do we not see that the treatment of It Girls translates to the treatment of all girls in our culture?

PARIS HILTON (2023)

For much of the aughts, the most popular pastime across culture and entertainment was watching and looking at women: on reality television, in pornography, in music videos, in magazines, in movies—all genres that were melding and merging and borrowing from one another with unnerving ease. An absurdist *Esquire* profile of Jessica Simpson from May 2008 assessed the singer from head to toe by way of introduction, as though to emulate the imagined reader's roving, greedy gaze: "Blond hair the way God meant, blond like Clorox sunshine. A caviar body, if you like your caviar lacquered in barbecue sauce. Breasts like plucked guinea hens, undercooked and overstuffed. . . . Cheerleader legs. Jackknifing legs that split the air like seesaws." On the cover of the magazine, Simpson posed topless, her hair teased into bombshell waves. Next to her was shaky text in all caps: "WE SHOT THIS IMAGE TO CATCH YOUR EYE SO YOU WILL PICK UP THIS ISSUE . . . AND IMMERSE YOURSELF IN THE MOST GRIPPING STORY YOU WILL READ THIS YEAR." Simpson, the magazine made clear, was the bait—the Trojan horse to sell a much more substantive piece of journalism about a soldier killed in Iraq, a story that actually mattered.

This cover by itself was telling. People wanted to peer at gorgeous young female stars; they were even willing to pay to do so. But more and more, they were resenting those women for making them look. Public prurience was, by this point, curdling into something darker and more hateful. And celebrity media was stuck in a loop: The more overexposed women sold, the more attention was paid to women in turn, provoking reactions that got yet more attention and led to yet more exposure.

By 2007, the most notorious women in the world were under unprecedented scrutiny, and many of them were buckling under the pressure. In January, the same month that Hillary Clinton announced she was running for president, the former child star Lindsay Lohan checked into rehab during the filming of *I Know Who Killed Me*, a garish torture-porn thriller in which she played identical twins. In February, Anna Nicole

Smith overdosed on prescription drugs at a hotel in Hollywood, Florida, resulting in a media feeding frenzy that led to video of Smith's corpse being captured for television and the contents of her fridge (methadone and SlimFast) being leaked online. Eight days later, Britney Spears, who by this point was the twenty-five-year-old mother of two young children, shaved her own head in full view of the paparazzi at a hair salon in the San Fernando Valley. The scene felt so shocking in part because Spears was attacking the thing that had made her so famous: her own presentation of desirable, covetable femininity. We had come to expect and anticipate chaos from young female stars, but not this—not such a flagrantly public display of self-disassembly.

In March, I had tickets to see twenty-three-year-old Amy Winehouse at the Shepherd's Bush Empire in London, and while I was having dinner with a friend nearby, I received a text message saying that the show had been canceled. Later, we were drinking at a hotel bar when in walked Amy herself, as tiny as a child in a black polo shirt and grubby denim cutoffs, almost catatonic, much more delicate in person than she was in pictures. She walked over to us, for some reason, and just *stared*, her eyes glassy and unfocused. She muttered something, but we couldn't understand it. A woman came over and apologized to us, hustling her away. Amy had just broken up with her boyfriend, she said, and was having a hard time. Soon she'd be reunited with the ex-lover who'd inspired her second album, *Back to Black*, a heroin addict whose chaotic relationship with her would culminate in a public brawl a few months later, bloodied ballet pumps and open wounds all over the news, jail time (for him), and, ultimately, her death in 2011 from what would be labeled "misadventure" by the coroner.

In April, Whitney Houston and Bobby Brown divorced, after a turbulent marriage marked by charges of battery and drug abuse, some of it captured or alluded to on the 2005 Bravo reality show *Being Bobby Brown*. During the same month, Kate Moss was photographed hanging dangerously out of a window, a lit cigarette in her mouth, while her boyfriend, the scandal-prone musician Pete Doherty, played guitar. (A few months earlier, an actor named Mark Blanco had died after seemingly falling from a balcony at a party where Doherty was present.) In May, Lohan was arrested for cocaine possession and driving under the influence of a controlled substance. In June, Paris Hilton began a forty-five-day jail sentence for violating her probation for an earlier reckless-driving charge; she was released after three days, then recalled to jail, sobbing, by a judge who ruled that her sentence had specified imprisonment. In July, Lohan was arrested again. In August, Nicole Richie announced that she was nearly four months pregnant, shortly before *she* was sent to jail—for a grand total of eighty-two minutes—on an earlier charge of driving under the influence.

In September, nudes of the eighteen-year-old actress and Disney star Vanessa Hudgens were leaked online, linked to without pixelation by gossip blogs including *Perez Hilton* even though (a) they had been stolen and (b) Hudgens was underage when they were taken. In December, the twenty-one-year-old actress Mischa Barton was arrested for driving under the influence of alcohol, almost two years after her character on *The*

O.C., Marissa Cooper, had been killed off *in a car crash*—in part because TV bloggers on a forum popular at the time hated her. Also in December, the sixteen-year-old Nickelodeon star Jamie Lynn Spears, Britney's sister, announced that she was pregnant.

It's hard to describe how dizzying this particular moment felt—being constantly bombarded with images and video and updates of celebrities breaking down in real time, cast members in a vast multiplatform soap opera they'd never officially signed up for. If you lived in London or Los Angeles or New York, you could even cross paths with them in real life, barhopping and shopping—I ran right into Paris Hilton outside Henri Bendel on Fifth Avenue in the fall of 2007—and posing for the omnipresent cameras, drawing us civilians into the drama. Between 9/11 and the financial crisis of 2008, celebrity media was at its febrile peak. For much of the twenty-first century, the rewards for being perpetually visible as a young famous woman had exceeded the costs: Celebrity during the aughts meant surrendering to surveillance, and many were willing to do it. "I always raised them to be exposed, and to be a part of everything," Kathy Hilton told *Vanity Fair* of her then-teenage daughters, Paris and Nicky, in 2000. But for others, who hadn't consented to nonstop scrutiny and withering detestation across brand-new kinds of media, it was fundamentally destabilizing. Some have never recovered.

I came to this project from the beginning because the cruelty and disdain expressed toward women during the aughts seemed to be more significant than it's often given credit for.

This was a moment in which every woman was presented as being available for critique and public dissection, from teenagers suffering mental health crises to the first female candidate for president. Early in 2008, when Hillary Clinton briefly welled up in a coffee shop after a bruising loss in the Iowa caucuses, the moment was interpreted as being both messily melodramatic enough for *TMZ* and a cynical ploy for sympathy and attention that eventually won her New Hampshire.

The nature of how women were being treated in mass media wasn't an aberration. Rather, it was the most logical place for postfeminism's ideals to lead. The women we were being conditioned to hate were too visible. (As they were often forced to be by the men who wouldn't stop taking pictures of them.) They were too sexual. (Which, it had been reiterated over and over again, was a woman's primary form of currency.) They were famous for nothing. (Thanks to a moment when the nature of celebrity had been upended, and women's bodies were considered to be in the public domain.) They were failing at the postfeminist project by taking its instructions, in the parlance of popular magazines, "too far." (They were too thin, too fake, too intoxicated, too narcissistic, too *much*.)

The celebrity coverage of the decade was where all the previous shifts and trends in popular culture over the aughts coalesced into something new: the end of privacy, a fixation on images, a brave new technological world of nonstop updates and constant exposure. In 2006, Kurt Andersen wrote that the gossip fixation of the age represented "postmodern democracy. The stars are brought down to the plebeians' level—but now the plebes are also provided with exhaustive instructions for achieving the hallucination that they are just like the stars." It's been well-documented by now that this particular decade was crushing for many of the women who lived through its lens, and they deserve reappraisal. But I'm interested, too, in what this moment did to those of us who were simply spectators: curious and even envious of the stars whose degradation was offered up to us as thrilling, perpetual, stakes-free entertainment. How did it condition us to see ourselves? And, maybe more crucially, what did it condition us to think about other women and what they might be capable of?

ONE OF THE REASONS celebrity coverage exploded during the aughts was that people craved distraction. In the immediate weeks after 9/11, American culture found itself scrambling to adapt to an entirely different world. Movies deemed to be violent, disturbing, or even abstractly iconoclastic were postponed or reedited before release; comedians found themselves wondering, in the words of Lorne Michaels on *Saturday Night Live*, whether it was appropriate to be funny against the context of such sharp national trauma. Awards ceremonies and sporting events ground to a halt. Celebrity coverage seemed impossibly trivial: In *TelevisionWeek*, Louis Chunovic wrote, "In the wake of the terrorist attack against the United States, it's hard to believe Americans once cared who would win *Big Brother 2*, or whether Anne Heche is crazy."

They had, though, and the dirty secret was that they still did. When the coronavirus pandemic began in 2020, I reported a story on how people were using popular culture to cope. A media psychologist told me that people tend to deal with stress and trauma in one of two ways—either by anesthetizing themselves with comforting fluff or by leaning fully toward the thing that scares them. (This is why so many people streamed *Outbreak* and *Contagion* during the spring of 2020, and also why *The Towering Inferno* felt newly relevant in the months after 9/11.) Celebrity coverage and reality competitions were, at this point, still comforting fluff. It wasn't a coincidence that some of the most enduring and influential reality shows—*American Idol*, *The Osbournes*, *The Bachelor*—debuted in 2002, as counterprogramming for a nation that craved placation.

At the same time, the media industry was reorienting itself more fully around stars: probing them on reality shows, analyzing their appeal, selling their lifestyles via attainable, mass-market knockoffs. In 2000, the publisher Jann Wenner had retooled *Us* from a monthly publication covering the entertainment industry to a weekly magazine with a focus on "friendly" celebrity coverage. By 2001, the strategy wasn't yet working, so Wenner sold a 50 percent stake in *Us Weekly* to Disney, setting up cross-promotional opportunities with shows on Disney-owned ABC. A year later, Wenner appointed the former women's-magazine editor Bonnie Fuller editor of *Us Weekly*, a move that would prove even more consequential. Fuller had an intuitive understanding of both what readers wanted and what would sell. "She's a vulgarizer and a titillator—but fashionably so," Michael Wolff wrote in 2002. "She's taking *Us*'s generic newsstand-celebrity approach and has begun to turn it into something truly and excitingly and originally tawdry."

This wasn't quite fair or true. Fuller was less reverent with celebrities than Wenner had originally wanted to be, but only because she sensed that readers wanted to feel more of a connection with the people they read about. She introduced a handful of new features—including "Stars—They're Just Like Us!," "Who Wore It Best?," and "Star Beauty"—that turned the minutiae of famous people's lives into snackable visual content. During her sixteen-month stint at *Us Weekly*, newsstand sales more than doubled, while a handful of competing titles (*In Touch Weekly* among them) jumped into the fray. Photographers suddenly had a lucrative new opportunity capturing candid photos of stars while they were shopping at the farmers' market or picking up a Frappuccino, any one of which could sell for thousands of dollars. And as rival magazines competed for "exclusives," it was easier to make money than it had ever been.

The competition among photographers led some to employ extreme tactics to get shots. Jennifer Lopez once revealed that during her wedding to Marc Anthony, the couple couldn't hear each other's vows because a paparazzi helicopter hovering overhead was so loud. Jennifer Aniston sued a photographer in 2002 after he scaled a neighbor's wall to snap her sunbathing topless in her garden. Photographers hid in bushes and sand dunes, rented all manner of aerial and aquatic vehicles, and often goaded stars with verbal abuse to try to get them to react. (The actress Keira Knightley has talked about how, early in her career, two dozen photographers could be posted outside her house at any one time, sometimes calling her a "whore" to her face to get her or her boyfriend to react.) Prior to 2013, when legislation was passed to protect the children of celebrities, whom readers often particularly wanted to see, there were no ethical or legal qualms about targeting them. That year, seven-year-old Suri Cruise was berated by a stranger as being a "bitch" and a "little brat" for complaining as photographers swarmed her car in New York City.

Technology was also starting to transform celebrity coverage and the business of media. In 2002, the former *Financial Times* journalist Nick Denton launched *Gawker*, an intentionally irreverent portal for gossip and media news that was ruder and more scathing than a mainstream publication had ever been before. *Gawker*'s sister site, the sex- and porn-oriented *Fleshbot*, debuted as a spin-off in November 2003, distinguishing itself by being one of the first places to publish Paris Hilton's sex tape. Two years later, the caustic blogger Mario Lavandeira, better known as Perez Hilton—named in "tribute" to the heiress—launched his own site for nonstop celebrity updates, distinguished by his habit of defacing agency photos of stars with profane doodles (penises, semen dripping from their mouths) and hand-scrawled nicknames so that he could claim "fair use." In 2005, the former lawyer and journalist Harvey Levin founded the gossip site TMZ, named for the "thirty-mile zone" around Los

Angeles used to determine employee benefits for Hollywood. TMZ's first scoop was a video of Paris Hilton and her then-boyfriend, Stavros Niarchos, leaving a nightclub, crashing into a parked car, and then fleeing the scene. (Given how pivotal Hilton was to the launch of three such influential media brands during the aughts, you have to wonder what gossip blogs would have done without her.)

It was around this time that paparazzi photography entered what the writer David Samuels described as its "industrial phase," prioritizing quantity of images over quality, and—in lieu of professional photographers—sending out roving squads of young men with digital cameras to literally stalk the stars who offered the best chance of return. The photo agency X17, which would become notorious for its relentless coverage of Spears, was founded in the late 1990s; by 2007, its Britney-related output was estimated to be worth $3 million a year, a quarter of the company's revenue. When the star shaved her head, the CBS show *Entertainment Tonight* paid a rumored $80,000 to X17 for rights to the photos for just one night.

The spike in celebrity news was so feverish, the profits so vast, and the access so unprecedented that it was easy for people to forget they were dealing with actual, vulnerable human beings. Stars had become more like characters—walking story-lines dealing with a litany of outlandish plot twists, from addictions and infidelity to arrests and shotgun marriages that were shorter in duration than the hangovers that followed them. Perez Hilton was particularly cruel: In 2008, he sold T-shirts after the actor Heath Ledger's death bearing the phrase "Why

Couldn't It Be Britney?" And his nicknames—the teenage daughter of Bruce Willis and Demi Moore was named "Potato Head"—picked on girls for no other reason than that they occasionally appeared out in public.

Tabloid magazines had led the way in offering a more unfiltered look at celebrity life. But blogs had no filters at all; they published anything they could get. It was around this time that photographers started actively pursuing what are now called "upskirt photos"—images of a woman's underwear or lack thereof. Adult men would lie on the ground while young female stars were stepping out of cars to try to capture what was essentially nonconsensual pornography, and when the photographers succeeded, it was unfailingly their subjects who were shamed. Lindsay Lohan, an ABC News story from 2006 lamented, had been caught "panty-less four times over the last two months." Perez Hilton, interviewed for comment, insisted that the celebrities were exposing themselves because they liked the attention, not because dozens of men were suddenly pointing telephoto lenses at their genitalia. The actress Emma Watson once explained how, as she was heading into her eighteenth birthday party in 2008, photographers positioned themselves way down on the ground to take upskirt pictures of her that would have been illegal to publish the previous day. In 2010, Perez Hilton was excoriated when he posted links to crotch shots of the Disney star Miley Cyrus while she was underage; Cyrus ultimately declined to press charges.

One of the first upskirt victims, as Sarah Ditum writes in her book *Toxic*, was the rapper Lil' Kim, who inadvertently ended up on the cover of the October 2004 issue of *Hustler* after her minidress rode up while she was performing onstage and a photographer managed to snap a picture of her exposed vulva. After that, it was open season on any woman unwise enough to wear a dress in public. Upskirt photos made literal the subtext of paparazzi shots: This was a business dedicated to turning famous women's bodies into profit, with sexually aggressive overtones. The photographers who haunted Princess Diana until her death in 1997 supposedly used violent language to describe their methods: they "blitzed her" as a group, "whacked her," "hose[d] her down." The overwhelmed princess once reportedly shouted at them to go "rape someone else." In her 2023 memoir, *The Woman in Me,* Spears describes the moment she shaved her head and how she flipped after a photographer repeatedly harassed her a few days later, attacking him with an umbrella. "Later, that paparazzo would say in a documentary about me, 'That was not a good night for her . . . But it *was* a good night for us—'cause we got the money shot.'"

IF PAPARAZZI PHOTOGRAPHERS seemed intent on capturing or provoking celebrity debasement, they were simply following a model that started on television. "There has never been a better time to be a has-been," Alessandra Stanley wrote in *The New York Times* in 2003. "Reality shows flooding the midseason schedule are tapping a new vein: loser chic. From the slimmest niche cable shows to the major networks, television producers are plumbing the backwaters of Hollywood for entertainers willing to resurrect their careers by flaunting their failures."

Around the beginning of the aughts, the nature of celebrity— what it meant to be famous, what a person could become famous *for*, how we in the general public understood and related to people with fame—began to change, in ways that would have striking repercussions. The academic Sharon Marcus has argued that fame during the nineteenth century fell into two categories: exemplarity and impudence. There were people who were famous for modeling exceptional standards or achievements and people who flaunted their refusal to conform. During the twenty-first century, fame seemed to follow a similar pattern: exemplarity and shamelessness. There were the old-school stars who resisted the paparazzi, avoided interviews, and offered themselves up to the public mostly through their work. Then there was the new guard, who studied fame, courted it assiduously, engaged with photographers, behaved in ways that sold newspapers, and successfully elevated their profiles in the process. Occasionally, stars managed to be both. Jennifer Lopez, her former publicist told the podcast *Just Like Us*, "knew how to step out of a car or an apartment or house and create a photograph. She also knew, too, that nothing she could say would be as interesting as the way she looked."

Reality television, almost from its inception, had created a strange new hinterland halfway between fame and obscurity. Stars whose profiles had faded could participate in shows as a way to revive their flagging careers, capitalizing on nostalgia and reminding the public of who they once had been. Often, this meant reinforcing the hierarchy between the A-list and the hustlers. "I don't think this is the type of show that you would want to necessarily cast, I don't know, Tom Cruise in," John Saade, an executive producer of ABC's *I'm a Celebrity, Get Me Out of Here!* told reporters in 2003. "I think that Melissa [Rivers] and Robin [Leach], these are perfect people for this show." (*I'm a Celebrity* also featured a pretransition Caitlyn Jenner, the first member of her family to engage with the genre; Tom Cruise did end up once appearing on a South Korean reality-variety show called *Running Man* in 2018, promoting the *Mission Impossible* franchise on a series that is hugely popular in China.)

But reality TV also created brand-new stars for a media firmament that badly needed them to fill space. Contestants who appeared on *The Bachelor* might soon appear on the cover of *Us Weekly*, thanks to both institutions' Disney parentage. In 2002, toward the end of the debut season of *American Idol,* Kelly Clarkson, Justin Guarini, and Nikki McKibbin appeared in *People* and on the cover of *Entertainment Weekly*; after Clarkson won, she made the cover of *Us Weekly.* By 2011, according to *The Wall Street Journal,* "people who owe their fame to reality TV accounted for about 40 percent of the covers of the six major celebrity weekly magazines." Janice Min, who became the editor of *Us Weekly* in 2003, correctly identified that members of the general public, and women in particular, loved to look at stars whose lives, trajectories, and beauty regimes seemed more accessible, more like their own. But as the communications professor Erin A. Meyers has argued, coverage of reality stars "did more than just fill pages. It also helped validate the performance of . . . ordinariness, or just being yourself, as a viable path to fame in ways that resonated across celebrity culture."

This media culture occasionally led to shows that renegotiated what fame actually meant even as we watched. In 2001, following the extraordinary success of the British *Big Brother*, producers experimented with a version of the show featuring celebrities that would ostensibly raise money for charity. Later, *Celebrity Big Brother* became so popular that it replaced the original concept altogether. In 2006, producers impishly set up contestants with a trick only viewers at home knew about: Ten of the housemates qualified as "celebrities"—including the basketball player Dennis Rodman and the *Baywatch* star Traci Bingham—but one, Chantelle Houghton, was a nobody masquerading as a pop star, tasked with persuading the assembled group that she was really one of their kind. To add extra levels of metatextuality, Houghton had once worked as a Paris Hilton look-alike. She successfully tricked the other stars and went on to be crowned the winner in the season finale, signing a six-figure deal for her first interview upon leaving the Big Brother house.

What distinguished Houghton, *The Guardian* argued, was her "daffy, upbeat personality," but also her "chutzpah"—the shamelessness required to successfully present yourself as famous in the twenty-first century. It was a quality that the most successful reality stars of the decade would all share, along with a willingness to cheerfully submit to potential humiliation and debasement. *The Simple Life,* which transported two supposedly spoiled and stuck-up heiresses from Beverly Hills to the "real" world of rural America, drew its appeal from the promise that Hilton and Nicole Richie would be made uncomfortable, humbled, forced to earn an honest living. "30 days, no money, no luxury, and no clue," a voice-over taunted at the beginning of the series. "Will they make it?" The theme song piled on: "They're both spoiled rotten / Will they cry when they hit bottom?"

Hilton knew, she writes in her memoir, that "there was huge potential for humiliation. I needed to partner with someone who had no fear of looking silly—no fear of *being* silly." The subtext was often sexual; over the course of the series, Hilton and Richie milked cows, made sausages, worked as maids at a nudist colony, and gave "butt readings" to male patrons of a storefront astrologer. In the second season, stranded at a service station with nothing but a pink pickup truck and an Airstream trailer, they were obliged to ask total strangers to give them gas money, with everything that setup implied. Pretending to work, Hilton writes, was actually work: For the first season, the stars were shooting eighteen-hour days for eighteen weeks in midsummer Arkansas. In the end, somewhat surprisingly, reviews were positive. "*The Simple Life* might not feel very fresh," a *Slate* analysis argued, "but it might pull off a reality show first, with public humiliation offering someone their best shot at redemption."

The reward for both women for having surrendered themselves to the cameras was more fame and more cameras. The leaking of Hilton's sex tape had momentarily disrupted things—and truly devastated the star, she writes—but she sensed that leaning into the scandal and refusing to be ashamed would neutralize its ability to hurt her. Appearing on *Saturday Night Live* to promote the show at the end of 2003, Hilton participated in a *Weekend Update* segment with Jimmy Fallon in which the comedian joked about the "Paris Hilton," how "roomy" it was, and whether he could get in through "the back entrance." ("It doesn't matter who you are," Hilton replied. "It's not gonna happen.") Her willingness to play up her reputation was extraordinarily successful: By 2004, her name was the number-two most Googled term in the entire world, second only to Britney Spears.

What was peculiar about Hilton's fame, and about the fame of other reality stars of this era, was how accessible it seemed, as though being captured on camera was itself enough to make someone famous. "My generation thinks of celebrities as their peers—like neighbors, or people you went to high school with," Janice Min said in a 2006 interview for a *New York* piece about "American celebrity mania." The emergence of new celebrity categories positioned awkwardly between A-listers and nobodies made the lines even blurrier. Hilton, an inveterate salesperson, sold jewelry, perfume, and cultural products that promised girls more proximity to her specific experience. In her 2004 book *Confessions of an Heiress*, part satire, part self-help guide, she offered readers advice on how to be just like her: "Channel your own inner heiress, create your own image, and project an extreme sense of confidence."

When Hilton was targeted by a string of robberies orchestrated by high schoolers in 2008 and 2009, the perpetrators— quickly nicknamed the "bling ring"—seemed to be motivated by aspiration. They wanted the dresses Hilton wore to clubs, the Gucci sunglasses and the jewelry and the Louis Vuitton totes. The possessions of celebrities by this point were being so thoroughly documented and scrutinized that owning them, it was implied, might redistribute their power. A detective told *Vanity Fair*, "It may be a stretch, but is wanting to wear somebody's clothes that different from wanting to wrap yourself up in their skin, like that guy in *The Silence of the Lambs?*" One senses that if covetous teenagers could have forcibly occupied Hilton's physicality and identity, they would have. For the first time, one of the most famous women in the world felt not like an alien breed but an upgraded, bedazzled version of a normal girl. "In their world of Facebook and Twitter, Instagram and TMZ, where everybody was a star of their own social universe, as well as being their own paparazzi, the suburban teenagers idolized the people they were [closest] to being themselves," Andrew O'Hagan later wrote in the *London Review of Books*.

One of the thieves, Alexis Neiers, was even filming an E! reality series, *Pretty Wild*, during the time of her arrest, executive produced by Chelsea Handler. The premise was that three wannabe stars were being raised by their mother, a former *Playboy* model, to manifest fame for themselves, in accordance with the teachings of *The Secret*. "At home, my mom and my sisters and I were getting up every morning and saying this affirmation together, saying essentially that we were going to have careers in the entertainment industry benefiting the world," Neiers told *The Cut* in 2020. Somewhat ironically, these affirmations did result in fame when Neiers was arrested for burglary, a moment that happened off camera but was later restaged by E! for scenes in the show. During her time in jail, she was briefly neighbors in protective custody with Lohan, whose home had been among those targeted. And in 2013, in a twist Neiers could never have envisioned, she was played by Emma Watson in *The Bling Ring*, a movie about the Hollywood burglaries directed by the auteur and Hollywood scion Sofia Coppola.

In an alternate world, and with more irony, *Pretty Wild* could have been a hit in the Kardashian mode; with more privilege and less substance abuse, it could have emulated *The Hills*. That MTV reality show, which ran from 2006 to 2010, was in some ways the apotheosis of how media in the aughts manufactured celebrities to best serve its needs, transforming ordinary high schoolers, Cinderella-style, into walking advertorials. Unlike the troubled Neiers or the tart Kardashian sisters, Lauren Conrad, the serene, wide-eyed star of the show, was a perfectly anodyne canvas upon which brands could showcase themselves. A 2019 *Los Angeles Times* retrospective argued that the show helped define the modern influencer, making consumption—labels viewers could buy, nightclubs they could try to get into to party alongside their favorite stars—as major a reason to watch the show as the melodramatic, often scripted storylines.

The parasocial relationship fans had with the reality stars of this moment was part of the whole construction. We'd been told for years that stars were, in fact, just like us, but now, for the first time, we could invert the order of things and be just like them. That Conrad enjoyed all the trappings of celebrity without seeming to identify as one herself was crucial. She was portrayed on the show actually *working* toward a specific career in fashion—first studying at the Fashion Institute of Design and Merchandising and then interning at *Teen Vogue*. Some reality fans, used to the outrageous antics and nonstop drama that had previously been required to succeed on television, griped that Conrad was boring—"one of the dullest major characters in reality-television history," as *Salon* once put it. But her blankness was the point. For viewers tired of trying to keep up with celebrities whose lives and looks were constantly changing, Conrad was so surface-level that people watching could project themselves right into her shoes. (Literally into her shoes—listed conveniently in *Us Weekly* as peep-toed $225 slingbacks from Anne Klein.) Being "relatable" had never been such a profitable asset.

IN 2008, a TV show debuted on VH1 that seemed to embody how the nature of fame had changed over the course of the decade. *Celebrity Rehab with Dr. Drew* was a series that combined the most prurient aspects of sensationalist TV—watching people struggle with addiction—with the by-any-means ethos of celebrity revival. The series was hosted by Dr. Drew Pinsky, a blandly handsome, capable presence who'd become famous for, as *The New York Times* put it, "navigating a precarious balance of professionalism and salaciousness." Pinsky's ability to indict people's most self-destructive impulses and behaviors while simultaneously turning them into entertainment—on a different show, he once commissioned a plastic surgeon to examine the seventeen-year-old tabloid sensation Courtney Stodden's breasts on camera to assess whether they were real—made him perfect for the moment.

Celebrity Rehab offered scenes of struggling stars at rock bottom doing hard drugs (the same kind of footage tabloids paid ridiculous amounts of money to publish), going through withdrawal, and openly discussing the traumatic events in their lives that had contributed to their addictions. Many were refugees from former reality shows: Brigitte Nielsen from VH1's *The Surreal Life*, Jessica Sierra from *American Idol*, Jason Wahler from *The Hills*. They came to rehab seeming desperate—not just for sobriety but also for attention and for a semblance of the lives and fame they'd once had. "I've had cameras on me the last ten years of my life," Seth Binzer, from the band Crazy Town, told *The New York Times*, which noted that he smoked crack on the show. "I'm comfortable around cameras."

What had begun on reality television as a simple trade, humiliation for exposure, was turning into something darker. The crueler online commentary got, the more clicks it seemed to receive in return. (In July 2007, when Lindsay Lohan was arrested, *Perez Hilton* reported sixty million page views.) The two pillars of cultural consumption after 9/11, celebrity fluff and violent spectacle, were colliding, and the incessant nature of celebrity coverage seemed to be having a dehumanizing effect, where certain people appeared less like human beings than symbols of decadent cultural decline. In a 2006 interview with *Salon*, Janice Min described Whitney Houston's addiction problems as celebrity "white noise," the kind you hardly notice because it's so omnipresent and so predictable. "She couldn't have been a bigger or more beloved star, and she was really the first black America's sweetheart," Min said. "Now she's not even worthy of *The Surreal Life*. She's fallen below the entertainment C-list level. It's almost too tragic to deal with."

That year, Houston's degradation had been put on display when Bobby Brown's sister sold pictures of the star's bathroom to the *National Enquirer*, along with an "insider" account of the depths of her drug addiction. The photos were striking in how sordid they were, tarnishing the singer's reputation more efficiently than any other medium could have managed. Glass pipes, lighters, and spoons covered in white powder sat on a countertop strewn with filthy plates, ashtrays, beer cans, and a copy of *Star* magazine with Jessica Simpson's face on the cover. By this point, Houston's problems had been well-documented. The *New York Post* reported in 2001 that MTV was collecting B-roll footage for a video obituary in case Houston overdosed. In 2002, she gave her infamous "crack is wack" interview to Diane Sawyer, who grilled Houston on her weight, drug use, and lackluster recent appearances and whether she was "tough enough" for show business. But the images of Houston's bathroom embodied a specific kind of horror. They provoked repulsion.

Disgust is one of the most powerful human responses and one of the least studied. The history of misogyny is defined by expressions of repulsion toward women and their bodies—pervasive ideas across culture, art, and religion that we are somehow unclean or putrid or, to use a term that was weaponized against Hillary Clinton, "nasty." Disgust is often triggered by fears of overt female sexuality: In the nineteenth century, a doctor in New Orleans who performed clitoridectomies on children described female masturbation as "moral leprosy." Over the past decade, social psychologists have also found that a person's sensitivity to disgust might be closely tied to their politics, impacting how they feel about gay rights, premarital sex, and gender equality. "When we experience disgust," Kathleen McAuliffe wrote in *The Atlantic* in 2019, "we tend to make harsher moral judgments."

Much of the coverage of certain celebrities during the second half of the aughts was written in ways that actively courted revulsion and condemnation. The website Hollywood-Tuna, which promised to give readers "a brutally honest perspective on the stench we call celebrities," published posts in a single month in 2005 titled "Alicia Keys Is Absolutely Disgusting," "Pedophile News: Heather Graham Considered Too Old," and "Pamela Anderson Spreading Her Disease." In a 2008 post about Miley Cyrus, Perez Hilton wrote, "Slutty needs to shut her hole." Of Amy Winehouse, Hilton noted that she'd neglected to wear underwear while performing a private concert, writing, "Grrrossss!!!!!!!!! Who needs to see cracked out snatch?" In 2006, when the oil heir Brandon Davis was doorstepped by photographers on his way out of a nightclub with Paris Hilton, he delighted them by referring to Lindsay Lohan, his ex, as "firecrotch." *The Hills* star Spencer Pratt, during his feud with Lauren Conrad, nicknamed her "beef curtains" in a blog post.

Throughout the aughts, the popular understanding of celebrity had rotated through cycles of idolization, jealousy, curiosity, and resentment. Disgust seemed to be the inevitable final phase, an "appropriate" response to stars who'd been gifted with talent, fame, and wealth only to flame out, and to women who'd supposedly courted attention throughout their careers only to turn around now and complain about being victimized. When Pink released the single "Stupid Girls" in 2006, excoriating the "porno paparazzi girls" who showed too much to photographers and whose ambitions were limited to sugar daddies and VIP rooms, the lyrics marshaled disgust by comparing young female stars to a contagion: "The disease is growing, it's epidemic / I'm scared that there ain't a cure / The world believes it, and I'm growing crazy / I cannot take any more."

It's hard not to deduce that the specific tone of celebrity coverage in this moment was also fueled by an ongoing cultural taste for degradation, the more extreme the better. In 2005, when Paris Hilton played a minor role in the horror remake *House of Wax*, a marketing campaign for the movie posted ads around Los Angeles with the tagline "See Paris Die!" (In the scene itself, she's impaled in the head with a spear, a nasty and discernibly sexualized end.) There was a certain kind of visual horror in images of famous women brutalized in movies and visibly disintegrating in real life that suited the moment.

Commentators seemed nonchalant, even sanguine, about the idea that some of the women whose antics occupied the cameras could die. By 2007, the psychological discomposure of Britney Spears had led many, as casually as if they were predicting the outcome of a football game, to anticipate when and how she might meet her end. "The exploitation is going on day in, day out," Pinsky, who hadn't treated her, said in an interview. "We're all watching Britney unravel and die in front of our eyes. . . . Even with good treatment, her probability of a positive response is 50/50." A cultural critic for *New York* analyzed the star's shaving her head not as a cry for help by a woman in crisis but as a work of outsider art that finally made her relevant to him and his cohort. "Spears's crack-up was the most interesting performance of her life," he wrote, wondering: "Will she OD or commit suicide like Monroe? Will she have a Grand Guignol death like the fat-obsessed Anna Nicole Smith? . . . That's what everyone wonders."

The logical extension of objectification is dehumanization. Since the late 1990s, young women in the public eye had been framed across media as sexy, entertaining, uncomplicated dolls, paid to entertain but never complain. Some understood the bargain. Hilton, who posed, smiling, next to those SEE PARIS DIE! signs, seemed on board with the reality that building a lucrative brand out of spun sugar and postfeminist presentation might result in people hating her. But for others, the cruelty with which they were being hounded by paparazzi and then dissected online was profoundly traumatic. In her memoir, Spears compares the photographers stalking her to "an army of zombies trying to get in every second." Nowhere, not even her home, was safe.

And the tone offered up by blogs was inevitably absorbed by the rest of us. "If Britney wasn't a joke before, she certainly is now because she apparently lost whatever talent she had that differentiated her from the other skanky starlets," one woman posted about Spears's "comeback" at the VMAs in 2007. "It may be because she is lazy or on drugs or both. . . . I wonder if she will even make it to 30." A Gawker commenter described the spectacle as "like watching a handicapped child at a state fair talent show. You really wanted to root for her, but it was just sad, and you ended up wondering who was cruel enough to let her do that to herself." This was the general inflection of the web in the late 2000s: cynical, performatively callous, perfectly indoctrinated by years of exposure into seeing stars as something less than human. In 2023, *The New York Times*' Amanda Hess revisited Britney's VMAs performance, remembering it as "disastrous and amusing," and was horrified by what she now saw. "It played like found footage in a horror movie," she wrote. "I saw a new mother being forced to do a sexy dance for America, and for the quality of her performance to inform whether she got to keep her children."

There was little public sympathy in this moment for anyone who suffered with addiction or had psychological issues or couldn't cope with being constantly besieged. Rather, women were eaten up by onlookers as the kind of archetypes that have been used to demonize them throughout history: sluts, whores, bad mothers, trainwrecks, manipulators, gluttons, wastrels. In 2011, when Winehouse died at the end of an evening spent watching videos of her old shows on YouTube, the moment seemed to strike many as not hopelessly tragic but somehow just—the logical conclusion to her hedonism and wasted talent. Seven months later, Houston also died, alone in a bathtub at the Beverly Hilton. Witnesses said she'd been behaving erratically beforehand, "skipping" around the hotel's ballroom like a child and doing handstands out by the pool—acting just like a girl who had no idea people were watching.

CHAPTER 8

Girl on *Girls*

The Confessional Auteur and Her Detractors

Who has not asked himself at some time or other: Am I
a monster or is this what it means to be a person?

Clarice Lispector (1977)

If I tell the story, I control the version.

Nora Ephron (1983)

Early in 2010, a twenty-three-year-old filmmaker debuted a work that circled, quietly, around a question that would preoccupy art over the next decade: What is a young woman worth? In Lena Dunham's *Tiny Furniture*, Dunham plays Aura, a recent Oberlin grad returning to her mother's austere Tribeca loft after her boyfriend breaks up with her. ("Something about having to build a shrine to his ancestors out of a dying tree.") She has no job, no money, and no prospects. Her creative portfolio amounts to a YouTube video with 357 hits in which she strips to her underwear and grooms herself in a campus fountain. *Tiny Furniture* is only a degree or two removed from reality: It was filmed in Dunham's parents' apartment, where she really did live at the time; her mother was played by her real-life mother, the artist Laurie Simmons, and her sibling (Cyrus Grace Dunham) by her real sibling; that fountain video really was one of her early works. Dunham wrote, directed, and staged scenes in the movie, but they amounted to a kind of self-portrait rendered in frank, sometimes excruciating detail.

With *Tiny Furniture*, Dunham seemed to be taking postfeminism's imperatives for women—that they surveil themselves and put themselves on display—to a seditious extreme. She exposed her own body, fleshier and paler than the kinds of figures typically tracked by cameras. She inverted the glamorizing lens of film and television to portray herself in a way that made her seem *more* abject, more clueless, more pitiful. The movie, as she told David Carr in 2010, is "about a period when someone doesn't know how to value yourself," and to me it captures the experience of a specific age, but also an era. Aura has two romantic interests, although both are politely disinterested at best: a mooching YouTube artist named Jed, who makes videos of himself quoting Nietzsche while riding a rocking horse, and a weaselly chef named Keith, who mostly prizes Aura for her access to prescription pills. Toward the end of the film, Keith has sex with Aura, doggy-style, inside a giant pipe on a construction site, and while the scene isn't traumatic for Aura, exactly, it is unsettling—grimy, pleasureless, unprotected. Afterward, Aura climbs into bed with her mother, coming to accept that she's figuring things out through experimentation. "In Dunham's world, there is no happy ending," Phillip Lopate wrote in an essay on *Tiny Furniture* for the Criterion Collection. "Only an enlightened realism."

Lopate compared Dunham's work to the fratty "loss-of-virginity" romps that had populated the aughts and argued that while she was similarly working within the realm of humiliation, hers was a "much more subtle and sophisticated comedy of chagrin." While her personal circumstances were different from those of most millennials—the privilege of her upbringing as the child of relatively well-known artists would become a sticking point for her detractors—the work she'd go on to create would be part of a growing movement of what the academic Maria San Filippo has called "provoc*auteurs*": women writers and filmmakers making spiky, troublesome, often darkly funny work intent on shading out new forms of truth.

By this point, there were more ways than ever to experiment with form and voice, and fewer gatekeepers or barriers to entry. A string of feminist blogs cropped up in the aughts: *Feministing, The F-Word, Racialicious, Jezebel, The Hairpin*—all sites that seemed informed by the tone and ambitions of riot-grrrl zines. These blogs grew passionate communities of readers, who debated each other in discussion threads inflected equally with pop-culture savvy and academic theory. The platforms kept coming. YouTube, born in 2005, gave amateur filmmakers a democratic showcase for their work. Twitter, which debuted as a "micro-blogging site" in 2006, rapidly became popular as a place for people to play with both a public-facing voice and the finessing of the self as a character. Tumblr, founded the following

year, offered more of the same: more space to write, more secrets and revelations, more images. What's fascinating to
me now about this moment was how much of it was mediated
through writing, after the insistently visual 1990s and 2000s.
Prior to Instagram (which launched in October 2010), Vine
(2013), and TikTok (2016), the quickest way to say something
publicly during the aughts was to type it out.

In 2010, the Canadian writer Sheila Heti published the first
iteration of *How Should a Person Be?*, a fragmented, experimental work of autofiction that was inspired, variously, by self-help
novels, online oversharing, and the MTV reality series *The Hills*.
When the book was published in the United States in 2012, it
roughly coincided with the premiere of Dunham's HBO show,
Girls, leading critics to compare the two artists' explorations of
sexual humiliation, delusional levels of artistic ambition, and
reckonings with the lack of clear cultural signposts for functional modern womanhood. Heti aspires in the book toward
creating both great art and a realistic portrayal of women, and
yet, at least as the novel's version of "Sheila," she doesn't know
any women and isn't particularly interested in them. The one
moment she seems to connect spiritually with another woman
is when she encounters the Paris Hilton sex tape. "Watching
her, I felt a kinship," Heti writes. "She was just another white
girl going through life with her clothes off."

Barack Obama's election in 2008 seemed to signal that the
future would be postracial and postfeminist—a progressive
America that was bruised by the Great Recession but optimis-
tic about the possibilities of a new intellectual age. Looking in-

ward for inspiration, writers offered up a new wave of prickly, difficult studies of the self. In 2011, the actress and comedian Issa Rae premiered her web series, *The Misadventures of Awkward Black Girl*, which carved out space for the kind of characters that Rae felt were totally missing from popular culture. With two major albums in quick succession, 2010's *Speak Now* and 2012's *Red*, Taylor Swift forced pop music to revert to *feeling* again, in all its messy, unreasonable intensity.

Many of these works seemed rooted in arrested development. Girlhood was no longer a temporary phase but a prolonged state that reached almost to midlife. But part of this stylized extended adolescence, it seems to me now, was about allowing room for experimentation. Girls are allowed to be vulnerable—to overshare, to overanalyze, to unburden themselves, to embarrass themselves, to fail. (The writer Leslie Jamison has observed the extent to which our language of confessional writing is steeped in the "liquid language" of female bodily experiences: *"gushing, vomiting, purging, bleeding."*) After a decade of being prized primarily as decoration, it seemed as though many women had minimal interest in their work's being pleasing or even palatable. What they wanted, as Ezra Pound wrote of modernism, was to create portrayals of life made wholly new.

Inevitably, there was backlash. The joyful claiming of *Girls* by some women as a cultural totem, "by us, for us," led to valid pushback by women who didn't see themselves represented on the show. The new proliferation of voices online also meant there was an unprecedented level of scrutiny directed at every single cultural product. "Because it was Dunham's fate to arrive on the cultural scene both grubby and unglamorous yet somehow already popular, she emerged, in some sense, pre-hated," Meghan Daum wrote in 2014. Swift's willingness to be what I can only describe now as *girly*, leaning all the way into fairy tales and vulnerability and princessy self-presentation, led *Jezebel*, Gawker's sister site, to agree with a writer in 2010 who branded the twenty-year-old "a feminist's nightmare." When Rachel Cusk published a memoir about her divorce, *Aftermath*, in 2012, she was labeled "a brittle little dominatrix and peerless narcissist" by *The Sunday Times* for turning her unhappy domestic life into literature.

Narcissism, in fact, was a general complaint—it's a word that no woman who insists on framing herself as a subject can escape. It was also a term that commentators on the right threw relentlessly at Obama, portraying him as an egoist presiding over a cult of personality—the avatar for an era of first-person bloggers and self-sold voices of a generation. The difference now was that the term was gradually being defanged by overuse, coming off as less of a clinical analysis and more of a projected millennial malaise. Deprived of many of the conventional markers of adulthood—houses, families, job security—a generation of artists were willing and able to scrutinize themselves for meaning instead. How should a person be? Or, as Chris Kraus wrote in 1997's *I Love Dick*, a work that anticipated the autofiction era by a dozen or so years, "If women have failed to make 'universal' art because we're trapped within the 'personal,' why not universalize the 'personal' and make it the subject of our art?"

When *Girls* debuted in 2012, it was very much in the shadow of *Sex and the City*, if only because all other HBO series during the aughts tended to be a sullen mire of intricately drawn, darkly violent men. *Girls* wasn't explicitly themed around sex: The first episode introduced Dunham's Hannah as a feckless, babyish, solipsistic recent graduate working on a memoir in essays called *Midnight Snack* and suggested that the series would be about the bruising process of finding out whether she, as an artist, had anything worth saying. But the second episode, "Vagina Panic," laid out all the pieces of a remarkably confident manifesto. *Sex and the City*, in spite of its title, had always been a show more interested in depicting consumption than pleasure. Its characters collected sexual experiences in the same way they did vintage couture, as items to be analyzed and admired over brunch. The show's interest in sex was anthropological, as per the conceit of Carrie Bradshaw's column, and mostly related to power. Everyone was beautiful and everything shimmered with easy money.

Girls, immediately, deflated that fantasy. There was nothing being sold here—not products, nor lifestyles, nor even New York as a backdrop. Sex wasn't a fun topic so much as a series of sharp and sour mortifications. "Vagina Panic" opens with Hannah having sex with Adam (Adam Driver), an intriguing but deeply strange man, in his gloomy apartment. "You like that?" he grunts, not as a question but as a ritualized exchange in a script. "I like everything . . . what you're doing," Hannah replies, timidly. "I knew when I found you that you wanted it this way," he blurts out, the sound of flesh slapping in the background as he thrusts. "You were a junkie, and you were only eleven, and you had your fuckin' Cabbage Patch lunchbox." Hannah, trying to be game, joins in. "And I was really scared when I saw you." Adam, getting closer, says, "You're a dirty little whore and I'm gonna send you home to your parents covered in come." Hannah, acting badly, cries: "Oh don't do that! They're gonna be so angry!" He rips off the condom, which we see flying onto the floor, and asks her where she wants it. "Uh, where?" Hannah replies. He puts his hand around her neck, shoves her head into the pillow, and ejaculates on her chest. We see only her face in close-up, unreadable in the dark. "That was really good. That was so good. I almost came," she says, meekly, as though to reassure him—not that he cares— that her lack of pleasure was her failure.

Throughout the aughts, it often felt as though girls were being conditioned by popular culture to perform sex for social kudos rather than explore it for their own fulfillment. "While it would be 'weird' for a teen girl to pursue sexual gratification," Ariel Levy wrote in *Female Chauvinist Pigs,* "it is crucial that she *seem* sexy—raunchy, willing, wild." Hannah, who explains later in the episode that she's only had sex with "two and a half men" and ends up Googling "diseases that come from no condom for one second," is an amateur trying to be a professional, a reality reinforced throughout the show by her childish demeanor, her oscillations between extreme politeness and absurd self-absorption, and her inability to take care of herself. She's not perturbed, necessarily, by Adam's role-playing but nor does she actually enjoy it. Abjection, for Hannah, will be a long and ongoing process that she understands, and is told, is necessary for becoming a writer. "Where's the sexual failure?" an editor asks her crankily in the show's second season, after reading a draft. "Where's the pudgy face slicked with semen and sadness?"

Dunham seemed to have concluded that men and women were approaching sex with different scripts. Women had an idealized conception of themselves as strong, curious, and intrepid adventurers that they'd absorbed from *Sex and the City*, and men had practices and dialogue that they'd ripped right from porn. "Guys my age watch *so* much pornography," Dunham told *The New York Times* in 2012, saying that she'd experienced aggressive positioning and "a lot of errant hair pulling" while thinking, "There's no way that you, young Jewish man from Chappaqua, taught this to yourself." *Sex and the City*, meanwhile, had been studied with Talmudic fervor by girls who saw it as part manual for empowered adulthood, part Myers–Briggs test. Shoshanna (played by Zosia Mamet), talking to her cousin, Jessa (Jemima Kirke), in the *Girls* pilot, characterizes her as "definitely a Carrie with, like, some Samantha aspects and Charlotte hair." Jessa, who's never seen the show, is characteristically unfazed. She's the only one of the four girls in the series who approaches sex entirely on her own terms, with an attitude steeped in confidence and defiance.

From its first episodes onward, *Girls* appeared to set itself up as a direct challenge to porn's tropes. Hannah is frequently naked on the show, and yet her body was often interpreted not as an object of desire but as an affront. Howard Stern, commenting on Dunham's frequent nude scenes in *Girls*, once said, on air: "It's a little fat girl who kinda looks like Jonah Hill and she keeps taking her clothes off and it kinda feels like rape. . . . I don't wanna see that." His comments spoke volumes: about Stern's insistence that all visible bodies in culture be calibrated to male desire and that all cultural products be oriented around what he wanted to see. (Just change the channel, Howard.) But his comments also underscored the reality that bodies like Dunham's, while the predominant form for women, were so rare on television at the time as to feel viscerally jarring. By objecting, Stern only seemed to strengthen Dunham's resolve. Hannah continued to be naked on *Girls*, not just as a political assertion of presence but also as a delineation of character. Being so exposed underscored her strangeness, but also her vulnerability.

With her nude scenes, Maria San Filippo argues, Dunham "detaches female nudity from women's heterosexualized desirability, repositioning it instead in contexts of naturalism and female intimacies." A comedy writer once supposedly told Dunham at a Halloween party, by way of unsolicited advice: "I don't want to see girls going to the fuckin' bathroom together. I want to see girls making out!" Dunham seemed to take it as a challenge: Hannah is often naked with her friends, but in a rigidly unerotic way—any potentially sexual energy in a scene where she shares a bath with Jessa is neutralized by Jessa's snot and Hannah's acknowledgment that she's peed in every bathtub she's ever been in.

At the same time, Dunham makes clear to what degree every character's sexual life has been influenced in one way or another by porn. In an early scene with the endearing grouch Ray (Alex Karpovsky), he's shown elaborating on a violent sexual fantasy about Marnie (Allison Williams), and how much he wants to "fuck her to teach her a lesson, just whip her." In the second-season episode "One Man's Trash," Hannah confesses to a lover that she once "asked someone to punch me in the chest and then come on that spot. Like, that was my idea. That came from my brain. And it's like, what makes me think I deserve that?" The women of *Sex and the City* once recoiled at a lover of Charlotte's who couldn't reach orgasm without screaming, "You fucking bitch, you fucking whore!" By the time *Girls* came around, that kind of language amounted to fairly standard pillow talk. (In season two, when Adam calls a new sexual partner "a dirty little whore," she replies, "I can like your cock and not be a whore," flummoxing him.)

In her 1993 essay "Feminism, Moralism, and Pornography," Ellen Willis argued that "women have learned, as a matter of survival, to be adept at shaping male fantasies to their own purposes." Some of Hannah's most cringeworthy moments arise when she seems to be trying to emulate scenarios from porn to make herself feel powerful. She makes a suggestive rape joke that sours one job interview, propositions her handsy boss, and later flashes her vagina at the principal of the school where she teaches. Dunham never flatly indicts porn, something that pro-sex feminists including Willis have long warned would only make many women ashamed of their sexual choices. Instead,

213

Girls appropriates porn's clichés and makes them wholly ridiculous. Dunham can't single-handedly reshape the visual and imaginative realm of sex altogether, but she can lead us to wonder what we actually find sexy and what's just been deeply imprinted on us by overexposure.

THE CULTURAL LANDSCAPE we inhabit shapes more than just fantasy—it also contours the ways in which we think, write, dream, create. The character of Sheila, at the beginning of *How Should a Person Be?*, is a kind of tabula rasa, an alien in female form studying humans to try to emulate them. The "great personalities" she considers—Andy Warhol, Oscar Wilde, Charles Darwin, Albert Einstein—are all male. "One good thing about being a woman," she writes, "is we haven't too many examples yet of what a genius looks like. It could be me." Her specialty, as it stands, is giving oral sex to men, which she commits to so enthusiastically that she once vomited midway, swallowed, and carried on going. "We live in an age of some really great blowjob artists," she concludes. "Every era has its art form. The nineteenth century, I know, was tops for the novel."

When I was thinking about *How Should a Person Be?* I stumbled across a Reddit post asking what to make of the novel. "Her thoughts seem so pretentious and self-important, while her actions are submissive and traditional," it read. Spanning a period of time starting in 2005 (when Heti was twenty-eight) up until 2012, when the US edition was published, the book runs headlong into exactly this contradiction: the collision of ambition with conformity, the lack of a road map in the aughts for female intellectual heft. Heti, commissioned by a theater to write a serious work of art about women, realizes she doesn't know any. "Ever since I was a teenager I had been drawn to men exclusively," she writes, "and they drew themselves to me—as lovers, as friends. . . . It was men I enjoyed talking to at parties, and whose opinions I was interested in hearing. It was men I wanted to grow close to and be influenced by." This is problematic for her work, because it makes anything she writes in a woman's voice seem odd or manufactured.

What she ends up creating, instead, is this "novel," a collage of flippant musings, transcribed conversations that happened in real life with her friend, the artist Margaux Williamson, and an extended sequence of baroque sexual gymnastics with an artist named Israel, the kind of man who writes her an email that begins, "hey Slut." Through realism, or at least a curated version of her own reality, Heti provides a fairly dismal rendering of modern womanhood. Initially, Sheila can't help concluding that the model for how a person should be is "a celebrity," which, Heti explained to *The Paris Review*, came from "thinking a lot about Paris Hilton and all those girls like Lindsay Lohan who were in the tabloids. I was wondering what I might have in common with them, to find the seeds of them in me, then think about those aspects, and emphasize those. I don't see their drive as being riches so much as fame. . . . Renown is something people have always wanted, but maybe what's modern is that it's considered a virtue, this desire, rather than a vice."

Chris Kraus, in a review, argued that *How Should a Person Be?* had more in common with *Don Quixote* than *Girls*, given that Heti's question was really this: "What is an epic quest for a girl?" Sheila does indeed go on a twenty-first-century odyssey, navigating Art Basel in Miami, a mysteriously sinister hairstylist, a trip to New York City, and a sadomasochistic relationship with Israel that threatens to become all-consuming—a land of the lotus-eaters where the fruit is sexual degradation. In one chapter, Sheila buys the same yellow dress as her friend Margaux's, which provokes a conflict between the two that feels ripped right out of *The Hills*, pointless drama manufactured for ratings. And yet the scene, at the same time, reveals how Margaux resents the way that Sheila is trying to cannibalize her personality and her art. "i really do need some of my own identity," Margaux writes to her, "and this is pretty simple and good for the head."

What Heti and Dunham both seemed to be grappling with during the early 2010s was how to make meaningful art in a cultural climate that ogled and sneered at women, and even loathed them. It's telling to me now that what offended people most about Dunham during her early years in television was her conviction that she had something worth saying. "For better or worse, I've never been obsessed with other people's perceptions of me," she told *The New Yorker* in 2024, "but I have always been obsessed with being able to do my thing." The character of Sheila, Heti told *The Paris Review*, "wants a perfect, beautiful, ideal self. That turns out to be ugly." A necessary process for women writers during this moment was acknowledging that the mythology of contemporary womanhood was entirely false, in order to create something less pretty and more truthful.

When Issa Rae debuted *The Misadventures of Awkward Black Girl* in 2011, it was in the hope of expanding the pantheon of Black female characters in popular culture. J, the central character—whom Rae described as sometimes 30 percent her, sometimes more like 60—is funny, misanthropic, frustrated, and awkward. Her televisual antecedents are from old-school situation comedy: Larry David, Elaine Benes, Dorothy Zbornak, Liz Lemon—all familiar, endearing grouches; all White. The series, as Jada Yuan wrote in 2016, amounts to Rae's "mission statement: to depict black women as imperfect subjects, worthy of fascination, with precise, observational humor. Or, more specifically, to depict the black women she knows, including some version of herself, as full-bodied human beings."

Awkward Black Girl, made on a shoestring budget and unartfully filmed in early episodes, has a low-fi feel that's immediately forgotten when Rae is on-screen, cringing and seething and performing terrible raps by herself in her bedroom. "My name is J and I'm awkward," she says in the first installment, gloomily looking at her reflection in the bathroom mirror. "And Black. Someone once told me those were the two worst things anyone could be." We then see a list of insulting descriptors scroll rapidly by. (It includes Pretentious Dying Insatiable Contagious Repugnant Old Gross Nasty Whorish Ugly; Awkward and Black are right there at the bottom). J works for a company selling a diet product named "Gutbusters," which, she explains, is basically "bulimia in pill form." Her White boss is "an offensive dumb fuck of an idiot" who wants to get cornrows together and obsesses over J's hair. Her work life is a series of elaborate mortifications: organized bonding sessions, racist commentary by an ethnically ambiguous coworker who turns out to be "100 percent Armenian"; anger-management therapy after J explodes when a snotty, sneezing colleague touches her stapler.

After *Girls* premiered, Rae was also often compared to Dunham, possibly because both were taking characters usually relegated to supporting status—the chubby sidekick, the Black best friend—and forcing them front and center. And both shows seemed to struggle with the burden of representation. *Girls* was criticized even before it debuted for featuring an all-White cast in one of the most racially and culturally diverse cities in America; *Awkward Black Girl* was seen as positioning Rae as a singular voice for Black women, something she chafed at because the point of her series was specificity. The problem wasn't with either woman (although Dunham's incautious sense of humor led to so many missteps that someone created a Lena Dunham Apology Generator on Twitter). The problem was that each had a platform to tell stories of distinct experience at a time when women writers and directors were so few and far between that their shows had to represent everyone.

When Rae debuted her second series, *Insecure*, in 2016, it was the first show created by and starring a Black woman in HBO's history.

Also in 2016, the academic and feminist theorist Rebecca Wanzo published a substantial examination of abjection as it's portrayed on *Awkward Black Girl* and *Girls*. Both J and Hannah, she argued, are shown to be creative people struggling professionally and economically in the wake of the Great Recession; both are in states of arrested development; and both are alienated from the world around them in a way that makes up much of their respective shows' humor. But while Hannah can play with bodily abjection in a way that's relatively new for White women on television, J is informed by the historical weight of how Black people have been dehumanized and humiliated in America. In making J such an identifiable part of sitcom tradition, Wanzo wrote, Rae is making tangible her desire "to see black women in genres often denied them." *Awkward Black Girl*, then, is a distinct, personal, small-scale story that also aims to crack wide open the segregated world of American comedy.

WHEN I WAS PITCHING this book to publishers, virtually every editor I met with had the same request: Could I make myself more of a presence? At first, I tried. But every time I wrote about myself while drafting this, I ended up deleting it, with a few exceptions. I lived through all the history covered in this book, and my interpretation of things is already informed by my personal experiences, limited and limiting as they are. What I wanted more than anything was to expand the ways in which I understand and think about this era, and inserting myself into it only ever seemed to be inhibiting my scope of vision.

And yet I understand why female first-person narrative is so enticing. At its best, either it provides a reassuringly familiar presence to guide the reader through the morass of contemporary experience or it offers a perspective so strange and deluded that it's thrilling to encounter out in the wild. Female confessional narrative seems to come in historical waves: During the 1990s, it soared after the publication of Elizabeth Wurtzel's *Prozac Nation*, peaked in extremity with Kathryn Harrison's *The Kiss* (a memoir about the author's incestuous relationship with her father), and waned as reality television offered a whole new medium for prurience during the aughts. Then, as the internet became more prominent a fixture in culture, interest in personal essays began to crest again in 2008, when the former *Gawker* writer Emily Gould published "Exposed," a *New York Times Magazine* story about the toll of an adult life spent revealing herself online.

Gould started working at *Gawker* in 2006, when she was twenty-four years old. She had a blog at the time, where she posted random ephemera for a couple hundred friends—the kinds of errant thoughts and cultural observations that sprawled across the internet before they found a home on Twitter. (For context: I wrote on my blog that same year about my dead father, Ugg boots, and Yoanna from Cycle 2 of *America's Next Top Model*.) Gould pointed out that bloggers had become preoccupied with oversharing, revealing personal details we'd never tell strangers in person because the remove of the internet seemed to create a distance that wasn't actually real. Encountering the most intensely personal details of someone's life, Gould wrote, was "enthralling." When she started at *Gawker*, an editor warned her not to read the comments, but also that the community of commenters craved personal details. What they wanted, more than information, was connection: the illusion of intimacy with a stranger behind a screen.

For women, self-revelation was both reassuringly familiar and excitingly political. "It's easy to draw parallels between what's going on online and what's going on in the rest of our media: the death of scripted TV, the endless parade of ordinary, heavily made-up faces that become vaguely familiar to us as they grin through their 15 minutes of reality-show fame," Gould wrote. "No wonder we're ready to confess our innermost thoughts to everyone: we're constantly being shown that the surest route to recognition is via humiliation in front of a panel of judges." Writing online was also a way to assert difference, in an environment where women seemed to all look and behave the same, and to refine the art of composing yourself as a character. The neologism "overshare," which emerged in the late 1990s and was popularized on an episode of *Buffy the Vampire Slayer*, was, by 2008, *Webster's New World Dictionary*'s Word of the Year. Millennial women had become well accustomed to publishing what amounted to diaries online: narratives that combined the most intimate details of their life with their attempts at crafting a literary voice—part Facebook post, part portfolio.

As readers became numbed by overexposure, their appetite for provocation grew. First-person essays, Laura Bennett wrote in 2015, became "the easiest way to jolt an increasingly jaded internet to attention." And for writers trying to make a name for themselves in a shrinking, precarious industry, a viral story could seem like a combustible calling card. In 2012, an unknown twenty-one-year-old student named Marie Calloway blew up the literary internet when she published "Adrien Brody," a long, experimental, almost violently honest account of her interactions with an older magazine editor. The piece begins with Calloway's first email to him, a fan letter of sorts in which she praises his writing and invites him to look at her Tumblr. They correspond, he admires her work—"read your pieces as critiques of narcissism and self-absorption, which are hard to make without embodying them to the nth degree"—and she announces that she's making a trip to New York and she'd love to sleep with him. He expresses similar interest. "I was relieved, and proud," Calloway writes, "that I was so attractive to him that it made him definitely want to see me."

When "Adrien Brody" was posted online, it contained a photo of Calloway with ejaculate on her face, an image whose starkness mirrored the nature of her work—she was letting us see everything, and yet it was hard to say exactly why. Her account of sex with the editor feels revelatory now for how it exposes the distance between what she says and what she means, what she does and what she wants to do. "I had never met a guy who liked doing it in missionary before," she writes. "I kind of even trained myself out of liking it, because most guys are so bored by it." At the same time, she constantly compares the editor's writing with how he behaves in reality, probing the gap between his online presentation of himself and the unfiltered version. The point of her own work, one senses, is for there to be no such gap at all, nothing that allows for self-flattery, self-embellishment, or even self-protection.

"When you see Calloway's pieces gathered together you recognize what this young woman has been doing, what her plan has been from the beginning, which she has executed, without error, right to the end," Stephen Marche wrote in *Esquire*. "She has been submitting herself to horrific sexual experiences *in order to write about them*." I'm not sure that this is entirely true; Calloway's writing reads to me now as part of a more radical canon that simply wanted more *honesty* in art—a stringently true account of what young women were feeling and thinking. In her subsequent book, *what purpose did i serve in your life*, she wrote about sex work, losing her virginity, and the men who wrote expressing fantasies about hurting her. Then, after drawing an extreme amount of attention, much of it brutal, she disappeared. It's hard for me not to compare her with Jennifer Ringley, another woman who seemed fascinated by the art and historical significance of her own self-exposure, until she realized how little it was giving her in return.

For the final season of *Girls*, Lena Dunham wrote an episode titled "American Bitch" that seems to have been drawn in part from Calloway's work and from the power imbalance in any relationship between a celebrated male artist and a young woman who craves some of his cachet. That gap, Dunham suggests, is too easy to exploit. And yet it's complicated by something Hannah has sensed since the show's beginning: Abjection for women in this era was also an assertion of their primacy and value as a subject. As Jessa says to Hannah when she's complaining about the success of a rival whose trauma memoir has become a cult success: "*Your* boyfriend should kill himself! You deserve it." But to be celebrated for all the ways in which one transcends the role of victim can become just another form of creative oppression.

This paradox, to me, provides some of the tension of the confessional writing of this moment. The genre was reckoning with what twenty-first-century postfeminism had wrought and forcing a more candid, discomfiting discussion of sex and power. Chuck Palmer, the celebrated, lupine novelist in "American Bitch," represents the laureate male author who's never had to suffer to find himself interesting, while Denise, the young woman who accuses him of a nonconsensual blow job on something he calls "Tumblr without an *e*," is only noteworthy to readers for the specific ways in which he has hurt her. "We see these wounded women everywhere," Leslie Jamison wrote in her 2014 essay "Grand Unified Theory of Female Pain." And, she argued, "the moment we start talking about wounded women, we risk transforming their suffering from an aspect of the female experience into an element of the female constitution—perhaps its finest, frailest consummation."

So much of the work that appeared in this era seems to me now to have been exploited in one way or another—for attention, for clicks, for the age-old project of turning women's pain and degradation into entertainment. Cat Marnell's columns about her drug addiction, published first at *xoJane* and then at *Vice*, were unsparingly frank and utterly unglamorous, and yet the editors commissioning them seemed to have understood them as the journalistic equivalent of a reality show—a vicarious window into a life in freefall. (JazzHate, the fictional website on *Girls* that commissions Hannah to "have a threesome with some people that you meet on Craigslist, or do a whole bunch of coke and then just write about it," feels like it was riffing on the existence of *xoJane*, an online magazine that only lived from 2011 to 2016 to sell women's humiliation to advertisers.)

But in some ways, too, the validation of narratives of intimate pain and trauma helped prepare people for what was coming in 2017, when *The New York Times* and *The New Yorker* published blockbuster reports on the megaproducer Harvey Weinstein. The #MeToo moment—named after an effort by the activist Tarana Burke to raise awareness regarding just how many women had firsthand experience of sexual harassment and assault—could not have happened without an upsurge in first-person writing that took women at their word. "There is nothing gutsier to me than a person announcing that their story is one that deserves to be told, especially if that person is a woman," Dunham wrote in her memoir in 2014. That we still haven't figured out how to prepare women for what happens after their testimony becomes public property—or to try to prevent it—is an indictment, but not of the women talking.

ONE OF THE REASONS I'm so conflicted over confessional writing is that women's stories are only a relatively recent addition to the literary canon—and that at their best, they demand not just sympathy but control. During the 1980s, when Nora Ephron decided to turn her husband's infidelity into a novel, the response was not kind. Ephron had been married to the Watergate reporter Carl Bernstein, so when the novel emerged, media reporters and gossip columnists combed through it with zeal trying to find allusions, parallels, and characters from real life rendered in fiction. *Heartburn* was criticized, in mealy-mouthed fashion, by men who saw the novel as a scorned wife's betrayal. "There are also those who say that *Heartburn*, though funny and sad, is a great misuse of talent, a book whose only point is to nail Carl Bernstein," Jesse Kornbluth wrote in *New York*. The literary critic Leon Wieseltier adopted a pseudonym ("Tristan Vox," possibly a play on the Latin for "sorrowful voice") to rail against the novel in *Vanity Fair*, arguing that Bernstein's infidelity was banal compared with "the infidelity of a mother toward her children" and that what Ephron had done in exposing her family was tantamount to child abuse.

Ephron knew better—she saw that what she was doing was motivated not by revenge but by self-preservation. "If I tell the story, I control the version," Rachel, her narrator, says in *Heartburn,* adding, "If I tell the story, it doesn't hurt as much." It's significant, I think, how often people interpret the narrativizing of an unfamiliar perspective as a threat. Men who write about their lives tend to be canonized as brave auteurs of the human experience; women who do the same are guilty of *oversharing.* Rachel Sykes, in a 2017 essay, described it this way: "Writers like Ben Lerner, Karl Ove Knausgård, and Tao Lin compose similarly autofictional accounts of their protagonists' inner life, body, and sexual activity, but reviewers often celebrate them as incarnations of Marcel Proust rather than literary oversharers." Or, as Ephron put it in 2004, "Philip Roth and John Updike picked away at the carcasses of their early marriages in book after book, but to the best of my knowledge they were never hit with the 'thinly disguised' thing."

Writing about Marie Calloway's "Adrien Brody" in 2011, Emily Gould identified the piece as part of a literary tradition without a name. I don't have a name for it either. But the writers I wanted to explore in this chapter all do the same things: re-create, with quite gnarly honesty, their experiences of twenty-first-century womanhood; probe the conditions they're living under; and force their way into an artistic realm that has not historically welcomed them. Most address a problem that, as Gould puts it, "at its most fundamental level, is the power imbalance inherent in heterosexuality." And, I'd add, in art.

What they received in return was quite a revealing amount

of vitriol. "*Girls* is a television program about the children of wealthy famous people and shitty music and Facebook and how hard it is to know who you are and Thought Catalog and sexually transmitted diseases and the exhaustion of ceaselessly dramatizing your own life while posing as someone who understands the fundamental emptiness and narcissism of that very self-dramatization," John Cook wrote in *Gawker*, one of the kinder critiques. *Jezebel* offered $10,000 for unretouched photos of Dunham's *Vogue* shoot with Annie Leibovitz—an attempt to comment on the body tyranny of fashion magazines that seemed to simultaneously shame Dunham for looking the way she did. It's worth noting here how differently *Girls* tends to be received now, both by millennials rewatching the series and younger viewers discovering it for the first time. What seemed in 2012 like the myopic narcissism of a privileged few now rings more like the first accurate—if incomplete—portrait of the internet generation.

But Dunham was by no means alone in how disproportionately she infuriated people. Gould was singled out in an eleven-thousand-word rant by a book critic about "middling millennials" that oozed with dehumanizing disgust: She was, the post insisted, a "minx whose head is . . . deeply deposited up her own slimy passage" and a "mangy dog about to be gassed at the pound." Why is male honesty in art seen as brave while female honesty is so repellent? In a first-season episode of *Girls*, Hannah tells Ray that she's planning on reading an essay about her brief relationship with a hoarder at a literary event. "Is there anything *real* you can write about?" he replies. Chuck Palmer puts it slightly differently: "You should be using your funny," he tells Hannah, "to tackle subjects that matter."

This kind of policing is about diminishment. In a 2013 profile of Taylor Swift, Jody Rosen pointed out the double standard at play in critiques of her songwriting—namely, the supposed triviality of her focus on feelings, and the idea that she's somehow betraying the privacy of the men who engage with her. "The tradition of musical score-settling stretches all the way back to medieval troubadours and lyre-plucking ancients; it's been a mainstay of American song at least since the first bluesman aimed an acidic twelve-bars at the woman who'd done him wrong," he writes. "Bob Dylan is an incorrigible, at times malicious, kisser-and-teller; for decades, rock critics have been quoting with admiration Elvis Costello's famous dictum: 'The only motivation points for me writing all these songs are revenge and guilt.'" Somehow, though, Swift became enshrined as the chronic oversharer, the tale-teller, the furious and vengeful woman scorned.

The ways in which Swift has engaged with autofiction in her music have overlapped intriguingly with cultural history. In 2006, the year she released her dreamy, earnest debut album, the year's best-selling records read like misogynist found poetry: "Gold Digger," "Money Maker," "Buttons," "My Humps," "Laffy Taffy," "Do It to It," "Shake That," "Smack That," "Gimme That."

By asserting how much she *felt*, Swift was underscoring her own humanity and that of girls everywhere. In 2010, *Speak Now* anticipated a decade of bruised, Tumblr-ready emotion, processing old wounds ("Innocent" appeared to take aim at Kanye West's interrupting her VMAs acceptance speech in 2009) and castigating a man—widely believed to be the musician John Mayer—whom she felt had taken advantage of her when she was "too young to be messed with." Swift's album *1989*, she acknowledged years later in a "prologue" accompanying her re-recorded version, was in part written as a response to the way she felt slut-shamed for dating in the public eye and to what she saw as widespread "trivialization of my songwriting as if it were a predatory act of a boy crazy psychopath." The album also aligned with a moment in which she publicly "came out" as a feminist and in which the f-word was suddenly being so widely discussed in popular culture that in 2014 *Time* magazine proposed banning it for overuse.

"These are the conditions," Emily Gould wrote in 2011. "Why wouldn't women want revenge?" Ultimately, it's not surprising that so many artists in the 2010s, having experienced a decade in which the most intimate details of women's turbulent lives were appropriated callously for entertainment, decided to claim ownership of their own narratives before others could do so. Or that they often chose to deconstruct storytelling itself to try to approximate the fragmented, chaotic nature of what being alive felt like. And yet, to me, the writing of this era was also doing something more productive: contouring reality to try to make space for something else and to imagine all the ways in which things could be, somehow, different.

CHAPTER 9

Girl Boss

The Making Over of Female Ambition

The master's tools will never dismantle the master's house. They may allow us temporarily to beat him at his own game, but they will never enable us to bring about genuine change.

AUDRE LORDE (1983)

You better work, bitch.

BRITNEY SPEARS (2013)

A t the end of 2008, I was finishing up a graduate degree in journalism at New York University that had cost me $48,000 in tuition, $25,000 in rent, and eighteen months of whatever mozzarella sticks and the cheapest wine cost at happy hour. I had three unpaid internships to my name (including one at *Vogue*, the most prestigious magazine in fashion publishing, where I was sent to stand in a twenty-person line at the Times Square Starbucks three times a day). I had so little money that I lived on braised eggplant and canned tomatoes, a dish that tastes insultingly bitter on day three of being reheated. I was about to lose my visa unless I could find a job, and I had an ovarian cyst the size of a grapefruit that required surgery and health insurance that was about to run out. To make matters worse, I was living on Wall Street in the middle of the financial crisis, where the assembled camera crews all served as a reminder of the end times I felt as if I were witnessing: the end of prosperity, the end of journalism, the end of the career hopes I'd wasted all my savings and a pile of personal debt on.

All this is just to say, by the time the 2010s rolled around, my class of graduates, aspiring journalists, and creative workers had become well habituated to the idea of hustle. As the critic Jennifer Wilson wrote of watching the first season of *The Real Housewives of New York City* during her senior year, "Little did I realize that a show about wealth was preparing me to live without it." We would all soon be busy pieces on a multiplatform professional chessboard, pitching and self-promoting and plotting three moves at a time. When I met my husband, he was working two unpaid internships and one part-time job while doing his master's degree, all to try to maximize what he could get out of the education he couldn't afford. When I was offered a lifeline—an internship at a magazine in Washington, DC, that paid minimum wage, or $7.50 an hour at the time—I jumped at it, supplementing the work with freelance copywriting first thing in the morning and babysitting gigs at night. None of this was aspirational; it was simply necessary. But the relentlessness of grinding away made it easier to see something clarifying or even virtuous in the manifestos of people who were winning out through work, affirming the idea that everything would pay off in the end if we just kept on pushing.

There are two historical events that, by my reading, had a more profound impact than anything else did on how women would live during this decade. One was the cratering of the global economy, an implosion of commerce, wealth, and industry that would filter insidiously into the trends and trajectories of the next decade. The other was the arrival in October 2010 of Instagram. Much as MTV transformed music from an aural art form into a multimedia spectacle, edging out artists who didn't quite look the part, Instagram turned everyday life into performance. It encouraged its users to live publicly, documenting the visual texture of everything from hair appointments to house renovations to health crises. Ordinary people built vast followings based on nothing more than a nose for opportunity and an eye for arrangement. Celebrities took back control of their own images from the photographers who'd spent the last decade hounding them. For women, Instagram was the apotheosis of postfeminist promise, a platform that rewarded femininity, self-surveillance, and consumerism with constant dopamine hits and, sometimes, fame and fortune.

Culturally, times were changing in other, more promising ways. For one thing, the cheerful, flagrant sexism of the aughts was no longer in fashion. When "Blurred Lines" was released in 2013, accompanied by a music video in which the fully clothed Robin Thicke, T.I., and Pharrell Williams leered and grinned at three virtually naked models, the tenor of the response signaled an undeniable shift in how women were willing to be treated. This kind of cartoonish, technicolor objectification seemed jarringly anachronistic now. Was it just five years earlier that Dov Charney, the CEO of American Apparel, had advertised his company with a photograph of a topless female model licking a crotch rumored to be Charney's own? Later in 2013, the twenty-year-old former Disney star Miley Cyrus, a tiny slip of a girl in a flesh-colored PVC bikini, twerked during a duet at the VMAs with Thicke, grinding against his crotch and sticking out her tongue while spectators including Drake and Rihanna watched, as stone-faced as nuns. One year later at the same awards show, as if to offer a palate cleanser and a sign of things to come, Beyoncé performed in front of a giant projection of the word "FEMINIST."

Jia Tolentino, in her book *Trick Mirror*, describes the specific shift that happened early in the 2010s as "a sea change that feels both epochal and underrecognized." Suddenly, she observed, it was "now completely normal for women to understand their lives, and the lives of other women, on feminist terms." None of this had happened just by accident. Rather, the glossy misogyny of the aughts coupled with the internet's flourishing pop-feminist spaces had led both to extensive discourse about how women were portrayed and perceived and to a roiling sense of discontent with the status quo. I can still remember reading a definitive blog post by Tressie McMillan Cottom titled "Brown Body, White Wonderland," which pointed out the historical context of Cyrus's VMA performance using Black dancers as sexualized props and the unspoken racial hierarchy of so many of our pop-culture spectacles. The quality of thought, the layers of analysis being added to every trending topic virtually in real time were richer and more erudite than they had ever been, and yet what did it all actually mean? Beyond the ways in which women thought about ourselves and other women, had anything substantively changed?

The year 2014, though, was revelatory. All the pieces of the past decade and a half were braided into phenomena such as the girlboss, the celebrity entrepreneurs of beauty and fast fashion, and the early days of influencer culture and affiliate marketing. It was the year of Nicki Minaj's "Anaconda" video and Kim Kardashian's *Paper* magazine cover—both jubilant, absurd fetishizations of women's bodies that used exploding champagne bottles, bananas, and unabashed product placement to emphasize how lucrative catering to male desire could be. But 2014 was also the year of Emma Sulkowicz's mattress protests at Columbia, of Gamergate, and of the Isla Vista killings—early harbingers of the activist movements, misogynist backlashes, and nihilist atrocities that the next ten years would bring.

Enabled by Instagram, women rapidly figured out all the ways in which they could turn the art of self-presentation into a lucrative side hustle, in a moment when jobs and livelihoods felt ever more precarious. My book club read *Lean In*. Virtually every White woman's book club read *Lean In*. What we were learning was that the onus was on us as individuals to optimize ourselves for our careers. Everywhere we looked, it seemed to be working: Actresses and reality stars were building business empires on "affordable" luxuries such as lipstick and ninety-eight-dollar bedazzled wedges. Ordinary women were becoming celebrities by making their lives look enticing in photographs. Our jobs were becoming our identities, and showcasing our identities online—surveilling ourselves for likes and followers— was fast becoming its own job. "In the postindustrial economy, feminism has been retooled as a vehicle for expression of the self," Susan Faludi wrote in 2013. But this new online self, she argued, was becoming just a "marketable consumer object, val- ued by how many times it's been bought—or, in our electronic age, how many times it's been clicked on." This was the mode of the moment; both backlash and burnout were inevitable.

IN 2013, EVEN THE VERY youngest millennials were finish- ing high school, and the first generation raised against the back- drop of the internet was firmly established in the workforce. Changes were trending positive—the wage gap for women aged twenty-five to thirty-four had narrowed to 93 percent in the United States, compared with 67 percent at the beginning of the 1980s. Millennial women were more likely than their male counterparts to have a college degree. They were also ambi- tious: 61 percent surveyed by Pew in 2013 said they aspired to become a boss or a manager one day, versus 41 percent of Gen X women and just one-fifth of boomers.

Ascending the career ladder was in some ways easier than it had ever been. What was harder, still, was wanting more from life than work. "Without a child, I could dance across the sexism of my era," the director and artist Miranda July writes in her 2024 novel *All Fours*, "whereas becoming a mother shoved my face right in it." In the Pew survey, more than half of women with children said becoming a parent had made advancing in the workplace significantly harder. Only 16 percent of men with kids said the same. In my late twenties, I started to see women I'd gone to graduate school with leave their jobs after having children because the cost of childcare was more than their salaries or because they didn't want to keep fighting at jobs they didn't particularly enjoy while missing everything but the first few weeks of their babies' lives. "I still strongly believe that women can 'have it all' (and that men can too)," the former State Department official and Princeton professor Anne-Marie Slaughter wrote in 2012, in a provocative feature for *The Atlantic* that became the most-read piece in the magazine's history at that time, drawing nearly two hundred thousand likes on Facebook. "I believe that we can 'have it all at the same time.' But not today, not with the way America's economy and society are currently structured."

Generationally, Slaughter noted, there was also a divide—fast becoming a chasm—between women in their forties and fifties and millennials, who were finding themselves reluctant to pursue professional elevation if it meant never spending time with their own children. In 1995, before she left law to become a novelist, Min Jin Lee had published an essay in the third-wave anthology *To Be Real*, where she noted that the dilemma of how to have children while pursuing careers in law consumed her female coworkers. "Lately, I have been contemplating the sheer irony of my fore-sisters demanding the right to get on the track . . . [only] for me to realize how brutal it is to stay on it when you want other things, too," she wrote. Seventeen years later, very little had actually changed. In her feature, Slaughter cited a viral commencement speech by the Facebook executive Sheryl Sandberg in which Sandberg pleaded with women not to leave their jobs if they didn't absolutely have to. "Although couched in terms of encouragement, Sandberg's exhortation contains more than a note of reproach," Slaughter wrote. "We who have made it to the top, or are striving to get there, are essentially saying to the women in the generation behind us: 'What's the matter with you?'"

Into this disaffected climate, in 2013, came *Lean In*. When it was published, Sandberg was forty-three years old and five years into her job as chief operating officer at Facebook. She was well aware that neither tech nor corporate America were particularly welcoming environments for women. In 2012, a former Facebook employee named Katherine Losse had published a book titled *The Boy Kings* in which Losse recounted a fraternity-like culture where female employees had to wear T-shirts emblazoned with Mark Zuckerberg's face to celebrate his birthday, and one man consistently asked younger women in the office for threesomes. (That Facebook, like Google Images and YouTube before it, was spawned out of the initial desire to assess the hotness of women online, is a fact always worth keeping in mind.) Sandberg herself recounted meetings in *Lean In* where no male executives knew where the women's bathrooms were (no woman had ever been important enough to ask) and said that while she was pregnant, an engineer told her he'd named something called "Project Whale" in her honor.

Changing workplace culture, though, wasn't Sandberg's objective. What she was advocating for was for women to claim more power for themselves, with the understanding that once they had, things would naturally have to change. As an ideology, it was nicknamed "trickle-down feminism" by some, with all the loaded connotations that term implied. "When more people get in the race, more records will be broken," Sandberg wrote. "And the achievements will extend beyond those individuals to benefit us all." Her advice for women was documented across eleven main ideas, like a PowerPoint presentation, and argued first and foremost that women needed to put themselves forward, ask for what they needed, seek out more powerful female mentors who could guide them, form "Lean In Circles" of like-minded women their age, and accept that success meant making some sacrifices.

For decades, feminism had focused on broad structural changes: the right to vote, the right to reproductive choice, the right to not face discrimination on the basis of sex. What Sandberg was arguing, though—just like the postfeminists and Spice Girls who preceded her—was that women should instead prioritize personal ascension. In the viral 2010 TED Talk from which *Lean In* sprang, Sandberg began by saying, "The problem is this: Women are not making it to the top of any profession anywhere in the world." They made up just 9 of 190 heads of state worldwide, she said, and only 13 percent of all people in parliament.

And while many companies were debating policies such as "flex time and mentoring and programs that companies should have to train women," she didn't want to talk about any of that. "Today, I want to focus on what we can do as individuals."

For a generation raised on postfeminist principles, TV shows preaching the gospel of self-improvement, and the necessity of outperforming an economic climate that they absolutely could not rely on, her message was like catnip. And for the corporate world, which had little desire to change and absolutely none to commit money to the cause of women, it was even better. Sandberg didn't waste her time on mandatory parental leave or subsidized childcare or wage parity or inclusion. It wasn't on companies to change to accommodate women. It was on women to force their way in by working harder. "This feminism is focused on encouraging educated middle-class women to 'lean in' and 'crack the glass ceiling'—in other words, to climb the corporate ladder," the philosopher Nancy Fraser argued in *The New York Times*. "By definition, then, its beneficiaries can only be women of the professional-managerial class. And absent structural changes in capitalist society, those women can only benefit by leaning on others—by offloading their own care work and housework onto low-waged, precarious workers, typically racialized and/or immigrant women. So this is not, and cannot be, a feminism for all women!"

Faludi noted that while *Lean In* was using capitalism to "advance the cause of women's equality," Sandberg was equally guilty of using feminism's newfound cultural energy to advocate for the free market. Redirecting feminist goals toward capitalist ends, Faludi argued, was nothing new for feminism or for the marketplace. We had heard this song before, a century ago. In 1920, shortly after the Nineteenth Amendment granted women the right to vote, a flourishing American economy "seized upon women's yearnings for independence and equality and redirected them to the marketplace," she wrote. "Over and over, mass merchandisers promised women an ersatz version of emancipation, the fulfillment of individual, and aspirational, desire." In effect, women were assured by advertising campaigns and persistent media messaging that there were instant ways to assert their new power that didn't involve tedious organizing or advocacy. Corporations including General Electric, General Motors, Hoover, and the American Tobacco Company ran ads affirming women's social and economic rights, most of which seemed to begin and end with buying their products. Hoover declared that its vacuum cleaner could help women celebrate "positive agitation" with its "revolutionary cleaning principle." (While they were at home, doing housework.) Lucky Strike targeted liberated young women by branding its cigarettes "torches of freedom."

One hundred years later, there were distinct parallels with a feminist movement that seemed stuck in a mire of Dove's Campaign for Real Beauty ads and branded conference tote bags. *Lean In* sold more than four million copies in five years, in part by seizing on the concerns and contradictions of a movement in flux. Women were exhausted by the cultural sexism of the aughts and frustrated by the ongoing aftershocks of the recession and the persistent failure of the American workplace to support them. But they needed more than an eleven-point plan on how to steamroll their way into a corner office. In 2013, Faludi noted, the fastest-growing occupations for women were care work, customer service, and food service—undervalued and underpaid sectors of the economy in which Lean In Circles and power poses would get employees short shrift. As Tolentino wrote, surveying the state of feminist energy in a *Jezebel* piece from 2015: "We have politicized and vindicated every possible manifestation of female narcissism without getting any legislative movement towards mandatory paid parental leave. Feminism is proliferating essentially as merchandise; we can buy anything that suits us and nothing that we really need."

A YEAR AFTER *Lean In* was published, another how-to book for wannabe women tycoons blasted its way onto the bestseller list. #*Girlboss*—hashtag and all—was a memoir of sorts by the Nasty Gal clothing-brand founder Sophia Amoruso, a rags-to-riches account of how Amoruso went from a dumpster-diving, shoplifting freegan anarchist to the CEO of a $100 million business. The real secret of her success, it turned out, was buried right toward the end, after a few hundred pages of slogans and advice about the "alchemy" of magical thinking. When Nasty Gal was pursuing funding to scale the brand, Amoruso wrote, "most of the venture capitalists I met with had recently and unanimously 'discovered' that women liked to buy things online. They were super-stoked on the idea of a female-run business that sold things to women. I happened to check a lot of the boxes that they were excited about at the time."

With her book, and with the help of an investor culture once again sensing the untapped power of women as a consumer base, Amoruso gave a name to a 2010s phenomenon that was coming into sharper focus: the girlboss. The word was freighted with implication in two short syllables, condescending to women in the workplace with the diminutive "girl," while implying they couldn't simply be "bosses" without a qualifier. Girlbosses were young. And they were cute—savvy, mediagenic entrepreneurs who became celebrities in their own right, courted in magazines for their business acumen, and worshipped on social media by the girls and women hoping to mimic their ascent. They were in charge, if only temporarily. By the time the paperback edition of #*Girlboss* came out, Amoruso had stepped down from her role as CEO, telling *Forbes*, "No one knows what it takes to be CEO, even CEOs. My advice would be to get some real management chops, work for some great companies, and know more than I did before you try to do what I've done."

Girlbosses were avatars for a cultural moment in which the female-oriented prosperity gospel preached by so many reality-TV franchises and self-help guides was reaching its zenith. Although the infamous Bravo stars were branded as Housewives, stay-at-home helpmeets enabling their husbands' careers, in reality they were themselves zealous hustlers and entrepreneurs, building small fortunes by selling wifedom-enhancing products to other women. Bethenny Frankel, who'd previously been a nanny for Paris Hilton and appeared on a Martha Stewart–hosted offshoot of *The Apprentice*, leveraged her *Housewives* fame into a line of diet books, workout DVDs, and low-calorie margarita mix, branded Skinnygirl. Lisa Vanderpump created her own sangria range. Other Housewives marketed shapewear, perfumes, bedsheets, and supplements.

In the aftermath of the recession, brands had products they needed to sell to women, and the girlboss was an ideal marketing tool. One pioneer was Gwyneth Paltrow, who had debuted her newsletter, Goop, in September 2008, right around the time that Lehman Brothers went bankrupt. Goop was originally a recommendations portal, a way for Paltrow to share restaurants she liked in Barcelona, recipes for banana-nut muffins, and the particular knitwear brand she was wearing that month. The tone conveyed intimacy—a connection with her fans and followers. But the name signaled ambition, mimicking the double-Os of massive tech companies such as Google and Yahoo. By 2012, Goop was an e-commerce platform selling offbeat luxury items with California flair: organic skincare, ninety-five-dollar T-shirts, baby-soft lilac hammam towels. In 2014, *The New York Times* noted that Goop's model was quickly being emulated by other entrepreneurial celebrities. Jessica Alba launched the Honest Company, a parent-oriented wellness brand selling "earth-conscious" diapers and baby soap, in 2012. Blake Lively followed, in 2014, with Preserve, a short-lived lifestyle site. "Celebrities are increasingly moving from endorsing products to being the product," John Demsey, the group president of

Estée Lauder, told *The New York Times*. "This is only going to get more common."

The girlbosses of the mid-2010s didn't necessarily have to be celebrities. They just had to carry themselves as though they were famous, summoning a requisite combination of poise, relentlessness, professionalism, and intrigue. Investors tended to be drawn to the same kind of figurehead—someone who was young, beautiful, connected, savvy with social media, and, usually, White. No one embodied the formula quite like Emily Weiss, the founder of the beauty brand Glossier. In a previous era, Weiss had appeared on the MTV reality show *The Hills* as herself, a no-nonsense "superintern" at *Teen Vogue* whose preternatural calm and expertise on everything from prints to peonies stood in sharp contrast to the more befuddled Lauren Conrad and Whitney Port. She already had a significant following and connections from her time as a writer at *Vogue* when she launched *Into the Gloss* in 2010, the beauty-focused lifestyle site that would spawn a billion-dollar company.

There was a particular reason why Glossier became so ubiquitous and why so many of the celebrity businesswomen of the 2010s would build sizable fortunes on the back of beauty brands. In times of financial struggle, we're innately drawn to products that signal opulence, pleasure, and proximity to the kinds of women whose lives we fantasize about living. Most of us can't afford to wear the $500 sweater that Jennifer Lopez works out in, but we can more easily justify spending $55 on the Tom Ford lipstick that Lupita Nyong'o wears at a premiere. As the journalist Marisa Meltzer writes in *Glossy*, her account of Glossier's rise, there's little about individual beauty products that distinguishes them from others on the market. Branding is the key to sales—the intangible hook that compels a consumer to buy one specific face cream or eyebrow wand instead of another. And in a business where profit margins can be as high as 90 percent, celebrity figureheads and genius marketers alike can stand to make enormous amounts of money.

The women we tend to associate with the girlboss era now, for better or worse, are inextricably linked with the rise of Instagram. They broadcast the aesthetic details of their lives as public figures, drawing significant numbers of followers for the ways in which they projected a distinctly feminine kind of power. But they also shrewdly capitalized on all the ways in which Instagram had commanded our attention. Away, the pastel-colored luggage startup founded in 2015 by two female executives from Warby Parker, drew on Instagram's appeal as a travel journal, in which you could follow along on your friend's glamorous jaunts and city breaks in real time. Shop Jeen, an online boutique founded in 2012 by the twenty-year-old Erin Yogasundram, used the visual language of Tumblr—neons and anime and quirky catchphrases—to sell streetwear and accessories to younger shoppers. The Wing, a women-centric coworking and social club founded in 2016 by Lauren Kassan and Audrey Gelman—the latter, formerly a political aide who'd been friends with Lena Dunham since high school, had guest-starred on *Girls*, and had previously dated Terry Richardson—provided spaces that both were functional and served as the ideal power-photo backdrop: muted rose walls, artfully curated bookshelves, lush greenery.

No industry, though, grasped the potential of our new shared visual realm quite as beauty did. Glossier managed to anticipate a moment in which beauty standards were newly informed by the selfie: high-focus, close-up, filtered images of women's faces that either showcased luminous "natural" skin or maximized the artifice of contouring and heavily overdrawn lips—both trends that the Kardashian family members were propagating on their own Instagram pages. In 2015, a few months after admitting on *Keeping Up with the Kardashians* that she'd had her lips augmented, the eighteen-year-old Kylie Jenner launched her first cosmetics product, the Kylie Lip Kit. Four years later, with Kylie Cosmetics having expanded to include concealer, eyeshadow, and skincare, *Forbes* declared Jenner to be the first "selfie-made billionaire." What had started out as insecurity— a boy reportedly once told Jenner he didn't think she'd be a good kisser, because her lips were too small—became a business empire, with endless ripples informing the ways in which we all understood beauty.

Many of the products the Kardashians promoted via Instagram during the 2010s were questionable at best. In 2018, Kim Kardashian drew widespread criticism after she touted "appetite-suppressant lollipops" as "literally unreal," alongside a photo of herself sucking on one. Her sister Khloe continued to promote the same diet-aid line, which advertised laxative teas and meal-replacement shakes as weight-loss products, in 2020. In 2014, Kim shared her love for a particular branded "waist trainer," a figure-cinching apparatus that's essentially a corset. (Fitness and health care experts have decried waist trainers for weakening core muscles, increasing the risks of heartburn and indigestion, and compressing quite pivotal internal organs.) By 2024, waist trainers were available to purchase via her signature shapewear brand, Skims, which is now worth an estimated $4 billion. That same year, Kardashian wore such a tightly cinched silver jacquard corset to the Met Gala that she appeared to be having trouble breathing.

In the meantime, hundreds of millions of women were internalizing everything—the new old ideals for femininity, the vast platforms being built on extremely limited kinds of images, the money being made in real time. The term "girlboss" is inherently tricky and loaded. "To be a girlboss was to make business cute—a boy boss is a completely moot point and absurd," Meltzer writes in *Glossy*. Because girlbosses had been elevated to lofty pedestals thanks to their appeal to women consumers and their supposed feminist authority, it was all too easy to pick them apart when they seemed to be acting just like regular old bosses. In 2015, a lawsuit claimed that Nasty Gal had fired four separate employees when they became pregnant. (The company described the lawsuit as "frivolous and without merit.") The same year, *Jezebel* reported that Yogasundram's management of Shop Jeen was chaotic—that she withheld money from vendors and treated employees with disdain. (Yogasundram told *Vogue* in 2022 that the company's success had been "a logistical nightmare behind the scenes.") In the national reckoning over institutionalized racism that followed the death of George Floyd in 2020, both the Wing and Glossier faced allegations that they failed to safeguard employees of color from

racist treatment at work; at the time, Gelman and Weiss publicly acknowledged certain ways in which they had failed to create what Weiss described as "an inclusive, safe environment."

But the girlboss was also cursed from the start because she
was essentially a figurehead—as much a branding tool as Mr
Muscle or Tony the Tiger. For much of the 2010s, feminism
was chic, and the empowering symbol of a woman succeeding
in business was the ultimate key to media attention, good PR,
and—most crucially—juiced-up sales. "If these women could
succeed while upholding feminist values and treating their employees humanely," Amanda Mull wrote in *The Atlantic* in
2020, "then maybe the patriarchy was just a choice that savvy
consumers could shop their way around. Maybe people could
vote for equality by buying a particular set of luggage or joining
a particular co-working space." That many female entrepreneurs were getting rich off items that capitalized on toxic beauty
standards or environmentally poisonous fast fashion was less of
an issue than was the revelation that many girlbosses operated
just like men—they weren't interested in the elevation of other
women at all.

VIRTUALLY FROM THE BEGINNING, there was an undercur-
rent of scamminess to the girlboss era, something that came into
sharper focus as the decade went by. In 2010, two entrepreneurs

named Don Ressler and Adam Goldenberg launched a new "online lifestyle clothing brand" called JustFabulous, a fast-fashion site with a twist: It was actually quite difficult to stop buying its products if you no longer wanted them. The pair had previously been involved in selling dubious weight-loss products online, including "flavor-enhancing" crystals called Sensa that were issued a $26.5 million fine from the Federal Trade Commission for deceptive advertising. JustFab followed the subscription model that Ressler and Goldenberg had established in the aughts, offering customers free or heavily discounted trial products while simultaneously signing them up for monthly payments that were buried in small print and challenging to cancel. (In 2015, a spokesperson for JustFab said the company's rapid growth had led to "inevitable bumps along the way," but that customer satisfaction was a "top priority"; Goldenberg and Ressler declined to comment.)

Subscription fashion sites relied on celebrities to lend them both credibility and cachet. Paying $39.95 a month for a PVC handbag or a pair of magenta yoga pants is easier to digest, it turns out, when it connotes some kind of emotional or aesthetic connection to a star. In 2009, Kim Kardashian had launched the service ShoeDazzle.com with Robert Shapiro, one of the lawyers who'd helped defend O. J. Simpson from murder charges alongside her father; four years later, the site, which offered customers a new pair of shoes each month for a regular fee, was acquired by JustFab. In 2011, JustFab signed up the designer and entrepreneur Kimora Lee Simmons as its president and creative director, spawning a partnership in which Simmons promoted JustFab items on her social-media pages, curated lists of her favorite items for the site, and even starred in a short-lived reality show, *Kimora: House of Fab*, about her work at the company. "I've always been at the forefront of fashion," she states early in the show. With Ressler and Goldenberg, she said, "my two partners in crime . . . we're gonna guide this company off into the promised land."

There's nothing inherently sketchy about a subscription service per se, although the United Nations Environment Programme has expressed concern about the ways in which they encourage "unsustainable consumption practices" and lead to more discarded clothing and single-use plastics in landfills. But subscription services that disguise how they truly operate with enticing offers for new members, then make it extremely difficult to cancel your monthly membership, exploit customers who tend not to read the small print. As early as 2010, the Florida attorney general's office began investigating JustFab after receiving hundreds of complaints from customers who thought they were making a single purchase, not committing to a yearly outlay of hundreds of dollars. On Reddit, JustFab customers have complained bitterly about the byzantine process of canceling their subscriptions: links that disappear when you try to click on them, customer-service agents who profess not to be able to hear the person calling. "It is by far one of the most deliberately difficult cancellation processes I have ever seen," one woman wrote.

None of this deterred stars from seizing an opportunity. In 2013, the actress Kate Hudson signed on as a partner for the

JustFab spin-off brand Fabletics, an athleisure subscription service that has an estimated company value of $5 billion. ("VIP membership money scam theft," "Scammers," and "Theft," read a few of the reviews posted over the years on the site Trustpilot. In 2015, Hudson told the *Daily Mail* that she was "very proud of Fabletics," but that she takes all customer feedback "very seriously.") But the biggest celebrity coup of all was that of Rihanna, who by 2018 was on her way to becoming a billionaire thanks to the astonishing success of her cosmetics line, Fenty Beauty. That year, she launched the lingerie line Savage X Fenty with JustFab—now renamed TechStyle. In 2019, Kaitlyn Tiffany described in *Vox* how a number of consumers appeared to be gradually realizing they'd been charged regularly for Savage X Fenty for the past year, to their chagrin. "Cool, I've actually been accidentally subscribed to a $50 monthly membership fee on Rihanna's bra website for four months without knowing it," one tweet read. "I NEVER would've knowingly signed up for it, I don't even have any idea what I'm paying for. Wasted so much money." What was almost more perplexing, as Tiffany noted, was that many of these shoppers' parasocial relationships to Rihanna made them reluctant to publicly complain or to implicate the singer in any way. On the same day the *Vox* story was published, Savage X Fenty announced an additional $50 million in funding from investors. Three years later, in 2022, it paid $1.2 million to settle a consumer-protection lawsuit accusing it of misleading customers about the recurring fees attached to its VIP membership program.

Women consumers tend to be disproportionately targeted

and hooked by subscription services and online scams, many of which use images of celebrities to tout endorsements that are wholly fake. The allure of the free-delivery miracle product is often too enticing not to fall for when you're facing middle age, burned out by work and parenting, and desperate for a quick fix. More recently, though, male influencers have been getting into the supplements game. In 2017, the business-news site *Quartz* published a side-by-side analysis of the vitamins and supplements promoted, respectively, by Gwyneth Paltrow and the conspiracy-theorist Alex Jones, demonstrating that the same ingredients were almost without exception being praised and sold by both: cordyceps mushroom for "mental power," maca root for "sexy energy" and "superior vitality," and selenium for antioxidants and fighting "free radicals," among others.

With regard to multilevel marketing schemes, though, women are still the focus—for good reason. Around 2010, I began to get invitations from friends to social events that had a vested interest in selling me something. One woman turned her loft apartment into a miniboutique for a costume-jewelry company. A Facebook friend who was in graduate school began heavily promoting diet-replacement shakes in her updates. People I knew mostly over Instagram were suddenly posting regularly about the shampoos, the beauty products, and the yoga pants they were "endorsing." None of this was new—these women were simply participating in the same MLM schemes that manifested during the 1950s and 1960s as Tupperware parties and home visits from Avon. MLMs follow a direct-sales model where participants make a percentage of profits both from the products they sell and from the sales of the people they recruit. This sounds more lucrative than it actually is: In one analysis of more than five hundred MLM companies in the United States, 99 percent of people recruited into a company ended up losing money over the long run.

And yet here were women I knew, posting exuberant updates in language that didn't sound remotely like theirs, riddled with words such as "empowering" and "hustle" and "choice." The language of popular 2010s feminism had been co-opted by an industry that overwhelmingly targets women, relying on their communities at school and church and now social media to provide fertile territory for recruitment. The aesthetics and technology had been updated for an era of Instagram and Facebook Live. But increasingly it felt as if the ultimate girlboss was now a stay-at-home mom, trying as hard as she absolutely could to fit full-time, flexible employment into the evening hours when her kids were asleep. In #Girlboss, Sophia Amoruso recalled her social-media strategies back in the days of MySpace, when she'd illicitly use friend-adding software to generate as many connections as she possibly could—all in service of gaining an outsized audience for her auctions of vintage clothing. Now, MLM recruits were following thousands of other women on Instagram, then messaging them to compliment their style and offer them an exciting new opportunity.

MLMs, in so many ways, are a symbol of corporate feminism's failure. "If you want to create incredible wealth, identify an underutilized resource," Mark Stidham, a cofounder of the notorious clothing MLM company LuLaRoe, explains in the documentary series *LuLaRich*. "And you know what? There is an underutilized resource of stay-at-home moms." According to 2020 figures from the Direct Selling Association, 75 percent of people selling products through their own homes or online are women. 87 percent are White, which speaks to the dynamic of who exactly in America is encouraged to stay home with their children and who's obligated to go out and work. MLMs have historically targeted the "three Ms": Mormons, moms, and military wives—all sectors of women who encounter the most obstacles to entering the workforce. Over the last decade, they've had substantial success recruiting women who are talented, creative, hardworking, and resourceful, and who—thanks to an absolute dearth of resources for working parents—can't find work that doesn't involve promoting dubious diet products on Instagram.

So many of the MLMs with the biggest cultural footprint for millennials have capitalized on varying vulnerabilities in modern womanhood. LuLaRoe—which sold "modest" brightly colored leggings and dresses to a ballooning community of women right up until complaints piled up about its quality-control issues—profited from people who wanted comfortable, joyful clothing even as their bodies changed after childbirth and their routines kept them largely at home. (The culture writer Anne Helen Petersen, in her viral essay about millennial burnout, noted that yoga pants are the motif for a generation of hustlers, transitioning from the gym to Skype calls to school pickup.) Isagenix and Herbalife claim to offer complete nutritional shakes and supplements for people with busy schedules or who live in food deserts yet still feel compelled to lose weight. Companies such as Younique, Monat, and the perennial Avon and Mary Kay post Glossier-influenced images of lip liners against a pink backdrop and reels taken by saleswomen of their seamless hair and makeup routines—all designed to allow for minimum effort and optimized impact on camera. "Our company was begun with only one objective," a 2024 Mary Kay post stated. "Girl power."

For women who've been conditioned since reaching adulthood to meticulously present themselves for mass approval and to perform the details of their lives as a kind of ongoing art project, MLMs check all the boxes. But the reality is that the structural blocks keeping women out of the workforce are as insurmountable as they were in 2013 and that individual ascension is a poor substitute for a society that actually wants, encourages, and enables women to work. Girlboss culture has conditioned us to see ourselves as lacking sufficient motivation or hustle, despite using all the tools in our arsenal to turn ourselves into products. It ignores all the ways in which the system is resolutely rigged against us.

What proved the final death knell for the girlboss was sunlight. Time after time, supposedly progressive companies and leaders faced allegations that they had betrayed their own values. Founders of companies including Away and the clothing line Reformation were accused of presiding over toxic work environments, especially for employees of color. The specific brand of empowerment feminism touted throughout the 2010s was disparaged in a viral meme: "gaslight, gatekeep, girlboss."

But the emptiness of girlbossery also helped spark a darker movement that increasingly advocates opting out of the workplace altogether. On TikTok, the algorithm tends to reward some of the most regressive advocates for modern womanhood. Tradwives sell a sanitized—and extremely White—nostalgic ideal of traditional gender roles that turns the performance of domestic work into a lucrative business. Stay-at-home girlfriends argue that a life of "feminine leisure" is the most rewarding thing a woman could aspire to. In the meantime, we're no closer to having made tangible improvements in the lives of women who want to work *and* have families. When my twins started day care in New York City in January 2021, the cost of full-time enrollment for both was $5,400 a month. I was grateful for the women who cared for my babies, as well as for the job I loved and the fact that by cutting back absolutely everywhere else, my husband and I could just about make things work. But it was harder than it had ever been to argue with the women I saw on social media selling things, endlessly hopeful and naturally fluent in the lingo of parenting, engagement, and positive thinking. "No one has kids to miss all the little moments," one woman I know posted a few years ago. "Making extra income while being at home is such a gift. This opportunity is such a win-win."

CHAPTER 10

Girls on Top

Rewriting a Path Toward Power

The point is simple but important: As far back as we can see in Western
history there is a radical separation—real, cultural, and imaginary—
between women and power.

MARY BEARD (2017)

What I want is outrageous: all the possible pleasures of freedom.

KATE MILLETT (1974)

Why does culture matter? What impact does it actually have on our lives, our finances, our status, and
our possibilities? I was trying to parse these questions recently when I happened upon an argument by the social
scientist Alice Evans that pulled together everything I'd long
suspected. Evans studies gender divergence: why some cultures
are more favorable to women than others are, why progress is
often followed by regression, how social norms change and
change again. One of the single biggest drivers of gender equality, she argues, is romantic love. In societies where love is actively disdained in favor of consolidating male networks of

power in which marriage is often a valuable bargaining chip, women tend to have much lower status. In Europe, the Protestant Reformation—which celebrated and emphasized marital love—led to more respect for women, more acknowledgment of their humanity, and more willingness to accept their elevation. One of the most crucial forces behind gender equality, Evans writes, may simply be "loving men who want women to thrive and be happy."

She doesn't explicitly tie this to art as a galvanizing force, but I will. The Romantic movement of the nineteenth century, which celebrated chivalry, beauty, love, and emotion, arguably set a path for twentieth-century feminism by encouraging the perception of women as full human beings, not just commodities. On the flip side, the waning of romantic comedies in the early 2000s—and the boom in movies that fetishized male bonding, fraternal quests, and juvenile misogyny—may have led to women's seeming less human and less worthy of love and respect. By extension, is it surprising that the creator of a reality series that treats women as interchangeable, identikit trophy brides was issued a restraining order for allegedly attacking his pregnant wife? Is it strange that a generation raised on violent, dehumanizing pornography has trouble forming meaningful intimate relationships and is increasingly eschewing both romantic love and sex altogether?

The act of "re-vision," as the Adrienne Rich quote from the beginning of this book reads, is "an act of survival. Until we can understand the assumptions in which we are drenched we cannot know ourselves." I came into this project wanting to understand where the cultural sexism and backlash against women that manifested in the twenty-first century came from. But what's become clearer since I started my research is that popular culture is a strikingly predictive and transformative force with regard to the status of women and other historically marginalized groups. The things we watch, listen to, read, wear, write, and share dictate in large part how we internalize and project what we're worth.

In the summer of 2016, I was living in Washington, DC, and working at *The Atlantic*, both places that were consumed with the presidential election later that year. The conventional wisdom—backed up by polling, news coverage, and rationality—was that Hillary Clinton would beat Donald Trump. At a work happy hour one evening, I remember talking with one of my then-bosses about what might actually change under a Clinton administration. Pragmatically, the answer was: Nothing much. (Sheryl Sandberg, for what it's worth, was hotly tipped to have been Clinton's treasury secretary—about as steadfast an ally to corporate America as any capitalist could have wished for.) Emotionally, though, the stakes felt astronomical. I can remember arguing that Clinton's inauguration would upend the way America thought about women—that seeing a woman elevated to the most powerful job in the world would overwrite decades of conditioning about who was allowed to have authority and what might be possible. The shifts would be seismic, I argued, even if they weren't immediately obvious. This was a moment when progress still felt inevitable.

All I can think now is, *How stupid.* That July, I'd written a piece about the reaction to Paul Feig's all-female adaptation of *Ghostbusters*, in which a swamp of aggrieved online commenters directed organized ire at the movie and misogynistic and racist abuse at one of its stars, Leslie Jones. If America wasn't ready to even temporarily cede a fictional world of hearse-driving, ectoplasm-dodging paranormal investigators to women, it could hardly have been expected to give one of us the nuclear codes. The signs of what was about to happen were all there in our cultural macrocosm. I just didn't want to see them.

Our culture teaches us everything. And what I keep coming back to now is how few cultural representations there still are of women seeking and wielding power. The author Tom Perrotta once told me that when he wrote *Election* in 1998, he had no idea that Tracy Flick would go on to become an archetype for earnest female ambition. What he came to realize, especially after Reese Witherspoon's indelible turn in the movie adaptation, was that Tracy stuck in people's minds because there were just no other meaningful fictional representations of women politicians. Tracy—intelligent, worthy, hugely unpopular— became the dominant stereotype for any woman in politics, from *Parks and Recreation*'s Leslie Knope all the way up to Clinton herself. Until *Veep* debuted on HBO in 2012, Tracy stood virtually alone.

There are obviously reasons why people didn't want to vote for Hillary Clinton that had nothing or little to do with her gender. But given the dearth of other women who've managed to make it to the top of the ticket, her trajectory is worth revisiting, especially given the cultural backdrop it played out against.

In his 2002 book *Striptease Culture,* which examines the mass proliferation during the late 1990s of sex and sexual imagery in modern life, the academic Brian McNair argued that Clinton's election to the US Senate in 2000 demonstrated how little this kind of cultural shift had hurt feminism. In that moment, he argued, "the idea of a female U.S. president no longer seemed outlandish." Never mind that women still made up just 13 percent of senators at the time. Clinton, and her success, was to be our token of what was possible.

In 2007, the year Clinton announced that she was running for president, popular culture was mostly engaged in a frenzied race to the tabloid bottom. Everywhere you looked, beautiful, vacuous women were falling apart, melting down, selling out, going off the rails. It's not difficult to interpret that this might have influenced how voters my age felt about a potential woman president—about her gravitas, her professionalism, her capacity for ethical decision-making and tough negotiation. Earlier, I wrote about how much of the language directed at women in the public eye in 2007 was characterized by disgust—something that dehumanized the celebrities in question and made it easier to hate them. The same kind of disgust has long been aimed at Clinton, Julia Gillard, and Angela Merkel—the most powerful women in the world during the aughts. (And, soon enough, that disgust would be redirected at Kamala Harris, via absurd sexualized smears pushed on social media.) "Will this country want to actually watch a woman get older before their eyes on a daily basis?" Rush Limbaugh asked on his radio show in 2007. In 2015, when Clinton took a bathroom break during a televised

Democratic debate, Donald Trump told a rally that her doing so was "disgusting." During his own debate with her a year later, he referred to her as "such a nasty woman."

It's no longer at all surprising to me that a capable and experienced woman lost to a reality-TV character and a virulent misogynist in 2016 (to say nothing of 2024). Every single cultural message Americans had absorbed during the decades leading up to the first race was enshrining the idea that women fundamentally lacked the qualities required to gain and exercise authority: intelligence, morality, dignity. (It's worth noting here that men don't have to meet all these barriers to entry because they have always been powerful and thus have nothing to prove.) At the same time, any women who managed to accumulate cultural power for themselves were rapidly undermined or replaced altogether. In music during the 1990s, women who railed against the system were switched out with girls who could be more easily packaged and sold. In fashion that same decade, Amazonian supermodels with power and self-possession were edged out by vulnerable, hunched, more easily exploited teenagers.

On film throughout the aughts, female characters were presented as ancillary objects, shrewish and vacuous at very best. And the new medium of reality television, virtually from its inception, propagated the idea that women were hysterical, money-grubbing idiots, scratching each other's eyes out for a prize none of them seemed to even want. The world of shows such as *The Bachelor* and *Flavor of Love* was one where women's only form of power was sexual and where, as the media-literacy educator Jennifer L. Pozner once told me, "women not only appeared to not have any choices, but appeared not to *want* to have choices." Later, as reality-TV celebrity became a more reliable and lucrative career path, a hothouse for proto-influencers selling us things, it set the model for how modern women were supposed to make themselves over and present themselves to the world, the success of which mattered infinitely more than that of any other aspirations they might have.

We each of us have decades of internal wiring informed by the works we grew up with. And so we need to expand our conception of what power for women looks like. We need to rewrite the archetypes and the narratives, all the way down to the bones. And in many ways, this rewriting is already happening.

HILLARY CLINTON TENDS to stand front and center regarding the topic of female political ambition this century, but there's another woman whose rapid, turbulent ascent connects with all the cultural trends of this era. In August 2008, when Senator John McCain announced Sarah Palin as his presidential running mate, the forty-four-year-old Alaska governor was virtually unheard of outside her state. She had minimal political experience: two terms as the mayor of Wasilla, a town with fewer than seven thousand residents at the time, and two years as governor. But she was a woman—which the McCain campaign hoped would energize voters—a conservative Christian, and a mother. An early profile of Palin in *The New York Times* highlighted the latter, offering a sense of her as someone who had never had political ambitions of her own but rather was drawn to office reluctantly, out of a pragmatic desire to share her skills. Her successor as mayor described her to the newspaper as just "a P.T.A. mom who got involved."

This kind of framing was crucial. In her 2017 book *Down Girl*, the philosopher Kate Manne writes that nothing triggers misogyny quite like a woman who aspires to a "masculine-coded" social role, "especially when it would come at the expense of rival male politicians." Palin consistently downplayed her ambition and emphasized her feminine credentials, stereotyping herself as a "hockey mom" and a "mama grizzly." Although she struggled to answer basic policy questions or articulate a vision for America beyond faith, family, and fossil fuels, she was telegenic and seemed to connect with a faction of voters who are often obliquely characterized as "real" rather than "White."

But, aptly for someone who emerged toward the end of the aughts, Palin also fit neatly into the decade's understanding of what a woman should be. As a teenager, she'd competed in beauty pageants, winning the title of "Miss Wasilla" in 1984 and placing as second runner-up in the Miss Alaska contest that year. Although she was conventionally feminine, even glamorous—wearing highlighted chestnut hair and suit jackets that tended to be lacy or belted—she was quickly subjected to an expensive makeover by the Republican National Committee, which spent more than $150,000 of campaign contributions on upgrading her clothing, hair, and makeup. During the gossip-fixated aughts, the messier details of her family life engaged both the tabloids and the public. On the first day of the Republican National Convention in September, Palin announced that her seventeen-year-old daughter, Bristol, was pregnant; in the months to come, political commentators would comb over old photos of the governor during her own most recent pregnancy with the fervor of *Us Weekly* assessing A-listers' baby bodies. After McCain lost the election, the Palin family elected to prolong their notoriety by opening up their lives for reality-TV cameras, first when Bristol appeared on *Dancing with the Stars* in 2010 and then with the Mark Burnett–produced TLC series *Sarah Palin's Alaska* later that year.

More crucially, though, Palin was conceivable as a sex object. Mere days after she'd addressed the Republican National Convention as a candidate for vice president—the first woman in history to do so—the porn producer Larry Flynt's production company posted an ad on Craigslist requesting a "Sarah Palin look-alike for an adult film to be shot in the next ten days." Flynt had a history of trying to unite porn and politics: In 1975, one year after launching *Hustler*, he published photographs of the former First Lady Jacqueline Kennedy Onassis sunbathing nude on vacation, and in 1984 he attempted to run for president himself as a Republican. *Who's Nailin' Paylin?*, which filmed over two days in October 2008, starred the porn performer Lisa Ann as "Serra Paylin," a malapropism-prone politician who thinks the earth is ten thousand years old, struggles to pronounce "absolutely," and participates in hardcore group scenes with satirical versions of Hillary Clinton and Condoleezza Rice.

The media reaction to *Who's Nailin' Paylin?* at the time was largely jaded and laced with schadenfreude. If Palin was going to be so hypocritical about sex, arguing for abstinence-only education while her teenage daughter reaped the consequences, what could be the harm in ridiculing her? Five women writers debated the movie in a discussion for *Salon*, critiquing its "lack of creativity," weak attempts at political commentary, and low-budget production values, but not the fact that American culture's immediate response to a woman's political ascent was to put her on her back. The details of *Who's Nailin' Paylin?* are also illuminating. "Serra" has sex with Russian soldiers who arrive at her home, with a college professor—in flashback—while a student at the University of "I-DA-HO," and with the two other most prominent women in American politics. The character of "Candilezza" also shares that she's done "things to some guys who look a lot like Cheney, Rove, Wolfowitz, and Chuck Norris." The subtext was clear: There was no public venue—not foreign policy, not education, and not the White House—within which a woman couldn't be reduced to a sexual caricature.

In an essay from the 2018 book *Pornographies*, the theorist Tim Gregory argues that both porn and conventional mass media produce narratives where desire and power are kept separate and distinct. *"Who's Nailin' Paylin?* is not opposed to Palin's attempt to gain power," he writes, "but rather it criticizes her attempt to become anything other than an autonomous, powerful object of desire." Gregory also points out how the movie flips the traditional structure of porn films—which typically begin with girl-on-girl scenes before ending with male-female penetration—to end instead with a three-way between female politicians, as if to suggest that the only logical conclusion of women having power and authority would be lesbianism and the displacement of men. In other words, however emphatically Palin tried to downplay her ambitions by identifying as a wife and mother, it wasn't enough to neutralize herself as a subconscious threat to the status quo.

Ever since, women running for office have tended to fall into the same traps that Clinton and Palin stumbled into. In July 2024, as Democrats coalesced around Harris as a replacement presidential candidate after Joe Biden's disastrous performance in a debate with Donald Trump, a shadowy conservative network began pushing a campaign of "lurid sexual jibes" about Harris on social media, the news site *Semafor* later reported. If candidates downplay their appearances and their ability to be read as sexual objects, they're met with disgust. If they groom themselves according to the uncanny aesthetic standards of the conservative media ecosystem, they undermine themselves and their ability to be taken seriously. You could argue that to some extent on the right, post-Trump, this no longer matters; it's more important to look a way that will get you booked on Fox News than to exude gravitas. Provocation has become a more desirable and more efficient tool than power itself. But Republican women, as Rebecca Traister pointed out in a 2024 cover story for *New York*, are still in a bind: "When your value is tied inextricably to sexualized standards contrived by white men, you will not be appreciated, sometimes not even *seen*, unless you meet those standards. Yet if you do hit their (often shifting) aesthetic marks, you risk being degraded by those same men, not taken seriously as their peers but rather understood as their ornament."

It's no coincidence that so many conservative women these days bear remarkable aesthetic similarities to reality-TV stars, with "glam" preeminent above all else and the dominant mode of self-presentation seeming so unnatural it hardly reads as human. For one thing, Trump set the visual standard for contemporary right-wing politics, and he's a reality-TV star himself with a yen for tacky, monstrous excess. But even before Trump's presidency, the women of Fox News had long looked alike: bleached blonde hair, tight jewel-toned skirt suits, heavy makeup. In part, this was to gratify the predilections of Roger Ailes, the network's chairman and CEO, who was accused in 2016 of having sexually harassed more than twenty women who worked for him. Still, the requirement that women on the right conform to highly feminine, sexualized standards of dress is also the logical outcome of an ideology that prizes women as wives and mothers above all else. To look any other way is to instantly diminish your own value. The overarching message is the same as it was in popular culture twenty-five years ago:

Power is sex, and sex is power. That the power in question isn't real is exactly the point.

ONE OF THE MOST FASCINATING things about the popular culture of the twenty-first century, to me, is the ways in which you can see women and nonbinary people grappling with the limitations imposed on them versus the stories they want to tell. In her 2017 book *Women & Power*, the historian Mary Beard analyzes "just how deeply embedded in Western culture are the mechanisms that silence women, that refuse to take them seriously, and that sever them . . . from the centers of power." She cites the immature Telemachus essentially telling his own mother to shut up at the beginning of *The Odyssey*, and also the images rendering both Hillary Clinton and Angela Merkel as Medusa, whose beheading by Perseus is "the classic myth in which the dominance of the male is violently reasserted." These kinds of stories are the cornerstones of our literature, our society, and our structures of governance and power. And their influence can be insidious, even now.

In the immediate aftermath of the aughts, a decade in which women appeared in movies primarily to nag, preen, or get splattered in their own gore, the 2010s were more hospitable to female leads. Executives seemed to be gradually realizing what marketers and brands had recently figured out: that the power of women as consumers wasn't being adequately tapped. In 2011, the Judd Apatow–produced *Bridesmaids*—a smart, crass, ferociously funny movie about female friendship and the wedding-industrial complex—grossed more than $300 million, or roughly ten times its budget, and was nominated for two Academy Awards. Over the next decade, a wave of women-oriented shows and movies would follow, many exploring a mode the writer Joy Press once called "slapstick feminism." Their characters were more fully realized than women on-screen had been in a while: endearing, difficult, jaded, troubled, joyful. I watched them all through problematic hookups and excruciating work pratfalls and STD tests and manic episodes, and it wasn't until recently that I could fully see the one thing they all had in common.

The 2010s, in culture, were the decade of the trainwreck. You could argue that this was progress—the kinds of beautiful, self-obsessed, car-crashing magnets we'd obsessed over and dehumanized during the aughts were now being given interiority, in narratives that offered them sympathy, backstory, and (limited) agency. Often, characters were fully self-aware and all too cognizant of their own limitations. In 2011's *Young Adult*, Charlize Theron played a prickly, narcissistic, extraordinarily beautiful fuckup, in a thought experiment on what happens to the bitchy queen bee who never moves on from high school. (In short, as one reviewer summarized things, "depression, alcoholism, and trichotillomania.") The same year, on Showtime, Claire Danes returned to episodic TV for the first time since

My So-Called Life as Carrie Mathison, a CIA officer with bipolar disorder who becomes fixated on a Marine whom she suspects of being a terrorist. *Homeland*'s thesis was that Carrie's instincts were exceptional, even as it continuously presented evidence of her instincts' being terrible: she mixed pills and booze, slept with her targets, and generally broke every rule in the CIA playbook.

In 2012, the year Mitt Romney declared that he had "binders full of women" during a presidential debate, TV had sheaves of its own—*Girls'* Hannah Horvath, *Scandal*'s Olivia Pope, *Veep*'s Selina Meyer, and *The Mindy Project*'s Mindy Lahiri among them. It was an extraordinary year for representation on television: *Scandal* was the first network TV drama with a Black female lead since the 1970s, and *The Mindy Project* was the first American television show to feature a lead of South Asian descent ever. But these characters, while smashing through barriers, were also uniformly presented as being hot messes. Mindy, as *The New Yorker*'s Emily Nussbaum wrote, was a successful doctor who was also "reflexively selfish, sometimes downright delusional, her internal monologue eternally threatening to spill over into full-on clinical narcissism." Over the course of six seasons, she got accidentally pregnant despite being an actual ob-gyn, was sued for sexual harassment, and almost lost her business after unwittingly committing years of tax fraud. Olivia, for her part, was a highly successful and uniquely ingenious Washington fixer who just happened to be disastrously in love with the (married) president of the United States.

Veep, which seemed at least partly inspired by the rise and fall of Sarah Palin, was a curious show, in that the fact that Selina Meyer—played by *Seinfeld*'s Julia Louis-Dreyfus—was a woman was totally incidental to its plot. The series had such overarching cynicism and contempt for politics and politicians that there was little space for characterization. Selina was a walking exercise in humiliation, a bitter chaser to the optimism of the early Obama years. And *Veep* was a series about a woman in American politics whose early seasons were written entirely by British men, which was clarifying: Selina was absurdly powerless not because she was a woman but because she was the *vice president*. Still, her tendency to fail spectacularly in the most public way imaginable made her distinctive. On the other hand, she was just as venal—if not more so—than any other male politician on the show, which had to be its own consolation.

Around the middle of the decade, the critical success of *Girls* and *Bridesmaids* helped spawn a series of raunchy, jubilant comedies about love and friendship. In *Broad City*, which premiered in 2014, Ilana Glazer and Abbi Jacobson played best friends and sweetly madcap stoners whose antics often felt like a gender-flipped version of the bro-comedies of the aughts. In 2015's *Trainwreck*, Amy Schumer starred in her own movie about a commitment-phobic journalist at a men's magazine, a female chauvinist pig with a heart of gold. The advent of streaming television also opened up a whole new era for creators and stories too unconventional for network TV and premium cable. Jenji Kohan's *Orange Is the New Black*, which debuted on Netflix in 2013, used the premise of a middle-class White woman in prison to tell the stories of a sprawling cast of characters much less frequently seen on TV: women of color who grew up in the foster system, immigrant women, trans women, older women. The series was messy, joyful, and groundbreaking. On Amazon, Joey Soloway's 2014 series *Transparent* probed the dynamics of a Los Angeles family after their parent decides to transition, exploring gender identity, connection, and legacy in a way that had never been done on TV before.

When the Dutch psychiatrist Bessel van der Kolk published *The Body Keeps the Score* in 2014, the book encapsulated a burgeoning fascination in popular culture with the subject of trauma. Although van der Kolk's theses were hotly debated and challenged by researchers, the book helped reframe the ways in which people made sense of themselves and interpreted their own lives. You can practically watch the shift play out on television, as the comedies of the second half of the decade took a mordant, introspective turn. "In the past five years or so, after decades of seeing women subsumed into highly regulated, rigidly prescribed roles, we've seen an explosion of dark, uncontained, shockingly human female characters," Carina Chocano observed in 2020. *Fleabag,* Phoebe Waller-Bridge's 2016 BBC series adapted from her play of the same name, presented a millennial protagonist floundering in a contemporary postfeminist hellscape. She's grieving the loss of both her mother and her best friend, and her father has formed a romantic relationship with her genteel, evil godmother. To compensate, he sends Fleabag and her sister to feminist lectures, where they're the only two women who enthusiastically raise their hands when an austere speaker asks who'd "trade five years of your life for the so-called perfect body."

Self-hatred is branded into Fleabag's core. ("I hate my body I hate my body I hate my body," her friend Boo shrieks, in flashback, from a fitting room.) "I'm not obsessed with sex," Fleabag explains to the camera. "I just can't stop thinking about it. The *performance* of it. The *drama* . . . Not so much the feeling of it." In the first episode alone, she has anal sex with a man with an enormous penis, masturbates to a YouTube clip of Barack Obama, propositions a ferrety stranger from the bus, and asks a blackout-drunk woman on the street to go home with her. "I have a horrible feeling I'm a greedy, perverted, selfish, apathetic, cynical, depraved, morally bankrupt woman who can't even call herself a feminist," she blurts out to her father. "Yes . . . well . . . you get all that from your mother," he replies.

Butting up against Fleabag's significant pain and grief is the absurd state of modern womanhood, which expects its adherents to be power-dressing corporate leaders, immaculately groomed sex dolls in Agent Provocateur lingerie, and emotionally stable caregivers all at once. On a weekend retreat, Fleabag and her sister are assigned the task of scrubbing floors in silent meditation, while their male counterparts scream misogynistic invective as a "therapeutic" exercise. The series is deeply funny, but also reads as a bleak dispatch from a woman who's spent her adult life identifying first and foremost as a sexual commodity, drawing all her self-esteem, ambitions, and worldview from her ability to be—however briefly and scathingly—desired. *Fleabag* was an unanticipated smash and a sign of where the winds were blowing. If the women-led comedies of the first half of the 2010s were goofy, crass, and uproarious, shows in the latter half of the decade no longer wanted to be quite so glib or quite so accepting.

In 2019's *This Way Up*, the Irish comedian Aisling Bea played a sweet, hapless woman named Aine who was recovering from "a teeny nervous breakdown." A year later, Michaela Coel premiered the riveting, audacious miniseries *I May Destroy You*, about a writer named Arabella who's drugged and sexually assaulted one night while out at a bar. Loosely based on Coel's own experiences, the show probed questions about denial, forgiveness, and consent. In 2015, Coel had made her first series, the lovable cringe comedy *Chewing Gum*, in which she played a gawky Christian teenager trying energetically to lose her virginity. While writing the show's second season, she'd woken up from a blackout typing out scripts, only to experience later flashbacks of an attack she couldn't remember and didn't want to acknowledge. *I May Destroy You* was her way of reckoning with it. The series, as the *New Yorker* writer Doreen St. Félix observed, is "a beguiling study of friendship and casual trauma and writing as a path—albeit not a simple one—to reinvention."

TRYING TO SEE THE 2010S as a holistic entity now, I find it hard not to be struck by the constant push-me-pull-you of progress and regression. Even advocating for the most basic, incremental improvements, as the Georgetown University law student Sandra Fluke did in 2012 when she testified to a House committee about birth control and women's health, could lead to a months-long onslaught of conservative radio hosts calling a woman a "slut" and a "prostitute." The chimeric rise of women as avatars of business leadership in 2014 was counterbalanced by Gamergate the same year, a strikingly virulent and obsessive campaign against women's perceived influence in the world of video games that anticipated where both the internet and American politics were heading. If nothing else, Gamergate was instructive: It showed how the fight for equality in the 2010s and beyond was going to be about who could claim power over our most deeply rooted and popular narratives.

A reckoning was also coming over the long-standing abuse of that power and how for decades it had pushed women artists out of the industry. In 2014, I recorded a CBC interview with the radio host Jian Ghomeshi about a story I'd written regarding clowns as a theme in horror. At the time, Ghomeshi was a venerated figure in Canada, a musician turned cultural broadcaster who gave meaningful consideration to the arts on his daily show, *Q*. After our conversation, he sent me a string of silly lower-case emails about sad clowns and the Queen of England and invited me to tea in Toronto. But the interview never aired. Two days later, he took a leave of absence after being accused by multiple women of nonconsensual rough sex, harassment, and assault. In her 2022 book *Run Towards the Danger*, the filmmaker Sarah Polley writes about her decision not to speak publicly about her own experiences with Ghomeshi during his 2016 criminal trial for sexual assault, for which he was found not guilty. He had choked her during sex when she was sixteen years old, she stated, and ignored her cries when she asked him to stop. As an adult, she later went on his radio show multiple times to promote her projects. "When I look at my interviews with Jian on *Q* many years later, I am taken aback by my demeanor," she writes. "I am bubbly and giggly. I try to make things normal even as he consistently tries to throw me off."

The accusations against Ghomeshi emerged almost exactly three years before *The New York Times*' Jodi Kantor and Megan Twohey published a series of stories about the producer Harvey Weinstein detailing myriad allegations of abuse, harassment, sexual misconduct, and rape. If Ghomeshi had been a gatekeeper of sorts for Canada's artists and literati, Weinstein was a godlike force in Hollywood. One of the reasons accusations had never publicly been made about him before, paradoxically, was his power. He was so successful, so influential, that he was allegedly able to prey even on women with significant clout of their own. Gwyneth Paltrow told *The New York Times* that when she was twenty-two, Weinstein called her for a meeting in his hotel suite, then invited her into his bedroom and asked for a massage. "I thought he was going to fire me," she said. Later, she won an Oscar for a movie he'd produced, *Shakespeare in Love*, and obligatorily posed next to him with her statuette on the red carpet. Reporters even dubbed her the "first lady of Miramax," Weinstein's production company, as though Paltrow were his muse.

The unveiling of Weinstein as a predator precipitated the #MeToo movement. Revelations rippled out across industries all over the world. Still, the accusations against men in the entertainment industry seemed particularly noteworthy to me, if only because these were the people defining the contours of our collective imagination. It was hard to watch heavyweight after heavyweight uncovered as an alleged predator without wondering how women had managed to make any creative headway in the industry at all.

The #MeToo movement was enormously influential—*The New York Times* calculated a year later that more than two hundred powerful men had lost their jobs as a result, around half of whom were replaced by women. But it was also immediately divisive. Virtually before ink had dried on the print edition of the first Weinstein exposé, people wondered aloud whether #MeToo had gone too far. Critics seemed to sense something retributive about it, as though it were all just a big overreaction to the fact that Donald Trump was president. And, in a way, they were right. The fact that voters had elected a man credibly accused by dozens of women of sexual assault—and later found liable in court for the sexual abuse and defamation of E. Jean Carroll—added a real sense of urgency to the effort of exposing men who were abusing their power.

And this, I suppose, is why recent history has often felt so whiplash-inducing. After the election of Trump came the corrective efforts of #MeToo, which were followed in turn by the dismantling in the United States of women's reproductive choice as a constitutional right. "If fear and loathing of feminism is a sort of perpetual viral condition in our culture, it is not always in an acute stage; its symptoms subside and resurface periodically," Susan Faludi wrote in *Backlash*, more than thirty years ago. If, she adds, "we trace these occurrences in American history . . . we find such flare-ups are hardly random; they have always been triggered by the perception—accurate or not—that women are making great strides."

In the months after #MeToo, one of the ways of assessing how seriously the entertainment industry was taking such a deluge of women's stories was by noting how many women it was willing to pay for the privilege of writing their own stories. A year after the allegations against Weinstein were first published, I assessed the list of upcoming TV shows to try to see signs of change. The vast majority of new series in 2018 were made by and about men: father-and-son narratives, detective stories, prison-break thrillers, two separate examinations of male grief. Some even included in their credits actors and writers who'd been accused of abusing their power over the past year. This reality seemed revelatory: Part of the reason why so many abusive men had been enabled and protected for so long was that the stories they told were seen to have extraordinary, even irreplaceable, value. It didn't seem to occur to anyone in power that maybe the narratives themselves also needed to change.

IN THE SUMMER OF 2024, old cycles repeated once again. When Joe Biden announced that he would no longer run for a second term as president, the immediate attacks on Vice President Kamala Harris, as his successor, followed all the same patterns. Donald Trump, at rallies, criticized Harris's laugh, calling her "crazy" and "nuts." Megyn Kelly, the former Fox News host, alleged on social media that Harris "did sleep her way" to the top in California politics, using the same disgust-engendering language that had once been directed at her. (In 2015, Trump derided Kelly as having had "blood coming out of her wherever" after she grilled him during a presidential debate.) Harris was reduced to a sexual stereotype, with one guest on Fox Business calling her "the OG Hawk Tuah Girl," referring to a viral meme about blow jobs. Figures on the right criticized Harris's personal life and the fact that—despite being adored by two stepchildren, who referred to her as "Momala"—she'd never had kids of her own, a line of attack that Merkel, Gillard, and Theresa May had all been subjected to before her.

At first none of it seemed to stick. Unlike Biden, whom *Politico* once described as "a cultural black hole," Harris was youthful and savvy enough to define herself. She deflected attacks on herself by calling them, simply, "weird." She—and her staff—courted and absorbed the pent-up energy of the perpetually online. In the end, though, Harris lost, and the cultural juggernaut of edgy right-wing podcasters, incel influencers, and alternative media seemed as much to blame as inflation. Most unnerving of all was the fact that male voters aged between ages eighteen and twenty-nine had shifted a stunning fifteen points to the right since 2020, swayed by a barrage of voices—YouTube pranksters, Twitch streamers, NFL players—all asserting that Trump would restore their status and power while sending women back to the kitchen.

I have no idea what happens next. But history suggests that women will be much harder to sideline than the Trump-Vance administration may anticipate. And that we'll soon be due yet another correction. The momentum of #MeToo had already stalled in 2022 when Amber Heard's almost total loss of a defamation lawsuit in which she and Johnny Depp claimed and counterclaimed against each other in a US court case revealed the ways in which new technology could be weaponized against individuals by anonymous parties using troll farms, bots, and targeted campaigning. When Megan Thee Stallion—one of the most prominent women in hip-hop—alleged and then testified that the rapper Tory Lanez had shot her in the foot, she became a punch line and a target for online harassment. "Time after time, women are bullied with backlash for speaking out against their attackers, especially when they're accusing someone who is famous and wealthy," she wrote in *Elle* in 2023. "They're often accused of lying or attempting to make money from their trauma. From firsthand experience, I know why a lot of women don't come forward. Any support and empathy that I received was drowned out by overwhelming doubt and criticism from so many others." Still, the ways in which her case became a starting point for discussions of "misogynoir"—a term coined by the feminist Moya Bailey to describe the racialized oppression Black women face in contemporary culture—*was* new, as was the staunchness with which her fans defended her. And the flood of accusations and lawsuits centering on the alleged behavior of

Sean "Diddy" Combs affirms that no one, no matter how well protected, is truly untouchable.

I wanted to write this book because I was truly stunned by the reversal of *Roe v. Wade* in 2022 and by the tacit confirmation that progress for women is not and never will be linear. I've been knocked out, once again, by the reelection of Donald Trump and the appeal of his messaging to both men and a sizable minority of women. But I still believe that by understanding all the ways in which women have been diminished and broken down in the recent past, we can identify and defuse those same attacks in the present. For everything I found in my research that felt bleak, or even horrifying, there was more that affirmed how culture can expand our understanding of the world and our sense of what's possible. And the more platforms we have, the greater the diversity of ideas we're exposed to. In moments when I'm galled by archaic trends given a modern twist—tradwives, bimbo chic, stay-at-home girlfriends, twelve-year-old skincare influencers—it's consoling to remember that most women watching have both newfound language and skepticism that I couldn't have dreamed of while watching *Girls Gone Wild* or the video for "Money Maker."

Our storytelling models have always been limiting. But I do fundamentally believe—and hope—that art can occasionally enable a top-to-bottom reconfiguration of everything we've ever found ourselves thinking. The kind of unlearning, in other words, with which power is real, change is necessary, and wholly new stories can begin.

Acknowledgments

This book simply would not have been written if I hadn't been lucky enough to have really excellent childcare. I'm so grateful for Marta Bet, Bethany Webber, Athanasia Mouladaki, Sarah Osei-Bonsu, Eulalia Gaylor, and all the other people who took care of my children with astonishing kindness and expertise while I was at work.

I'm also in debt to so many people at *The Atlantic* who are brilliant, generous colleagues and friends. Thank you Jeffrey Goldberg and Adrienne LaFrance for all kinds of support all of the time; Jane Kim and Ann Hulbert for the best editing and guidance; Rebecca Rosen, Megan Garber, Spencer Kornhaber, and David Sims for friendship and solidarity. Thank you to all my BB2 people for absorbing all kinds of book questions and moods, and for making remote work feel much less remote. While I was working on *Girl on Girl*, John Hendrickson patiently fielded so many of my queries about how books actually get done and how to get through the endless daunt. I hope to be able to pay it forward in the future.

Special thanks to Maria Jose Baptista for being the kind of cheerleader people dream of; to Elizabeth Direnfeld for literal and spiritual flowers; to Hannah Giorgis and Lauren Williams for outstanding group-chat support; and to Daisy Gilbert, who always gets the cultural references and always makes me laugh.

Thank you to my agent, Elyse Cheney, who saw this book's potential given only a very short list of themes and a quick Zoom, and then made it happen. I'm forever grateful. And thank you to Isabel Mendía for helping me figure out the chapter I least wanted to write, and to Beniamino Ambrosi, Natasha Fairweather, and Grace Johnson.

My amazing editor, Kiara Barrow, has been instrumental in helping me to figure this book out, and her guidance, ideas, and encouragement have made it so much stronger and more cohesive. I'm also really grateful to Abigail Scruby at John Murray Press for her insightful and sharp suggestions. Thank you so much to Morgan Ome, my fact-checker, for the meticulous work and the joyful Google Doc comments, and for not being deterred when I threw you in at the deep end with chapter 6. Thank you also to Plaegian Alexander for the thoughtful copy edits, and to Natalie Coleman and everyone at Penguin Press for helping to make this a real book in the world.

I started pitching this project when I had two-year-old twins, which was ambitious at best. None of it would have been possible without John, who for the best part of two decades has been my very best reader and absolute best friend. Thank you, always and forever.

Notes

INTRODUCTION

x **the Spears profile:** Steven Daly, "Britney Spears, Teen Queen: Rolling Stone's 1999 Cover Story," *Rolling Stone*, April 15, 1999, rollingstone.com/music/music-news/britney-spears-teen-queen-rolling-stones-1999-cover-story-254871.

xi **"soft, feminine life":** Monica Hesse, "Tradwives, Stay-at-Home Girlfriends and the Dream of Feminine Leisure," *Washington Post*, April 10, 2024, washingtonpost.com/style/power/2024/04/10/tradwives-stay-at-home-girlfriends-modern-couples.

xiv **A smear campaign:** Susan Bolotin, "Voices from the Post-Feminist Generation," *New York Times Magazine*, October 17, 1982, nytimes.com/1982/10/17/magazine/voices-from-the-post-feminist-generation.html.

xiv **hypercommercialized Spice Girls:** Caity Weaver, "The Rise of the Spice Girls Generation," *New York Times*, July 20, 2019, nytimes.com/2019/07/19/style/spice-girls-reunion.html.

xv **paradox of postfeminism:** Elizabeth Gleick, "A V. Fine Mess," Style, *New York Times*, May 31, 1998, archive.nytimes.com/www.nytimes.com/books/98/05/31/reviews/980531.31gleickt.html.

xv **"airbrushed, highly sexualized":** Natasha Walter, *Living Dolls: The Return of Sexism* (Virago, 2015).

xvi **"Totally Raining Teens":** Krista Smith and James Wolcott, "It's Raining Teens," *Vanity Fair*, July 7, 2008, vanityfair.com/news/2003/07/teens-portfolio200307.

xviii **Amia Srinivasan wrote:** Amia Srinivasan, *The Right to Sex* (Bloomsbury, 2021), 64.

xviii **prone to self-objectification:** Rachel M. Calogero, "Objects Don't Object: Evidence That Self-Objectification Disrupts Women's Social Activism," *Psychological Science* 24, no. 3 (January 22, 2013): 312–18, doi.org/10.1177/0956797612452574.

CHAPTER 1: GIRL POWER, BOY RAGE: MUSIC AND FEMINISM IN THE 1990S

1 **"Girls in emo songs":** Jessica Hopper, "Classic Jessica Hopper: 'Emo Comes Off like Rimbaud at the Food Court,'" *Literary Hub*, May 22, 2017, lithub.com/classic-jessica-hopper-emo-comes-off-like-rimbaud-at -the-food-court.

3 **more than 120,000:** New York City AIDS Memorial, "HIV/AIDS Time-line," New York City AIDS Memorial, 2011, nycaidsmemorial.org/timeline.

3 **the New Traditionalism:** Marcy Darnovsky, "The New Traditional-ism: Repackaging Ms. Consumer," *Social Text*, no. 29 (1991): 72, doi .org/10.2307/466300.

3 **the New Voyeurism:** John Leland, "Madonna's 'Sex' Book: The New Voyeurism," *Newsweek*, November 1, 1992, newsweek.com/madonnas -sex-book-new-voyeurism-196758.

5 **shown on MTV:** Richard C. Vincent, Dennis K. Davis, and Lilly Ann Boruszkowski, "Sexism on MTV: The Portrayal of Women in Rock Vid-eos," *Journalism Quarterly* 64, no. 4 (December 1987): 750–941, doi.org /10.1177/107769908706400410.

6 **author Mary Gabriel:** Mary Gabriel, *Madonna* (Hachette UK, 2023), 378.

6 **her 2024 autobiography:** Kathleen Hanna, *Rebel Girl* (HarperCollins, 2024), 142.

7 **"The Revolution Starts Here":** Olivia Laing, "The Art and Politics of Riot Grrrl—in Pictures," *Guardian* (London), June 29, 2013, theguard ian.com/music/gallery/2013/jun/30/punk-music.

7 **"frivolous, vapid, superficial":** Laing, "Art and Politics."

9 **"Riot Grrrl Manifesto":** Kathleen Hanna, "Riot Grrrl Manifesto," History Is a Weapon, 1991, historyisaweapon.com/defcon1/riotgrrrlma nifesto.html.

9 **earliest political acts:** Emily White, "Revolution Girl-Style Now!," *Chicago Reader*, September 24, 1992, chicagoreader.com/news-politics /revolution-girl-style-now.

NOTES

9 **musician Ramdasha Bikceem:** Ramdasha Bikceem, *GUNK*, vol. 4, 1994.

11 **self-categorize as types:** Spice Girls, *Girl Power!* (Citadel, 1997), 72.

11 **to neutralize feminism:** Jessica K. Taft, "Girl Power Politics: Pop-Culture Barriers and Organizational Resistance," in *All About the Girl: Culture, Power, and Identity*, ed. Anita Harris (Routledge, 2004), 71.

13 **"Spice Girls version of it":** David Plotz, "The Spice Girls," *Slate*, November 16, 1997, slate.com/articles/news_and_politics/assessment/1997/11/the_spice_girls.html.

14 **Florida judge declared:** Chuck Philips, "Florida Judge Rules 'Nasty' Album Obscene," *Los Angeles Times*, June 7, 1990, latimes.com/archives/la-xpm-1990-06-07-ca-1689-story.html.

14 **"a parodic exaggeration":** Henry Louis Gates Jr., "2 Live Crew, Decoded," *New York Times*, June 19, 1990, nytimes.com/1990/06/19/opinion/2-live-crew-decoded.html.

15 **"The first time I listened":** Kimberlé Crenshaw, "Beyond Racism and Misogyny," *Boston Review*, December 1, 1991, bostonreview.net/articles/kimberle-w-crenshaw-beyond-racism-and-misogyny.

16 **adult-film rentals:** Eric Schlosser, "The Business of Pornography," *U.S. News and World Report*, February 2, 1997.

16 **"basically a locker-room":** Michele Wallace, "When Black Feminism Faces the Music, and the Music Is Rap," Arts, *New York Times*, July 29, 1990, nytimes.com/1990/07/29/arts/pop-view-when-black-feminism-faces-the-music-and-the-music-is-rap.html.

17 **sharks started mating:** Dave Simpson, "How We Made Salt-N-Pepa's Push It," Culture, *Guardian* (London), August 7, 2017, theguardian.com/culture/2017/aug/07/how-we-made-salt-n-pepa-push-it.

17 **"verbal and mental abuse":** dream hampton, "R-E-S-P-E-C-T," dream hampton, July 15, 2022, dreamhampton.com/post/r-e-s-p-e-c-t.

17 **Spike Lee offered:** Spencer Kornhaber, "Hip-Hop's Fiercest Critic," *Atlantic*, September 6, 2023, theatlantic.com/magazine/archive/2023/10/dream-hampton-music-journalism-hip-hop-notorious-big/675115.

17 **"harass Anita Hill":** Rebecca Walker, "Becoming the 3rd Wave," *Ms.*, January 1992.

17 **outright hateful tracks:** Kathy Iandoli, *God Save the Queens: The Essential History of Women in Hip-Hop* (HarperCollins, 2019), 87.

18 **"expressing virulent forms":** bell hooks, *Outlaw Culture: Resisting Representations* (Routledge, 1994), 137.

18 **"to chastise misogyny":** Wallace, "Black Feminism."

19 **"I needed a feminism":** Joan Morgan, *When Chickenheads Come Home to Roost: A Hip-Hop Feminist Breaks It Down* (Simon & Schuster, 1999), 36.

20 **characterized the era:** Ann Powers, *Women Who Rock*, Epix, dir. Jessica Hopper, season 1, episode 3, "Power" (2022).

22 **thoughts of vengeance:** Peter Fischer and Tobias Greitemeyer, "Music and Aggression: The Impact of Sexual-Aggressive Song Lyrics on Aggression-Related Thoughts, Emotions, and Behavior Toward the Same and the Opposite Sex," *Personality and Social Psychology Bulletin* 32, no. 9 (September 2006): 1165–76, doi.org/10.1177/0146167206288670.

22 **the original Woodstock:** Ellen Willis, "The Not-So-Groovy Side of Woodstock," *New Yorker*, August 30, 1969, newyorker.com/magazine /1969/09/06/ellen-willis-the-not-so-groovy-side-of-woodstock.

23 **"into our 30s":** Wire Reports, "People in the News," *Greensboro News & Record*, April 27, 1999, greensboro.com/people-in-the-news/article_1ffa 579c-aef5-53e9-8419-f3795f826920.html.

23 **"no women at all":** Jessica Hopper with Sasha Geffen and Jenn Pelly, "Building a Mystery: An Oral History of Lilith Fair," *Vanity Fair*, September 30, 2019, vanityfair.com/style/2019/09/an-oral-history-of-lilith-fair.

24 **Music channels were:** Meredith Levande, "Women, Pop Music, and Pornography," *Meridians* 8, no. 1 (2008): 293–321, jstor.org/stable/4033 8921.

25 **reclaiming power over:** bell hooks, "Hardcore Honey: Bell Hooks Goes on the Down Low with Lil' Kim," *Paper Magazine*, July 11, 2018, papermag.com/lil-kim-bell-hooks-cover#rebelltitem62.

26 **"system of control":** Clover Hope, *The Motherlode* (Abrams, 2021), 16.

CHAPTER 2: SHOW GIRL:
OVEREXPOSURE IN THE NEW MILLENNIUM

28 **"the most subversive thing":** Terry Richardson, *Terryworld* (Taschen, 2004), 10.

29 **parade of A-listers:** Guy Trebay, "What Fashion Owes to XXX," Style, *New York Times*, September 12, 2004, nytimes.com/2004/09/12 /fashion/shows/what-fashion-owes-to-xxx.html.

29 **"influence on fashion":** Trebay, "What Fashion Owes to XXX."

30 **championing porno chic:** Trebay, "What Fashion Owes to XXX."

31 **high-profile models:** David Bailey and John Rankin Waddell, "Rankin + Bailey: Down Under," 2003, https://web.archive.org/web/20030802061130 %20/http://www.baileyrankin.com/startnew.html.

32 **"mainstream cultural artifact":** Brian McNair, *Striptease Culture: Sex, Media and the Democratization of Desire* (Routledge, 2002), 61.

33 **"out of hand":** Cass Bird, "Is Terry Richardson an Artist or a Predator?," *Cut*, June 15, 2014, thecut.com/2014/06/terry-richardson-interview.html.

33 **for wannabe models:** Alani Nelson and Mira Olivia Milla, "A Brief History of Terry Richardson Being the Absolute Worst," *Complex*, August 14, 2014, complex.com/style/a/nelsonalanie/a-brief-history-of-terry -richardsons-worst-moments.

33 **Gaga's "anesthetized" body:** Claire Lobenfeld, "Lady Gaga: ARTPOP," *Pitchfork*, August 14, 2022, pitchfork.com/reviews/albums/lady -gaga-artpop.

35 **"just having fun":** "The 3rd Summer of Love," The Face, April 17, 2019, theface.com/archive/kate-moss-summer-of-love.

35 **"vulnerable and scared":** S Moda, "Kate Moss: 'I Was Only 15 and He Said, "Top Off" and I Could Feel There Was Something Wrong,'" *EL PAÍS English*, July 26, 2022, english.elpais.com/society/2022-07-26/kate -moss-i-was-only-15-and-he-said-take-your-top-off-and-i-could-feel -there-was-something-wrong.html#.

36 **"very straight shape":** Rebecca Arnold, *Fashion, Desire and Anxiety: Image and Morality in the 20th Century* (I.B. Tauris, 2001), 93.

36 **"creeping moral cowardice":** "Life Lessons from Drew Barrymore," *Interview*, December 27, 2021, interviewmagazine.com/film/life-lessons -from-drew-barrymore.

37 **"new '90s feeling":** Lucy Handley, "The Vanity Fair Photo of a Pregnant, Naked Demi Moore Was Never Meant to Appear in Public," CNBC, May 9, 2018, cnbc.com/2018/05/09/demi-moore-naked-vanity -fair-cover-was-not-meant-to-be-seen-in-public.html.

38 **"beauty and pleasure":** Camille Paglia, "Madonna—Finally, a Real Feminist," Opinion, *New York Times*, December 14, 1990, nytimes.com /1990/12/14/opinion/madonna-finally-a-real-feminist.html.

40 **"fantasy, a dream":** Madonna, *Sex* (Vade Retro, 1992).

41 **wondered whether Koons:** Roberta Smith, "That Was No Lady, That Was My Wife," *New York Times*, October 13, 2010, nytimes.com/2010 /10/14/arts/design/14koons.html.

41 **"puerile and sensationalistic"**: Calvin Tomkins, "Cindy Sherman's Secret Identities," *New Yorker*, May 8, 2000, newyorker.com/magazine /2000/05/15/her-secret-identities.

42 **"to lose anymore"**: Christopher Ciccone and Wendy Leigh, *Life with My Sister Madonna* (Pocket Books, 2009), 111.

43 **"no way unconventional"**: bell hooks, *Black Looks: Race and Representation* (Routledge, 1992), 164.

43 **promote an alternative**: Eva Wiseman, "Still Dazed at 20: The Gang Who Changed Pop Culture," *Guardian* (London), November 5, 2011, theguardian.com/media/2011/nov/05/dazed-confused-gang-still-cool.

44 **"wolf in sheep's clothing"**: Thom Waite, "Look Back on Rankin's Iconic 90s Archive, Starring Björk, Bowie, and More," *Dazed*, May 31, 2024, dazeddigital.com/art-photography/article/62753/1/look-back-rankin -iconic-90s-dazed-archive-starring-bjork-bowie-thom-yorke.

44 **One psychologist argued**: Roger Tredre, "Magazine in Row over 'Child Porn' Fashion Photos: 'Vogue' Is Accused of Projecting Women as Sexually Vulnerable," *Telegraph*, May 22, 1993, independent.co.uk /news/uk/magazine-in-row-over-child-porn-fashion-photos-vogue-is -accused-of-projecting-women-as-sexually-vulnerable-roger-tredre -reports-2324353.html.

45 **featuring upskirt images**: Laura M. Holson, "The Naughty Knave of Fashion's Court," *New York Times*, March 2, 2012, nytimes.com/2012 /03/04/fashion/terry-richardsons-photographs-provoke-and-reveal.html.

45 **"heavy-handed humour"**: Valerie Steele, "Identity Parade," *Frieze*, September 9, 1996, frieze.com/article/identity-parade.

46 **"emblem to eroticism"**: Arnold, *Fashion, Desire and Anxiety*, 78.

46 **"containing self-fisting yanks"**: McNair, *Striptease Culture*, 78.

47 **"Felix Dennis school"**: Andrew Ross Sorkin, "Building a Web Media Empire on a Daily Dose of Fresh Links," *New York Times*, November 17, 2003, nytimes.com/2003/11/17/business/building-a-web-media-empire -on-a-daily-dose-of-fresh-links.html.

47 **"enables the audience"**: "Terry Richardson and Sisley on Show in Berlin," Benetton Group, 2003, benettongroup.com/en/media-press/press -releases-and-statements/terry-richardson-and-sisley-on-show-in-berlin.

48 **"then completely naked"**: Greg Friedler, *Naked London* (W. W. Norton, 2000).

49 **"I couldn't walk"**: Tony Romando, "Jenna Jameson," *A&F Quarterly Christmas Issue*, 1999.

49 **sales had increased:** Stacy Perman, "Abercrombie's Beefcake Brigade," *Time*, February 14, 2000, time.com/archive/6740354/abercrom bies-beefcake-brigade.

51 **A Getty caption:** "Snoop Dogg Observes the Leash Law as He and His Dates Arrive," Getty Images, August 28, 2003, gettyimages.co.uk/de tail/news-photo/snoop-dogg-observes-the-leash-law-as-he-and-his -dates-news-photo/97304745.

CHAPTER 3: GIRLS ON FILM:
SEX COMEDIES FROM THE MULTIPLEX
TO THE MANOSPHERE

58 **"more hedonistic quest":** Bill Osgerby, *American Pie: The Anatomy of Vulgar Teen Comedy* (Routledge, 2019), 56.

58 **"girls got drunk":** Wesley Morris, "In '80s Comedies, Boys Had It Made: Girls Were the Joke," *New York Times*, October 4, 2018, nytimes .com/2018/10/04/movies/brett-kavanaugh-80s-teen-comedies.html.

59 **"mildly insouciant siren":** Michael Musto, "Alicia in Wonderland," *Vanity Fair*, August 1995, archive.vanityfair.com/article/1995/8/alicia -in-wonderland.

60 **a dubious sidebar:** Karina Longworth, "90s Lolitas, Volume 1: Drew Barrymore, Amy Fisher and Alicia Silverstone," *You Must Remember This*, May 15, 2023, youmustrememberthispodcast.com/episodes/90s -lolitas-volume-1-drew-barrymore-amy-fisher-and-alicia-silverstone -erotic-90s-part-8.

61 **"trying to bone Rosario":** Eric Hynes, "'Kids': The Oral History of the 90s' Most Controversial Film," *Rolling Stone*, July 16, 2015, rolling stone.com/feature/kids-the-oral-history-of-the-most-controversial -film-of-the-nineties-105069/8.

66 **"instances of misogyny":** "The Pie Who Loved Me," *Guardian* (London), October 1, 1999, theguardian.com/film/1999/oct/01/2.

66 **"teen-comedy stereotypes":** Robert Siegel, "The Story Behind American Pie," Blu-ray.com, March 16, 2012, blu-ray.com/news/?id=8343.

66 **this is a nice idea:** Osgerby, *American Pie*, 58.

69 **"made by men":** Tad Friend, "Funny like a Guy," *New Yorker*, April 4, 2011, newyorker.com/magazine/2011/04/11/funny-like-a-guy.

69 **worth $172 billion:** "Perfectcents Number 10," *The Mint*, accessed September 19, 2024, themint.org/pdf/Perfectcents_10.pdf.

69 **a new category:** Osgerby, *American Pie*, 95.

72 **"few women-centric genres":** Beatriz Oria, "We Found Love in a Hopeless Place: Romantic Comedy in the Post-Romantic Era," in *After "Happily Ever After": Romantic Comedy in the Post-Romantic Age*, ed. Maria San Filippo (Wayne State University Press, 2021), 24–46.

72 **"a little sexist":** Leslie Bennetts, "Heigl's Anatomy," *Vanity Fair*, January 2008, vanityfair.com/news/2008/01/heigl200801.

75 **"regressive male comedies":** Dave Itzkoff, "Finding the Fun in Eternal Frat Boys," Movies, *New York Times*, May 28, 2009, nytimes.com /2009/05/31/movies/31itz.html.

75 **"30 million people":** Joe Hagan, "'I Fucking Love My Life': Joaquin Phoenix on the Joker Controversy, Rooney Mara, and His Late Brother," *Vanity Fair*, October 1, 2019, vanityfair.com/hollywood/2019/10/joaquin -phoenix-cover-story.

76 **"a homicidal narcissist":** David Ehrlich, "'Joker' Review: For Better or Worse, Superhero Movies Will Never Be the Same," *IndieWire*, August 31, 2019, indiewire.com/criticism/movies/joker-review-joaquin-phoenix -1202170236.

76 **a certain kind of sexless man:** Srinivasan, *Right to Sex*, 73.

77 **"luridly literal form":** Ann Hornaday, "In a Final Videotaped Message, a Sad Reflection of the Sexist Stories We So Often See on Screen," *Washington Post*, May 25, 2014, washingtonpost.com/lifestyle/style/in-a -final-videotaped-message-a-sad-reflection-of-the-sexist-stories -we-so-often-see-on-screen/2014/05/25/dec7e7ea-e40d-11e3-afc6-a1dd 9407abcf_story.html.

77 **Apatow accusing her:** Judd Apatow (@JuddApatow) "'@Sethrogen: @ AnnHornaday I find your article horribly insulting and misinformed.' She uses tragedy to promote herself with idiotic thoughts," Twitter (now X), May 26, 2014, x.com/JuddApatow/status/471088853814505472.

78 **"the ultimate evil":** "The Manifesto of Elliot Rodger," U.S., *New York Times*, May 25, 2014, nytimes.com/interactive/2014/05/25/us/shooting -document.html.

78 **"girls ultimately decide":** Siegel, "The Story Behind American Pie."

79 **porn use and violence:** "The Relationship between Pornography Use and Harmful Sexual Behaviours," Government Equalities Office, January 15, 2021, gov.uk/government/publications/the-relationship-between -pornography-use-and-harmful-sexual-behaviours/the-relationship- between-pornography-use-and-harmful-sexual-behaviours.

79 **employed to dehumanize:** Alessia Tranchese and Lisa Sugiura, "'I Don't Hate All Women, Just Those Stuck-Up Bitches': How Incels and Mainstream Pornography Speak the Same Extreme Language of Misogyny," *Violence Against Women* 27, no. 14 (March 22, 2021): 2709–34, doi .org/10.1177/1077801221996453.

80 **"rot in loneliness":** Megan Garvey, "Transcript of the Disturbing Video 'Elliot Rodger's Retribution,'" *Los Angeles Times*, May 24, 2014, www.latimes.com/local/lanow/la-me-ln-transcript-ucsb-shootings -video-20140524-story.html.

80 **"mode of magical thinking":** Shannan Palma, "Entitled to a Happy Ending: Fairy-Tale Logic from 'Beauty and the Beast' to the Incel Movement," *Marvels & Tales* 33, no. 2 (2019): 319, doi.org/10.13110/marvels tales.33.2.0319.

80 **young French girls:** Maria Tatar, *Beauty and the Beast: Classic Tales About Animal Brides and Grooms from Around the World* (Penguin, 2017).

81 **a "nerd's fantasy":** Sharon Waxman, "Giving the Last Laugh to Life's Losers," *New York Times*, May 6, 2007, nytimes.com/2007/05/06/mov ies/moviesspecial/06waxm.html.

81 **"potential for *violence*":** Palma, "Entitled to a Happy Ending," 333.

CHAPTER 4: GIRL FIGHT: REGRESSION AND REPRESENTATION IN THE EARLY YEARS OF REALITY TELEVISION

85 **"that much attention":** Ira Glass, "Tale from the Net," *This American Life* (Chicago Public Media, June 6, 1997), thisamericanlife.org/66/tales -from-the-net.

85 **"completely alone":** Glass, "Tale from the Net."

86 **terrain of cam artists:** Brooke A. Knight, "Watch Me! Webcams and the Public Exposure of Private Lives," *Art Journal* 59, no. 4 (2000), doi .org/10.2307/778117.

87 **"troubling and captivating":** Simon Firth, "21st: Live! from My Bedroom," *Salon*, January 8, 1998, salon.com/1998/01/08/feature_354.

87 **David Letterman predicted:** Alex Goldman, "Jennicam," *Reply All* (Gimlet Media, December 14, 2014), gimletmedia.com/shows/reply-all /8whoja.

88 **"You amoral man-trapper!":** Libby Copeland, "All a Woman Can Bare," *Washington Post*, August 26, 2000, washingtonpost.com/archive

/lifestyle/2000/08/26/all-a-woman-can-bare/f104e1fc-7cc1-47ca-acad
-53193eb1c18b.

89 **anthropologist Margaret Mead:** Dennis Lim, "Reality-TV Originals, in Drama's Lens," Arts, *New York Times*, April 15, 2011, nytimes.com/2011 /04/17/arts/television/hbos-cinema-verite-looks-at-american-family.html.

90 **"the middle-class dream":** Lim, "Reality-TV Originals."

90 **"four negative shots":** Steven V. Roberts, "An American Family Sees Itself on TV," *New York Times*, January 13, 1973, nytimes.com/1973/01 /13/archives/an-american-family-sees-itself-on-tv-we-were-misled -getting-the.html.

93 **formal written complaint:** Cahal Milmo, "Psychologists in Trouble for 'Big Brother,'" *Independent*, August 1, 2000, independent.co.uk/news /media/psychologists-in-trouble-for-big-brother-711122.html.

94 **"women are socialized":** Danielle J. Lindemann, *True Story: What Reality TV Says About Us* (Farrar, Straus and Giroux, 2022), 223.

95 **"post-feminist overstretched woman":** Nigella Lawson, *How to Be a Domestic Goddess: Baking and the Art of Comfort Cooking* (Hyperion, 2005), vii.

96 **"all the terror":** Gary R. Edgerton and Jeffrey P. Jones, *The Essential HBO Reader* (University Press of Kentucky, 2008), 278.

96 **2.8 million people:** Molly Langmuir, "Masturbation, Nudists, and Street Interviews: An Oral History of HBO's 'Real Sex,'" *Vulture*, July 30, 2013, vulture.com/2013/07/hbo-real-sex-oral-history-masturbation -nudists-street-interviews.html.

97 **"what they deserve":** Langmuir, "Oral History."

98 **"most controversial show":** Mark Seal, "The Story Behind the Reality TV Golden Era," *Vanity Fair*, January 24, 2014, vanityfair.com/news /2003/07/reality-tv-golden-era.

99 **"pop cultural backlash":** Jennifer L. Pozner, *Reality Bites Back: The Troubling Truth About Guilty Pleasure TV* (Seal Press, 2010), 13.

100 **"smoke and mirrors":** Seal, "Reality TV Golden Era."

100 **Melissa Gorga explained:** Jennifer Wilson, "The Real Message of 'The Real Housewives,'" *New Yorker*, September 22, 2023, newyorker.com /culture/cultural-comment/the-real-message-of-the-real-housewives.

101 **her male clients:** Brenna Egan, "Dating Guru Patti Stanger Spills Her Newest Dating Dos & Don'ts," *Refinery29*, September 7, 2012, refinery 29.com/en-us/millionaire-matchmaker-interview.

101 **four posed topless:** Walter, *Living Dolls*, 30.

101 **active sexual subjects:** Rosalind Gill, "Postfeminist Media Culture: Elements of a Sensibility," *European Journal of Cultural Studies* 10, no. 2 (2007): 147–66, doi.org/10.1177/1367549407075898.

102 **"have revolutionized television":** Seal, "Reality TV Golden Era."

103 **"A poorly executed":** Michael Speier, "Are You Hot?," *Variety*, February 13, 2003, variety.com/2003/tv/reviews/are-you-hot-1200543466/.

103 **battling with ABC:** Allison Hope Weiner, "'Are You Hot?'s Producer Addresses His Critics," *Entertainment Weekly*, February 14, 2003, ew .com/article/2003/02/14/are-you-hots-producer-addresses-his-critics.

103 **"Clean is clean":** Alessandra Stanley, "The TV Watch: It's All About Hottitude and Tweaking 'Reality,'" *New York Times*, February 13, 2003, nytimes.com/2003/02/13/arts/the-tv-watch-it-s-all-about-hottitude -and-tweaking-reality.html.

104 **"marked by marginalization":** Pozner, *Reality Bites Back*, 162.

105 **"white people learn":** Justin Simien, "Dear White People: Reality TV Is the New Blackface," *Vulture*, November 11, 2014, vulture.com/2014 /11/why-reality-tv-is-the-new-blackface.html.

105 **better perform femininity:** Melvin L. Williams, "My Job Is to Be a Bad Bitch: Locating Women of Color in Postfeminist Media Culture on Love and Hip-Hop: Atlanta," *Race, Gender & Class* 23, no. 3–4 (2016): 68–88, jstor.org/stable/26529209.

106 **"satire of *The Bachelor*":** Racquel J. Gates, *Double Negative: The Black Image and Popular Culture* (Duke University Press, 2018), 2.

106 **"operations of patriarchy":** Racquel J. Gates, "What Snooki and Joseline Taught Me About Race, Motherhood, and Reality TV," *Los Angeles Review of Books*, October 21, 2017, lareviewofbooks.org/article/what -snooki-and-joseline-taught-me-about-race-motherhood-and-reality-tv.

108 **"thrown me away":** Joel Stein, "Television: Anna Goes Prime Time," *Time*, July 22, 2002, content.time.com/time/subscriber/article/0,33009, 1002903-1,00.html.

109 **"waited for marriage":** Ariel Levy, "Queen of the Boob Tube," *Blender*, April 2004.

110 **"a posh life":** Paris Hilton, *Paris* (HarperCollins, 2023), 241.

111 **"decisive turn toward":** Joshua Gamson, "The Unwatched Life Is Not Worth Living: The Elevation of the Ordinary in Celebrity Culture," *PMLA* 126, no. 4 (October 2011): 1061–69, doi.org/10.1632/pmla.2011 .126.4.1061.

112 **"glamorously or not":** Gamson, "The Unwatched Life."

NOTES

CHAPTER 5: BEAUTIFUL GIRL: THE GOLDMINE OF IMPOSSIBLE EXPECTATIONS

116 **"publicity image steals":** John Berger, *Ways of Seeing* (Penguin, 1972), 134.

116 **up 69 percent:** *2010 Report of the 2009 Statistics: National Clearinghouse of Plastic Surgery Statistics* (American Society of Plastic Surgeons, 2010), plasticsurgery.org/documents/News/Statistics/2009/plastic-surgery -statistics-full-report-2009.pdf.

116 **"that American Dream":** Alex Kuczynski, *Beauty Junkies: Inside Our $15 Billion Obsession with Cosmetic Surgery* (Doubleday, 2006), 6.

117 **"a fat-farm place":** Pandora Sykes and Sirin Kale, "The Makeover Era: The Swan and What Not to Wear," May 17, 2022, in *Unreal*, produced by Hannah Hufford, podcast, radio, 54:00, www.bbc.co.uk/pro grammes/p0c71k7k.

119 **"Doesn't everybody want":** Anderson Cooper, *Anderson*, season 1, episode 146, "Cohost Monday with Kristen Johnston," aired on April 30, 2012, on CNN.

119 **"women's calculated deployment":** Susan J. Douglas, *The Rise of Enlightened Sexism: How Pop Culture Took Us from Girl Power to Girls Gone Wild* (St. Martin's Griffin, 2011), 10.

119 **Florida chili cook-off:** Johanna Piazza, "Turning Pounds into Dollars," *The Daily Beast*, February 5, 2009, thedailybeast.com/turning -pounds-into-dollars.

120 **"probed, painted, suctioned":** Elizabeth Atwood Gailey, "Self-Made Women: Cosmetic Surgery Shows and the Construction of Female Psychopathology," in *Makeover Television: Realities Remodelled*, ed. Dana Heller (I.B. Tauris, 2007), 107–18.

120 **"an inflatable doll":** Hilary Mantel, "Some Girls Want Out," *London Review of Books*, March 4, 2004, lrb.co.uk/the-paper/v26/n05/hilary -mantel/some-girls-want-out.

120 **"learned to pose":** Brenda R. Weber, *Makeover TV: Selfhood, Citizenship, and Celebrity* (Duke University Press, 2010), 24.

121 **"Plastic surgery means":** Dodai Stewart, "Plastic Surgery Means Many Beauty Queens, but Only One Kind of Face," *Jezebel*, April 25, 2013, www.jezebel.com/plastic-surgery-means-many-beauty-queens-but -only-one-480929886.

122 **"the real hungers":** Caroline Knapp, *Appetites: Why Women Want* (Counterpoint, 2003), 47.

123 **"gentlemen never do":** Mark Binelli, "Lindsay Lohan: Confessions of a Teenage Drama Queen," *Rolling Stone*, August 19, 2004, rollingstone .com/tv-movies/tv-movie-features/lindsay-lohan-confessions-of-a -teenage-drama-queen-227834.

123 **focused on weight:** Sonia Weiser, "Tabloid Reporters of the 2000s Fueled an Obsession with Weight Loss: Some Say They Regret It," *Slate*, July 6, 2022, slate.com/business/2022/07/celebrity-weight-loss-health -media-body-image.html.

124 **pulled a photo:** Kate Betts, "The Tyranny of Skinny, Fashion's Insider Secret," Style, *New York Times*, March 31, 2002, nytimes.com/2002/03 /31/style/the-tyranny-of-skinny-fashion-s-insider-secret.html.

125 *Skinny Bitch*'s **dedication:** Rory Freedman and Kim Barnouin, *Skinny Bitch* (Running Press, 2005), 6.

126 **A 2023 study:** Jasmine Fardouly, Amy Slater, Jade Parnell, and Phillippa C. Diedrichs, "Can Following Body Positive or Appearance Neutral Facebook Pages Improve Young Women's Body Image and Mood? Testing Novel Social Media Micro-Interventions," *Body Image* 44 (March 2023): 136–47, doi.org/10.1016/j.bodyim.2022.12.008.

128 **deprived his body:** Edward Wyatt, "On 'The Biggest Loser,' Health Can Take Back Seat," *New York Times*, November 24, 2009, nytimes .com/2009/11/25/business/media/25loser.html.

130 **"assessing physical beauty":** E. Alex Jung, "Why America's Next Top Model Was Never Better Than Its First Cycle," *Vulture*, December 4, 2015, vulture.com/2015/12/americas-next-top-model-first-cycle-was -the-best.html.

130 **"One can re-create":** Naomi Wolf, *The Beauty Myth: How Images of Beauty Are Used Against Women* (William Morrow, 1991), 252.

131 **one promotional photo:** Brian Moylan, *The Housewives* (Flatiron Books, 2021), 1.

132 **"as spectacularized works":** Misha Kavka, "Reality TV and the Gendered Politics of Flaunting," in *Reality Gendervision: Sexuality and Gender on Transatlantic Reality Television*, ed. Brenda Weber (Duke University Press, 2014), 58.

133 **"smooth our foreheads":** Carole Radziwill, "Carole Radziwill: Glam Isn't Always so Pretty," *Allure*, November 11, 2020, allure.com/story /carole-radziwill-real-housewives-beauty-essay.

133 **"is now embedded":** Louis Staples, "The Great Real Housewives Glam-Squad Divide," *Cut*, May 31, 2022, thecut.com/2022/05/real -housewives-glam-squad-debate.html.

133 **separate beauty brands:** Aubrey Noble, "A Definitive Guide to Every Beauty Brand Founded by One of the 'Real Housewives,'" *Bustle*, November 28, 2022, bustle.com/style/the-real-housewives-beauty-brands.

134 **cursed time capsule:** Alessandra Stanley, "Shop as if There's No Tomorrow," Arts, *New York Times*, October 9, 2008, nytimes.com/2008/10 /10/arts/television/10watc.html.

134 **signs of grooming:** Anita Bhagwandas, *Ugly* (Kings Road, 2022), 189.

135 **"a codified hyper-feminine":** Kavka, "Reality TV," 59.

135 **"negotiating their value":** Anna Shechtman, "Wages for Housewives," *New York Review of Books*, May 14, 2023, nybooks.com/online /2023/05/14/wages-for-housewives.

136 *RuPaul's Drag Race:* Lindemann, *True Story*, 189.

138 **"highly idealized images":** Imani Perry, "Who(se) Am I? The Identity and Image of Women in Hip-Hop," in *Gender, Race, and Class in Media*, ed. Gail Dines and Jean M. Humez (Sage, 2003), 141.

138 **a fivefold increase:** Aisha Durham, "'Check on It': Beyonce, Southern Booty, and Black Femininities in Music Video," *Feminist Media Studies* 12, no. 1 (March 2012): 35–49, doi.org/10.1080/14680777.2011.558346.

142 **"as sexualized signifiers":** Maria Pramaggiore and Diane Negra, "Keeping up with the Aspirations: Commercial Family Values and the Kardashian Brand," in *Reality Gendervision: Sexuality and Gender on Transatlantic Reality Television*, ed. Brenda Weber (Duke University Press, 2014), 83.

142 **called "midriff advertising":** Rosalind Gill, "Empowerment/Sexism: Figuring Female Sexual Agency in Contemporary Advertising," *Feminism & Psychology* 18, no. 1 (February 2008): 35–60.

144 **jumped 3,233 percent:** Jonathan D. Tijerina, Shane D. Morrison, Ian T. Nolan, Matthew J. Parham, Michael T. Richardson, and Rahim Nazerali, "Celebrity Influence Affecting Public Interest in Plastic Surgery Procedures: Google Trends Analysis," *Aesthetic Plastic Surgery* 43, no. 6 (August 7, 2019): 1669–80, doi.org/10.1007/s00266-019-01466-7.

144 **there were 61,387:** Sandra E. Garcia, "Butt Lifts Are Booming: Healing Is No Joke," *New York Times Magazine*, May 11, 2022, nytimes.com /interactive/2022/05/11/magazine/brazilian-butt-lift.html.

145 **increased by 70 percent:** Sierra Leone Starks, "'Inclusivity' Has Never Topped the List of Plastic Surgery Trends—It's Time for a Shake-Up," *Allure*, March 22, 2023, allure.com/story/plastic-surgery -trends-inclusivity.

145 **"single, cyborgian face":** Jia Tolentino, "The Age of Instagram Face," *New Yorker*, December 12, 2019, newyorker.com/culture/decade-in-review /the-age-of-instagram-face.

CHAPTER 6: FINAL GIRL: EXTREME SEX, ART, AND VIOLENCE IN POST-9/11 AMERICA

148 **Sex and sadism:** David Edelstein, "Now Playing at Your Local Multiplex: Torture Porn," *New York Magazine*, January 26, 2006, nymag.com /movies/features/15622.

149 **"capitalism gone awry":** John Patterson, "Putting the Gory in to Allegory," *Guardian* (London), June 23, 2007, theguardian.com/film/2007 /jun/23/1.

149 **promote *Hostel 2*:** Peter Sciretta, "Eli Roth Poses 'Nude' to Promote Hostel 2," *SlashFilm*, June 4, 2007, slashfilm.com/496361/eli-roth-poses -nude-to-promote-hostel-2.

150 **the film's plot:** Nicole Sperling, "Curtain Falls Quickly on 'Captivity' Ad Campaign," *Hollywood Reporter*, March 20, 2007, hollywoodreporter .com/business/business-news/curtain-falls-quickly-captivity-ad-132376.

150 **"The new element":** Martin Amis, "A Rough Trade," *Guardian* (London), March 16, 2001, theguardian.com/books/2001/mar/17/society.mar tinamis1.

151 **"the triumphant woman":** Christopher Sharrett, "The Problem of Saw: 'Torture Porn' and the Conservatism of Contemporary Horror Films," *Cinéaste* 35, no. 1 (2009): 32–37, jstor.org/stable/41690851.

154 **"typical Max Hardcore":** Evan Wright, "Maxed Out," *Salon*, January 18, 2000, salon.com/2000/01/18/hustler.

155 **"from Bosch's *Garden*":** David Foster Wallace, *Consider the Lobster* (Little, Brown, 2005), 25.

156 **most profitable studio:** Schlosser, "Business of Pornography."

156 **comparing price points**: Janice Turner, "Dirty Young Men," *Guardian* (London), October 21, 2005, theguardian.com/theguardian/2005 /oct/22/weekend7.weekend3.

156 **distinguish between derogatory quotes:** Miranda A. H. Horvath, Peter Hegarty, Suzannah Tyler, and Sophie Mansfield, "'Lights On at the End of the Party': Are Lads' Mags Mainstreaming Dangerous Sexism?," *British Journal of Psychology* 103, no. 4 (December 13, 2011): 454–71, doi.org/10.1111/j.2044-8295.2011.02086.x.

NOTES

157 **"You can hear"**: Amis, "Rough Trade."

157 **"the Freddie Krueger"**: William Bredderman, "Los Angeles Real Estate Tycoon Mark Handel Exposed as 'Boogeyman of Porn' Khan Tusion," *Daily Beast*, November 25, 2022, thedailybeast.com/los-angeles -real-estate-tycoon-mark-handel-exposed-as-boogeyman-of-porn-khan -tusion.

157 **"new French Extremity"**: James Quandt, "Flesh & Blood: Sex and Violence in Recent French Cinema," *Artforum*, February 2004, artfo rum.com/features/flesh-blood-sex-and-violence-in-recent-french -cinema-168041.

158 **Despentes once said:** Elizabeth Day, "Femmes Fatales Fight Back with Sex and Violence," Film, *Guardian* (London), January 17, 2009, theguardian.com/film/2009/jan/18/french-feminism-despentes -catherine-millet.

159 **"not in my films"**: Michael Nordine, "Catherine Breillat Says Asia Argento Is a 'Traitor,' Harvey Weinstein Isn't That Bad, and She's Against #MeToo," *IndieWire*, March 29, 2018, indiewire.com/features/general /catherine-breillat-asia-argento-harvey-weinstein-jessica-chastain -me-too-1201945040.

160 **"critique of pornography"**: Maria San Filippo, *Provocauteurs and Provocations* (Indiana University Press, 2021), 169.

160 **as speculation mounted:** "Culture: Is It Art or Porn? The Sequel," *The Sunday Times* (London), July 18, 2004, thetimes.com/article/culture -is-it-art-or-porn-the-sequel-rgp5fbsmc59.

160 **"exhume the unspeakable"**: Catherine Breillat, *Pornocracy* (MIT Press, 2008), 8.

161 **"all things female"**: Breillat, *Pornocracy*, 11.

161 **essentially a discourse:** Erika Lust, "It's Time for Porn to Change," posted December 3, 2014, by TEDx Talks, YouTube, 12 min., 55 sec., youtu.be/Z9LaQtfpP_8?si=C5Hd1c8l0RLpjBLn.

162 **relishing her reduction:** Catherine Millet, *The Sexual Life of Catherine M.* (Grove, 2003), 118.

162 **"calmness and availability"**: Millet, *The Sexual Life*, 52.

163 **"Chereau means it"**: Alan A. Stone, "Desperately Seeking Sex," *Boston Review*, February 1, 2002, bostonreview.net/articles/alan-stone-des perately-seeking-sex.

163 **an ongoing puzzle:** Alexandra Kleeman, "Provocative Sex Is Back at the Movies: But Are We Ready for It?," *New York Times Magazine*,

December 12, 2023, nytimes.com/2023/12/12/magazine/sex-movies-may -december.html.

165 **fifty-three-page secret report:** Seymour Hersh, "Torture at Abu Ghraib," *New Yorker*, April 30, 2004, newyorker.com/magazine/2004/05 /10/torture-at-abu-ghraib.

165 **"making prisoners masturbate":** Richardson, *Terryworld*, 9.

166 **a "pyramide humaine":** Keely Shinners, "A Young Feminist's Perspective on Twenty Years of American Apparel Ads," *Autre Magazine*, January 29, 2016, autre.love/this-and-that-main/2016/1/29/a-young-fem inists-perspective-on-a-decade-of-american-apparel-ads.

166 **"scene straight out":** Carmine Sarracino and Kevin M. Scott, *The Porning of America: The Rise of Porn Culture, What It Means, and Where We Go from Here* (Beacon, 2008), 146.

167 **"hegemonic American manliness":** Laura Sjoberg, *Gender, Justice, and the Wars in Iraq: A Feminist Reformulation of Just War Theory* (Lexington Books, 2006), 143.

167 **"The pictures taken":** Susan Sontag, "Regarding the Torture of Others," *New York Times Magazine*, May 23, 2004, nytimes.com/2004/05/23 /magazine/regarding-the-torture-of-others.html.

168 **the Abu Ghraib pictures:** Sontag, "Regarding the Torture."

169 **"pale, adolescent looks":** Dave Gardetta, "The Teenager & the Porn Star," *Los Angeles Magazine*, November 1, 2006, lamag.com/news/the -teenager-the-porn-star.

170 **"black hair and tattoos":** Vanessa Grigoriadis, "The Dirtiest Girl in the World," *Rolling Stone*, May 14, 2009, https://www.rollingstone.com /culture/culture-news/the-dirtiest-girl-in-the-world-38931/.

171 **88 percent contained:** Ana J. Bridges, Robert Wosnitzer, Erica Scharrer, Chyng Sun, and Rachael Liberman, "Aggression and Sexual Behavior in Best-Selling Pornography Videos: A Content Analysis Update," *Violence Against Women* 16, no. 10 (October 2010): 1065–85, doi.org/10 .1177/1077801210382866.

171 **experienced unwanted slapping:** "Has Violence During Consensual Sex Become 'Normalised'?," BBC, November 28, 2019, bbc.co.uk/sounds /play/p07wbvzg.

172 **"heartbreaking as it is":** Grigoriadis, "Dirtiest Girl."

173 **Adult Video Awards:** Benjamin Wallace, "The Geek-Kings of Smut," *New York Magazine*, January 28, 2011, nymag.com/news/features/70985 /index4.html.

174 **in their fifties:** Kate Dennett and Nola Ojomu, "The Stars Baring All for the Big Bucks!," *Daily Mail*, August 25, 2023, dailymail.co.uk /tvshowbiz/article-12444747/Celebrities-MILLIONS-OnlyFans -Sopranos-Drea-Matteo.html.

CHAPTER 7: GOSSIP GIRLS: THE DEGRADATION OF WOMEN AND FAME IN TWENTY-FIRST-CENTURY MEDIA

176 **"Jackknifing legs that":** Lisa Taddeo, "The Case for Jessica Simpson," *Esquire*, October 6, 2008, esquire.com/entertainment/a4456/jessica -simpson-0508.

179 **Paris and Nicky:** Nancy Jo Sales, "Hip-Hop Debs," *Vanity Fair*, September 1, 2000, vanityfair.com/culture/2000/09/hiltons200009.

180 **Early in 2008:** Maureen Dowd, "Can Hillary Cry Her Way Back to the White House?," *New York Times*, January 9, 2008, nytimes.com/2008 /01/09/opinion/08dowd.html.

180 **"the plebeians' level":** Kurt Andersen, "Celebrity Death Watch," *New York Magazine*, January 25, 2006, nymag.com/news/imperialcity/16493.

181 **seemed impossibly trivial:** Louis Chunovic, "Will TV News—or Its Audience—Finally Grow Up?," *TelevisionWeek*, September 24, 2001, tvweek.com/in-depth/2001/09/editorial-will-tv-news-or-its.

182 **A media psychologist:** Sophie Gilbert, "Why You Can't Stop Streaming 'Seinfeld.' Or 'Frasier.' Or 'Bones,'" *Atlantic*, March 22, 2020, the atlantic.com/culture/archive/2020/03/seinfeld-frasier-and-the -psychology-of-comfort-tv/608497.

183 **"generic newsstand-celebrity approach":** Michael Wolff, "The Odd Couple," *New York Magazine*, May 20, 2002, nymag.com/nymetro/news /media/columns/medialife/6029.

185 **$80,000 to X17:** David Samuels, "Shooting Britney," *Atlantic*, April 2008, theatlantic.com/magazine/archive/2008/04/shooting-britney/306735/.

186 **"panty-less four times":** "Britney Spears Flashes Privates, Gets Press," ABC News, November 22, 2008, abcnews.go.com/Entertainment/Spe cialConcert/story?id=2681885&page=1.

186 **first upskirt victims:** Sarah Ditum, *Toxic* (Little, Brown, 2024), 110.

187 **describe their methods:** Shawn Hubler, William D. Montalbano, and Ann W. O'Neill, "Money Drives Paparazzi to Pursue till End," *Los An-*

geles Times, September 1, 1997, latimes.com/archives/la-xpm-1997-sep
-01-mn-27861-story.html.

187 **"paparazzo would say"**: Britney Spears, *The Woman in Me* (Simon and Schuster, 2023), 153.

188 **"plumbing the backwaters"**: Alessandra Stanley, "Forgotten Stars Never Die; They Show up in Reality TV," *New York Times*, January 18, 2003, nytimes.com/2003/01/18/arts/forgotten-stars-never-die-they-show -up-in-reality-tv.html.

188 **argued that fame:** Sharon Marcus, "Salomé!! Sarah Bernhardt, Oscar Wilde, and the Drama of Celebrity," *PMLA* 126, no. 4 (October 2011): 999–1021, doi.org/10.1632/pmla.2011.126.4.999.

188 **"be as interesting"**: Clare Malone, "How Jennifer Lopez and Ben Affleck Helped Launch the 2000s Tabloid Boom," *Ringer*, February 14, 2022, theringer.com/2022/2/14/22932644/just-like-us-episode-1-tabloids -podcast-jennifer-lopez-ben-affleck-bennifer.

189 **"are perfect people"**: Stanley, "Forgotten Stars Never Die."

189 **"owe their fame"**: Russell Adams, "Hot Covers! One Prince, Three Sisters, Lots of Breakups," *Wall Street Journal*, February 8, 2012, wsj .com/articles/SB10001424052970204136404577209122444911332.

190 **"a viable path"**: Erin A. Meyers, *Extraordinarily Ordinary: Us Weekly and the Rise of Reality Television Celebrity* (Rutgers University Press, 2020).

190 **"daffy, upbeat personality"**: Julia Day, "Chantelle Banks Exclusive Interview," *Guardian* (London), January 27, 2006, theguardian.com /media/2006/jan/27/dailystar.pressandpublishing.

191 **"fear of looking"**: Hilton, *Paris*, 235.

191 **"public humiliation offering"**: Dennis Cass, "Embarrassing Riches," *Slate*, December 3, 2003, slate.com/culture/2003/12/green-acres-a-go -go.html.

192 **"My generation thinks"**: Andersen, "Celebrity Death Watch."

193 **"own inner heiress"**: "Confessions of an Heiress: A Tongue-in-Chic Peek Behind the Pose by Paris Hilton," *Publishers Weekly*, 2004, publish ersweekly.com/9780743266642.

193 **"wear somebody's clothes"**: Nancy Jo Sales, "The Suspects Wore Louboutins," *Vanity Fair*, March 2010, archive.vanityfair.com/article /share/e9cc0cc3-dbf1-4fab-8367-5fc7c05608e6#.

193 **"own social universe"**: Andrew O'Hagan, "So Many Handbags, So

Little Time," *London Review of Books*, June 20, 2013, lrb.co.uk/the-paper/v35/n12/andrew-o-hagan/so-many-handbags-so-little-time.

194 **"saying this affirmation"**: Ilana Kaplan, "And So It Is," *Cut*, March 13, 2020, thecut.com/2020/03/pretty-wild-oral-history.html.

194 **show helped define:** Yvonne Villarreal, "'The Hills' Helped Invent the Social Media Influencer: Now What?," *Los Angeles Times*, June 24, 2019, latimes.com/entertainment/tv/la-et-st-the-hills-mtv-20190624-story.html.

195 **"dullest major characters"**: Thomas Rogers, "The Unbearable Lightness of Lauren Conrad," *Salon*, June 19, 2009, salon.com/2009/06/19/lauren_conrad.

196 **"a precarious balance"**: Kara Jesella, "Detox for the Camera: Doctor's Order!," *New York Times*, February 3, 2008, nytimes.com/2008/02/03/fashion/03drew.html.

196 **"I'm comfortable around"**: Jesella, "Detox for the Camera."

197 **"almost too tragic"**: Rebecca Traister, "Didn't She Almost Have It All?," *Salon*, February 12, 2012, salon.com/2012/02/12/didnt_she_almost_have_it_all.

198 **"we experience disgust"**: Kathleen McAuliffe, "Conservatives React Differently to Disgusting Pictures," *Atlantic*, March 2019, theatlantic.com/magazine/archive/2019/03/the-yuck-factor/580465.

199 **her "beef curtains"**: Mitchell Sunderland, "Spencer Pratt Reflects on His Iconic Feud with Lauren Conrad 10 Years Later," *Vice*, August 8, 2017, www.vice.com/en/article/spencer-pratt-reflects-on-his-iconic-feud-with-lauren-conrad-10-years-later/; https://web.archive.org/web/20070806120446/http://spencerpratt.com/board/index.php?showtopic=16.

200 **"a positive response"**: "Celebrity Rehab with Dr. Drew: Drugs Worse Than Cancer?," posted January 15, 2008, by PIX11 News, YouTube, 4 min., 48 sec., youtube.com/watch?v=ACMCLZkrLOo.

200 **"Grand Guignol death"**: Mark Stevens, "Britney Spears, Outsider Artist," *New York Magazine*, February 23, 2007, nymag.com/news/intelligencer/features/28528.

201 **"army of zombies"**: Spears, *Woman in Me*, 134.

201 **"other skanky starlets"**: Alan Sepinwall, "The Obligatory Bash Britney Post," *What's Alan Watching?*, September 10, 2007, sepinwall.blogspot.com/2007/09/obligatory-bash-britney-post.html.

201 **"was just sad"**: Mathew Ingram, "Performance Was 'like Watching the Fat Elvis,'" *Globe and Mail*, September 11, 2007, theglobeandmail

.com/technology/performance-was-like-watching-the-fat-elvis/arti
cle725315.

201 **"disastrous and amusing"**: Amanda Hess, "Watching Britney Spears, as a Girl and a Woman," *New York Times*, October 30, 2023, nytimes .com/2023/10/30/arts/music/britney-spears-woman-in-me.html.

CHAPTER 8: GIRL ON *GIRLS*:
THE CONFESSIONAL AUTEUR AND HER DETRACTORS

204 **"to value yourself"**: David Carr, "Lena Dunham Finds Her Worth in 'Tiny Furniture,'" *New York Times*, March 19, 2010, nytimes.com/2010 /03/20/movies/20tiny.html.

204 **"In Dunham's world"**: Phillip Lopate, "'Tiny Furniture': Out There," Criterion Collection, February 15, 2012, criterion.com/current/posts /2149-tiny-furniture-out-there.

205 **Dunham's work:** Lopate, "Out There."

206 **"another white girl"**: Sheila Heti, *How Should a Person Be?* (Henry Holt, 2012), 105.

207 **female bodily experiences:** Leslie Jamison, "This Female Consciousness: On Chris Kraus," *New Yorker*, April 9, 2015, newyorker.com/cul ture/cultural-comment/this-female-consciousness-on-chris-kraus.

208 **"grubby and unglamorous"**: Meghan Daum, "Lena Dunham Is Not Done Confessing," *New York Times*, September 10, 2014, nytimes.com /2014/09/14/magazine/lena-dunham.html.

208 **"a feminist's nightmare"**: Dodai Stewart, "'Taylor Swift Is a Feminist's Nightmare,'" *Jezebel*, February 8, 2010, jezebel.com/taylor-swift -is-a-feminists-nightmare-5466685.

208 **"brittle little dominatrix"**: Camilla Long, "Aftermath: On Marriage and Separation by Rachel Cusk," *Sunday Times*, March 4, 2012, the times.com/article/aftermath-on-marriage-and-separation-by-rachel -cusk-xn0xgt0lsp9.

208 **"make 'universal' art"**: Chris Kraus, *I Love Dick* (Semiotext(e), 1997), 211.

210 **"pursue sexual gratification"**: Ariel Levy, *Female Chauvinist Pigs: Women and the Rise of Raunch Culture* (Free Press, 2005), 148.

211 **"errant hair pulling"**: Frank Bruni, "The Bleaker Sex," *New York Times*, March 31, 2012, nytimes.com/2012/04/01/opinion/sunday/bruni -the-bleaker-sex.html.

NOTES

212 **"little fat girl"**: Brian Moylan, "A Complete Timeline of All the Controversies 'Girls' Started," *Vulture*, February 12, 2017, vulture.com/2017 /02/hbos-girls-a-complete-controversy-timeline.html.

212 **"detaches female nudity"**: San Filippo, *Provocauteurs and Provocations*, 211.

213 **"women have learned"**: Ellen Willis, "Feminism, Moralism, and Pornography," *NYLS Law Review* 38, no. 1 (January 1993): 351–58, digi talcommons.nyls.edu/cgi/viewcontent.cgi?article=2126&context=nyls _law_review.

214 **"great blow-job artists"**: Heti, *How Should a Person Be?*, 3.

215 **"men I wanted"**: Heti, *How Should a Person Be?*, 32.

216 **"considered a virtue"**: Thessaly La Force, "Sheila Heti on 'How Should a Person Be?,'" *Paris Review*, June 18, 2012, theparisreview.org /blog/2012/06/18/sheila-heti-on-how-should-a-person-be.

216 **"other people's perceptions"**: Rachel Syme, "Lena Dunham's Change of Pace," *New Yorker*, July 9, 2024, newyorker.com/culture/the-new -yorker-interview/lena-dunhams-change-of-pace.

217 **"perfect, beautiful, ideal"**: La Force, "Sheila Heti."

217 **"precise, observational humor"**: Jada Yuan, "'Awkward Black Girl' Goes to Hollywood," *Vulture*, October 9, 2016, vulture.com/2016/10 /awkward-black-girl-issa-rae-hollywood-c-v-r.html.

219 **examination of abjection**: Rebecca Wanzo, "Precarious-Girl Comedy: Issa Rae, Lena Dunham, and Abjection Aesthetics," *Camera Obscura: Feminism, Culture, and Media Studies* 31, no. 2 (2016): 27–59, doi .org/10.1215/02705346-3592565.

220 **writer Emily Gould**: Emily Gould, "Exposed," *New York Times Magazine*, May 25, 2008, nytimes.com/ 2008/ 05/ 25/ magazine/ 25internet-t .html.

221 **"route to recognition"**: Gould, "Exposed."

222 **"increasingly jaded internet"**: Laura Bennett, "The First-Person Industrial Complex," *Slate*, September 14, 2015, slate.com/articles/life /technology/2015/09/the_first_person_industrial_complex_how_the _harrowing_personal_essay_took.html.

222 **unknown twenty-one-year-old student**: Marie Calloway, "Adrien Brody," Muumuuhouse.com, muumuuhouse.com/mc.fiction1.html.

222 **Her account of sex**: Calloway, "Adrien Brody."

223 **"Calloway's pieces gathered"**: Stephen Marche, "The New Bad Kids

of Fiction," *Esquire*, June 10, 2013, esquire.com/entertainment/books /a23000/marie-calloway-tao-lin.

224 **"wounded women everywhere"**: Leslie Jamison, "Grand Unified Theory of Female Pain," *VQR*, April 2, 2014, vqronline.org/spring -2014/essays/grand-unified-theory-female-pain.

225 **"There is nothing gutsier"**: Lena Dunham, *Not That Kind of Girl: A Young Woman Tells You What She's "Learned"* (Random House, 2014), xxiv.

226 **"misuse of talent"**: Jesse Kornbluth, "Scenes from a Marriage," *New York Magazine*, March 13, 1983.

226 **against the novel:** Tristan Vox, "Carl and Nora and Jack and Meryl," *Vanity Fair*, October 1985, archive.vanityfair.com/article/1985/10/carl -and-nora-and-jack-and-meryl.

227 **"control the version"**: Nora Ephron, *Heartburn* (Alfred A. Knopf, 1983), 177.

227 **"of Marcel Proust"**: Rachel Sykes, "'Who Gets to Speak and Why?' Oversharing in Contemporary North American Women's Writing," *Signs* 43, no. 1 (2017): 151–74, jstor.org/stable/26552985.

227 **"their early marriages"**: Nora Ephron, "Forget the Hamsters," *Guardian* (London), November 5, 2004, theguardian.com/books/2004/nov/06 /featuresreviews.guardianreview33.

227 **"power imbalance inherent"**: Emily Gould, "Our Graffiti," *Emily Magazine*, November 29, 2011, emilymagazine.com/?p=827.

228 **"emptiness and narcissism"**: Amanda Dobbins, "Anatomy of a Back-lash: Tracking the Arguments About 'Girls,'" *Vulture*, April 16, 2012, vulture.com/2012/04/anatomy-of-a-backlash-tracking-the-arguments -about-girls.html.

228 ***Jezebel* offered $10,000:** Jessica Coen, "We're Offering $10,000 for Unretouched Images of Lena Dunham in 'Vogue,'" *Jezebel*, January 16, 2014, jezebel.com/were-offering-10-000-for-unretouched-images-of-lena -d-1502000514.

228 **"own slimy passage"** . . . **"gassed at the pound"**: Laura Bennett, "'Bring It Sad Sick Dudes': Emily Gould Isn't Sorry about Anything," *Salon*, July 14, 2014, www.salon.com/2014/07/14/bring_it_sad_sick _dudes_emily_gould_isnt_sorry_about_anything/; www.vox.com/culture /2017/12/5/16724110/emma-cline-chaz-reetz-laiolo-plagiarism-lawsuit.

229 **in critiques of her songwriting:** Jody Rosen, "Why Taylor Swift Is the Reigning Queen of Pop," *Vulture*, November 17, 2013, vulture.com /2013/11/taylor-swift-reigning-queen-of-pop.html.

230 **"trivialization of my songwriting"**: Hannah Dailey, "Taylor Swift Reflects on Rumors of Her Sexuality & Defends Her Squad in '1989 (Taylor's Version)' Prologue," *Billboard*, October 27, 2023, www.bill board.com/music/music-news/taylor-swift-sexuality-rumors-squad -1989-taylors-version-prologue-1235456748/; https://lareviewofbooks.org /article/i-had-become-the-target-on-taylor-swift-and-the-power-of -revisionism/.

CHAPTER 9: GIRL BOSS: THE MAKING OVER OF FEMALE AMBITION

232 **"show about wealth"**: Jennifer Wilson, "The Real Message of 'The Real Housewives,'" *New Yorker*, September 22, 2023, newyorker.com /culture/cultural-comment/the-real-message-of-the-real-housewives.

234 **the specific shift:** Jia Tolentino, *Trick Mirror: Reflections on Self-Delusion* (Random House, 2019), 235.

234 **Cyrus's VMA performance:** Tressie McMillan Cottom, "Brown Body, White Wonderland," *Slate*, August 29, 2013, slate.com/human -interest/2013/08/miley-cyrus-vma-performance-white-appropriation -of-black-bodies.html?pay=1723759163669&support_journalism =please.

236 **"the postindustrial economy"**: Susan Faludi, "Facebook Feminism, Like It or Not," *Baffler*, August 2013, thebaffler.com/salvos/facebook -feminism-like-it-or-not.

236 **were trending positive:** "Chapter 1: Trends from Government Data," Pew Research Center, December 11, 2013, pewresearch.org/social-trends /2013/12/11/chapter-1-trends-from-government-data.

236 **were also ambitious:** Anna Brown, "Perceptions About Women Bosses Improve, but Gap Remains," Pew Research Center, August 7, 2014, pewresearch.org/short-reads/2014/08/07/perceptions-about-women -leaders-improve-but-gap-remains.

237 **"Without a child"**: Miranda July, *All Fours* (Riverhead, 2024), 15.

237 **Anne-Marie Slaughter wrote:** Anne-Marie Slaughter, "Why Women Still Can't Have It All," *Atlantic*, June 13, 2012, theatlantic.com/maga zine/archive/2012/07/why-women-still-cant-have-it-all/309020.

238 **"the sheer irony"**: Rebecca Walker, ed., *To Be Real: Telling the Truth and Changing the Face of Feminism* (Anchor Books, 1995), 100.

238 **a viral commencement speech:** Slaughter, "Why Women Still Can't Have It All."

239 **the loaded connotations:** Sarah Jaffe, "Trickle-Down Feminism," *Dissent*, 2013, dissentmagazine.org/article/trickle-down-feminism.

239 **"achievements will extend":** Sheryl Sandberg, *Lean In: Women, Work, and the Will to Lead* (Alfred A. Knopf, 2013), 7.

239 **2010 TED Talk:** Sheryl Sandberg, "Why We Have Too Few Women Leaders," TED Talk, December 21, 2010, 14 min., 41 sec., ted.com /talks/sheryl_sandberg_why_we_have_too_few_women_leaders/tran script?subtitle=en.

240 **"educated middle-class women":** Gary Gutting and Nancy Fraser, "A Feminism Where 'Lean In' Means Leaning on Others," *New York Times*, October 15, 2015, archive.nytimes.com/opinionator.blogs.nytimes .com/2015/10/15/a-feminism-where-leaning-in-means-leaning-on -others.

241 **"version of emancipation":** Faludi, "Facebook Feminism."

242 **the fastest-growing occupations:** Faludi, "Facebook Feminism."

242 **"Feminism is proliferating":** Jia Tolentino, "No Offense," *Jezebel*, December 23, 2015, jezebel.com/no-offense-1749221642.

243 **"were excited about":** Sophia Amoruso, *#Girlboss* (Penguin, 2014), 191.

243 **"real management chops":** Dan Schawbel, "Sophia Amoruso: Work for a Company Then Become an Entrepreneur," *Forbes*, September 29, 2015, forbes.com/sites/danschawbel/2015/09/29/sophia-amoruso-work-for -a-company-then-become-an-entrepreneur.

244 **"being the product":** Vanessa Friedman, "How Gwyneth Paltrow's Goop Has Become a Role Model for Other Celebrities," Fashion, *New York Times*, November 14, 2014, nytimes.com/2014/11/16/fashion/how -gwyneth-paltrow-goop-has-become-a-role-model-for-other-celebrities .html.

246 **individual beauty products:** Marisa Meltzer, *Glossy* (Simon and Schuster, 2023), 76.

247 ***Forbes* declared Jenner:** Natalie Robehmed, "At 21, Kylie Jenner Becomes the Youngest Self-Made Billionaire Ever," *Forbes*, March 7, 2019, www.forbes.com/sites/natalierobehmed/2019/03/05/at-21-kylie-jenner -becomes-the-youngest-self-made-billionaire-ever/.

248 **"make business cute":** Meltzer, *Glossy*, 103.

248 **In 2015, a lawsuit:** Sam Reed, "Nasty Gal Responds to Pregnancy-Discrimination Lawsuit," *Hollywood Reporter*, June 9, 2015, www.holly woodreporter.com/news/general-news/nasty-gal-responds-pregnancy -discrimination-801304/.

249 **Gelman and Weiss publicly acknowledged:** Sara Ashley O'Brien, "Glossier, a Billion-Dollar Beauty Brand, Apologizes to Former Retail Workers after Racism Allegations," CNN, August 18, 2020, edition. cnn.com/2020/08/18/tech/glossier-apology-retail-workers/index.html.

249 **"buying a particular set":** Amanda Mull, "The Girlboss Has Left the Building," *Atlantic*, June 25, 2020, theatlantic.com/health/archive/2020 /06/girlbosses-what-comes-next/613519.

252 **"VIP membership money scam":** Emily James, "Kate Hudson's Fitness Brand Fabletics Is Accused of Scamming Members." Mail Online, September 29, 2015, www.dailymail.co.uk/femail/article-3253569/Kate -Hudson-s-activewear-brand-Fabletics-slated-customers-claim -scammed-deceptive-ads.html.

252 **been charged regularly:** Kaitlyn Tiffany, "We May Never Know How Many People Have Accidentally Signed up to Pay Rihanna $50 a Month," *Vox*, August 28, 2019, vox.com/the-goods/2019/8/28/20833663 /rihanna-savage-fenty-vip-membership-fee-fabletics.

253 **a side-by-side analysis:** Nikhil Sonnad, "All the 'Wellness' Products Americans Love to Buy Are Sold on Both Infowars and Goop," *Quartz*, June 29, 2017, qz.com/1010684/all-the-wellness-products-american-love -to-buy-are-sold-on-both-infowars-and-goop.

254 **99 percent of people:** Jon Taylor, "The Case (for and) against Multi-Level Marketing," 1999, ftc.gov/sites/default/files/documents/pub lic_comments/trade-regulation-rule-disclosure-requirements-and -prohibitions-concerning-business-opportunities-ftc.r511993-00008 %C2%A0/00008-57281.pdf.

255 **87 percent are White:** *Direct Selling in the United States: 2020 Industry Overview* (Direct Selling Association, 2021), dsa.org/docs/default-source /research/dsa-industry-overview-fact-sheetd601b69c41746fcd88eaff00 0002c0f4.pdf.

255 **about millennial burnout:** Anne Helen Petersen, "How Millennials Became the Burnout Generation," *BuzzFeed News*, January 5, 2019, buzzfeednews.com/article/annehelenpetersen/millennials-burnout -generation-debt-work.

CHAPTER 10: GIRLS ON TOP: REWRITING A PATH TOWARD POWER

260 **behind gender equality:** Alice Evans, "Romantic Love Is an Under-Rated Driver of Gender Equality," The Great Gender Divergence, March 7, 2024, ggd.world/p/romantic-love-is-an-under-rated-driver.

260 **"understand the assumptions"**: Adrienne Rich, "When We Dead Awaken: Writing as Re-Vision," *College English* 34, no. 1 (1972): 18–30, doi.org/10.2307/375215.

263 **"female U.S. president"**: McNair, *Striptease Culture*, 9.

263 **just 13 percent**: "History of Women in the U.S. Congress," Rutgers University Center for American Women and Politics, 2023, cawp.rut gers.edu/facts/levels-office/congress/history-women-us-congress.

264 **form of power**: Sophie Gilbert, "The Real Housewives of Jane Austen," *Atlantic*, May 31, 2016, theatlantic.com/entertainment/archive/2016/05 /the-real-housewives-of-jane-austen/484748.

266 **"a P.T.A. mom"**: William Yardley, "Sarah Heath Palin, an Outsider Who Charms," *New York Times*, August 29, 2008, nytimes.com/2008 /08/30/us/politics/30palin.html?hp.

266 **nothing triggers misogyny**: Kate Manne, *Down Girl: The Logic of Misogyny* (Oxford University Press, 2018), 103.

268 **"lack of creativity"**: Tracy Clark-Flory, "Sneak Peek: The Palin Porno," *Salon*, October 20, 2008, salon.com/2008/10/20/palin_porn.

268 **2018 book *Pornographies***: Tim Gregory, "The Aestheticisation of the Real Body in Politics and Pornography," in *Pornographies: Critical Positions*, ed. Katherine Harrison and Cassandra A. Ogden (University of Chester Press, 2018), 193–219.

269 **"lurid sexual jibes"**: Kadia Goba, Ellie Hall, and David Weigel, "Mysterious Influencer Network Pushed Sexual Smears of Harris," *Semafor*, September 8, 2024, semafor.com/article/09/08/2024/mysterious -influencer-network-pushed-sexual-smears-of-harris.

270 **"risk being degraded"**: Rebecca Traister, "How Did Republican Women End Up like This?," *New York Magazine*, June 17, 2024, nymag.com/in telligencer/article/conservatives-republican-party-women-rebecca -traister.html.

271 **"that silence women"**: Mary Beard, *Women & Power: A Manifesto* (Profile, 2017), xii.

272 **wave of women-oriented shows**: Joy Press, "The Secret Weapons of 'Broad City' Make Fine Art from Crude Humor," *New York Times*, February 12, 2016, nytimes.com/2016/02/14/arts/television/the-secret -weapons-of-broad-city-makefine-art-fromcrude-humor.html.

273 **"sometimes downright delusional"**: Emily Nussbaum, "Mindy's Happy Ending," *New Yorker*, December 9, 2015, newyorker.com/culture /culture-desk/mindys-happy-ending.

275 **"rigidly prescribed roles":** Carina Chocano, "Emerald Fennell's Dark, Jaded, Funny, Furious Fables of Female Revenge," *New York Times Magazine*, December 17, 2020, nytimes.com/2020/12/17/magazine/promising-young-woman-emerald-fennell.html.

277 **"a beguiling study":** Doreen St. Félix, "Michaela Coel's Chaos and Charisma in 'I May Destroy You,'" *New Yorker*, June 29, 2020, newyorker.com/magazine/2020/07/06/michaela-coels-chaos-and-charisma-in-i-may-destroy-you.

279 **"make things normal":** Sarah Polley, *Run Towards the Danger* (Penguin, 2022), 87.

279 **"first lady of Miramax":** Jodi Kantor and Rachel Abrams, "Gwyneth Paltrow, Angelina Jolie and Others Say Weinstein Harassed Them," U.S., *New York Times*, October 10, 2017, nytimes.com/2017/10/10/us/gwyneth-paltrow-angelina-jolie-harvey-weinstein.html.

280 **two hundred powerful men:** Audrey Carlsen, Maya Salam, Claire Cain Miller, Denise Lu, Ash Ngu, Jugal K. Patel, and Zach Wichter, "#MeToo Brought Down 201 Powerful Men. Nearly Half of Their Replacements Are Women," *New York Times*, October 29, 2018, nytimes.com/interactive/2018/10/23/us/metoo-replacements.html.

280 **"subside and resurface":** Susan Faludi, *Backlash: The Undeclared War Against Women* (Crown, 1991), xix.

281 **upcoming TV shows:** Sophie Gilbert, "The Men of #MeToo Go Back to Work," *Atlantic*, October 12, 2018, theatlantic.com/entertainment/archive/2018/10/has-metoo-actually-changed-hollywood/572815.

282 **"cultural black hole":** Sophie Haigney, "How the Biden Presidency Became a Cultural Black Hole," *Politico*, January 30, 2022, politico.com/news/magazine/2022/01/30/biden-aesthetics-presidents-bland-00003265.

283 **"bullied with backlash":** Megan Thee Stallion, "'Nobody Can Take Your Power': Megan Thee Stallion in Her Own Words," *Elle*, April 18, 2023, elle.com/culture/celebrities/a43567508/megan-thee-stallion-tory-lanez-case-interview-2023.

283 **feminist Moya Bailey:** Stephen J. Lewis, "From the Combination of Racism and Sexism, Here Is the Story of a New Word," *Northwestern Now*, May 4, 2023, news.northwestern.edu/stories/2023/05/professor-coins-new-word-misogynoir/; www.moyabailey.com/about/.

Index

INDEX

INDEX

INDEX

INDEX

INDEX

INDEX

INDEX

INDEX

327

INDEX

INDEX